'This is the most remarkable memoir . . . If you have never read a book about Nazi Germany before, or if you have already read a thousand, I would urge you to read *Defying Hitler*. It sings with wisdom and understanding, and, through a deft patchwork of the historical and the personal, manages somehow to explain the inexplicable'   Craig Brown, *Mail on Sunday*

'It is nothing less than a clear-eyed autobiographical analysis of the German character as it appeared to the writer, and who experienced it, in his own heart and mind . . . It is raw, revelatory stuff . . . Haffner distils the essence of the Weimar Republic: its snapshot scenes are little nuggets of pure sensation informed by sensibility. If it were to be a movie, it would be the German equivalent of *Les Quatre-Cents Coups*'
Iain Finlayson, *The Times*

'This raw, passionate . . . account . . . The book has already topped the bestseller list in Germany for a year. No wonder: it reads as compellingly as a top-class thriller. The outstanding impression you get as Haffner takes you from day to day through early 1933 is how easy it was for Hitler, beginning in such small ways, to turn a civilised, intelligent people into a helpless, penned-in flock of sheep'   Peter Lewis, *Daily Mail*

'Each of us sometimes asks what we would have done if we had been young and German in 1933. There could scarcely be a better way to explore this question than to read Haffner's book . . . He is vivid, concise, lucid, penetrating, humane, brave, playful and profound: a representative of the German civilisation which thuggish German nationalsists tried to destroy'
Andrew Gimson, *Evening Standard*

'A brilliant, moving and terrifying evocation of the destruction of civilisation in Germany by the Nazis'
Anthony Daniels, *Sunday Telegraph*

'An unforgettable memoir of life in Germany during the rise of the Nazis, a mesmerising study of the way a generation surrendered to Hitler'   Robert McCrum, *Observer*

'Episodes from everyday life provide memorable illustrations of what was happening throughout the country ... This is a riveting story, which the translator helpfully continues in a brief Afterword to satisfy the reader's curiosity about Haffner's life after we leave him in the final chapter'
Theo Richmond, *Spectator*

'As gripping as any thriller I've ever read'
Miriam Gross, *Sunday Telegraph*

'Haffner's outstanding gifts of observation and imagination enabled him to reconstruct, vividly and convincingly, the state of mind of the German people during the tumultuous decades before 1933'   Roger Morgan, *TLS*

Sebastian Haffner was born in 1907 in Berlin, where he studied law and graduated in 1933, before leaving for Paris. He returned to Berlin in 1934 and then left Germany in 1938 for Britain, where he worked for the *Observer*. He went back to live in Germany in 1954, and wrote for *Die Welt* and for *Stern* magazine. He was the author of several historical bestsellers, including *The Rise and Fall of Prussia*, *From Bismarck to Hitler* and *The Meaning of Hitler*, which has sold nearly a million copies. He died in 1999.

Defying Hitler

A MEMOIR

Sebastian Haffner

Translated by Oliver Pretzel

PHOENIX

A PHOENIX PAPERBACK

First published in Great Britain in 2002
by Weidenfeld & Nicolson
This paperback edition published in 2003
by Phoenix,
an imprint of Orion Books Ltd,
Orion House, 5 Upper St Martin's Lane,
London WC2H 9EA

Originally published as *Geschichte eines Deutschen*

Revised edition

A CIP catalogue record for this book
is available from the British Library.

ISBN 1 84212 660 1

Typeset by Deltatype Ltd, Birkenhead, Merseyside
Printed and bound in Great Britain by
Clays Ltd, St Ives plc

Germany is nothing, each individual German is everything.   GOETHE (1808)

But first the most important thing:
'What are you doing in these great times?

Great I say; for times seem great
to me, when each man, driven
half to death by the era's hate,
and standing in the place he's given,

Must willy-nilly contemplate
no less a thing than his own BEING!
A little breath, a second's wait
may well suffice – you catch my meaning?'

PETER GAN (1935)

Contents

Photographs

1 Mary Evans Picture Library
2 Illustrated London News Picture Library
3 Anthony Potter Collection/Hulton Archive
4 Hulton Archive
The remaining photographs were supplied by Oliver Pretzel

Introduction

My father, Sebastian Haffner, might not have been pleased to see this book published. He died in 1999 at the age of ninety-one, a celebrated German author and historical journalist, with a reputation for books containing highly original, coolly and lucidly argued insights into the history of Germany in the twentieth century. This book, the first political book he wrote, was started in exile in England early in 1939. Abandoned in the autumn of that year, it may be original and lucid, but it is not cool. It is the passionate outburst of a young man whose career has been cut off and whose life has been turned inside out by his own countrymen, following a leader and an ideology he views only with contempt and disgust. In his old age, my father tended to be slightly ashamed of the early works he had published in England. What would he have thought of this one, unfinished, raw, and revealing so much of his inner self?

It describes his life and the political events in Germany from 1914, when he was seven years old, until 1933. The original plan was to continue the narrative up to the time of his emigration to England in August 1938, but the advent of the war caused him to stop working on the book, presumably because its theme is the question of how it was possible for the Nazis to come to power. Instead he started another one, whose subject was the more urgent question of how to deal with Nazi Germany.

The memoir deliberately avoids the use of my father's real name, Raimund Pretzel, and so it seemed reasonable to publish it under his pseudonym, Sebastian Haffner. It is a mixture of autobiography and political analysis. I have added footnotes to explain some of the political references that may not be familiar to present-day readers. They will, I hope, assist the narrative without interrupting the flow.

Today the very reason that caused my father to lay it aside, its closeness to the events it describes, and its evocation of the predicament he faced, seem to me to give it its particular interest.

Oliver Pretzel
November 2001
London

Revised edition
May 2003

PROLOGUE

One

This is the story of a duel.

It is a duel between two very unequal adversaries: an exceedingly powerful, formidable and ruthless state and an insignificant, unknown private individual. The duel does not take place in what is commonly known as the sphere of politics; the individual is by no means a politician, still less a conspirator, or an enemy of the state. Throughout, he finds himself very much on the defensive. He only wishes to preserve what he considers his integrity, his private life and his personal honour. These are under constant attack by the Government of the country he lives in, and by the most brutal, but often also clumsy, means.

With fearful menace the state demands that the individual give up his friends, abandon his lovers, renounce his beliefs and assume new, prescribed ones. He must use a new form of greeting, eat and drink in ways he does not fancy, employ his leisure in occupations he abhors, make himself available for activities he despises, and deny his past and his individuality. For all this, he must constantly express extreme enthusiasm and gratitude.

The individual is opposed to all of that, but he is ill-prepared for the onslaught. He was not born a hero, still less a martyr. He is just an ordinary man with many weaknesses, having grown up in vulnerable times. He is nevertheless stubbornly antagonistic. So he enters into the duel – without enthusiasm, shrugging his shoulders but with a quiet determination not to yield. He is, of course, much weaker than his opponent, but rather more agile. You will see him duck and weave, dodge his foe and dart back, evading crushing blows by a whisker. You will have to admit that, for someone who is neither a hero nor a martyr, he manages to put up a good fight. Finally, however, you will see him compelled to abandon the struggle or, if you will, transfer it to another plane.

The state is the German Reich and I am the individual. Our fight may be interesting to watch, like any fight (indeed I hope it will be), but I am not recounting it just for entertainment. There is another purpose, closer to my heart.

My private duel with the Third Reich is not an isolated encounter. Thousands, maybe hundreds of thousands of such duels, in which an individual tries to defend his integrity and his personal honour against a formidably hostile state, have been fought in Germany during the last six years. Each is waged in total isolation and out of public view. Many of the duellists, greater heroes or martyrs by nature, have taken the fight further than I – as far as the concentration camp or the gallows – and may perhaps be honoured by a future monument. Others were defeated much earlier and are now silent grumblers in the ranks of SA reservists or NSV *Blockwarts* (block wardens).*

One might well consider my case as typical. From it, you can easily judge the chances for mankind in Germany today.

You will see that they are pretty slim. They need not have been quite so hopeless if the outside world had intervened. It is still in the world's interest, I believe, for these chances to be improved. It is too late to avoid a war, but it might shorten the war by a year or two. Those Germans of goodwill who are fighting to defend their private peace and their private liberty, are fighting, without knowing it, for the peace and liberty of the whole world.

Thus it still seems worth while to me to draw the attention of the world to the unknown events inside Germany.

The book will tell a story, not preach a sermon; but it has a moral which, like that 'other and greater theme' in Elgar's

---

* SA (Sturm-Abteilung), Nazi storm troopers; NSV (National-Sozialistische Volkfursorge), National Socialist Society for the Welfare of the People.

Enigma Variations, silently 'runs through and over the whole'. I will not mind if, after reading the book, you forget all the adventures and incidents that I recount; but I would be pleased if you did not forget the underlying moral.

Two

ven before the totalitarian state advanced on me with threats and challenges, and taught me what it meant to experience history in person, I had already lived through a fair number of 'historical events'. All Europeans of the present generation can make that claim, and none more so than the Germans.

Those events have naturally left their mark on me, as on all my compatriots. If one fails to appreciate this, one will not be able to understand what happened later. There is, however, an important difference between what happened before 1933 and what came afterwards. We watched the earlier events unfold. They occupied and excited us, sometimes they even killed one or other of us or ruined him; but they did not confront us with ultimate decisions of conscience. Our innermost being remained untouched. We gained experience, acquired convictions, but remained basically the same people. However, no one who has, willingly or reluctantly, been caught up in the machine of the Third Reich can honestly say that of himself.

Clearly historical events have varying degrees of intensity. Some may almost fail to impinge on true reality, that is, on the central, most personal part of a person's life. Others can wreak such havoc there that nothing is left standing. The usual way in which history is written fails to reveal this. '1890: Wilhelm II dismisses Bismarck.' Certainly a key event in German history, but scarcely an event at all in the biography of any German outside its small circle of protagonists. Life went on as before. No family was torn apart, no friendship broke up, no one fled their country. Not even a rendezvous was missed or an opera performance cancelled. Those in love, whether happily or not, remained so; the poor remained poor, and the rich rich. Now compare that with '1933: Hindenburg sends for Hitler.' An earthquake shatters sixty-six million lives.

Official, academic history has, as I said, nothing to tell us about the differences in intensity of historical occurrences. To learn about that, you must read biographies, not those of statesmen but the all too rare ones of unknown individuals. There you will see that one historical event passes over the private (real) lives of people like a cloud over a lake. Nothing stirs, there is only a fleeting shadow. Another event whips up the lake as if in a thunderstorm. For a while it is scarcely recognisable. A third may, perhaps, drain the lake completely.

I believe history is misunderstood if this aspect is forgotten (and it usually is forgotten). So before I reach my proper theme, let me tell you my version of twenty years of German history – the history of Germany as a part of my private story. It will not take long, and it will make what follows easier to understand. Besides, it may help us get to know each other a little better.

Three

My conscious life started with the outbreak of the Great War. It found me, like most Europeans, on my summer holidays. Indeed, the worst thing the war did to me was to spoil those holidays. With what merciful suddenness the last war began, compared with the slow, tortured approach of the one that is now imminent! On the 1st of August 1914, we had just decided not to take the matter very seriously, and to continue our holidays. We were on a farm estate in eastern Pomerania, lost to the world, in the midst of woods which I, as a small boy, knew and loved like nothing else in the world. The return from those woods to town, which usually took place in the middle of August, was the saddest and most unbearable event of the year for me; comparable, perhaps, only to the dismantling and burning of the Christmas tree after the New Year.

On the 1st of August that return was still two weeks away. A few days earlier, some disquieting things had happened. The newspaper contained something never seen before: headlines. My father read it longer than usual, looked very worried, and cursed the Austrians when he put it down. On one occasion the headline was 'WAR?' I kept hearing new words which I did not understand, but which were soon to be explained by events: ultimatum, mobilisation, alliance, Entente. A major who was staying on the same estate, and with whose daughters I was on terms of teasing conflict, suddenly received an 'order' – another of those new words – and departed precipitately. One of our host's sons was also called up. As he drove off to the station in a gig, we all ran after him shouting, 'Be brave!', 'Take care of yourself!', 'Come back soon!' Someone called, 'Thrash the Serbs!' and I, remembering what my father had said after reading the newspaper, shouted 'And the Austrians!' I was very surprised when everyone burst out laughing.

It made a far deeper impression on me to hear that the best horses on the estate, Hanne and Wachtel, were being taken away because (what a quantity of words to be explained!) they belonged to the 'cavalry reserve'. I loved each and every horse on the estate, and the fact that two of the finest were suddenly leaving was a great blow.

Most depressing of all was hearing the word 'return' every now and then. 'Perhaps we shall have to return tomorrow.' That sounded to me exactly as if someone had said 'Perhaps we shall die tomorrow.' Tomorrow – and not after an eternity of two weeks!

In those days there was no wireless, of course, and the papers arrived in our woods with twenty-four hours' delay. They also contained far less than nowadays. The diplomats were much more discreet. So it came about that, on the 1st of August 1914, we decided that there was not going to be a war, and that we were going to stay put.

I shall never forget that 1st of August. The memory of that day will always instil in me a profound feeling of calm, of suspense resolved, of 'all's well again'. It was a Saturday, with all the wonderful stillness that a Saturday produces in the country. The day's work was done. Bells of cattle returning home tinkled through the air. Peace and quiet reigned over the entire farm. The farmhands and girls were in their rooms scrubbing themselves for an evening dance.

Downstairs, in the hall, with its hunting trophies on the walls and a row of pewter jugs and bright earthenware plates ranged along a high shelf, I found my father and our host, the owner of the estate, seated in deep armchairs, solemnly and weightily discussing the situation. Of course I did not understand much of what they were saying and I can recall no details. But I have not forgotten how calm and consoling their voices sounded, my father's higher tones against the deep bass of our host; how reassuring the sight of their leisurely manner was, the fragrant smoke of their cigars rising above them in slender columns; and how, the longer they talked, the clearer, the better and the more comforting everything became. Until, finally, it was irrefutably clear that war was quite *impossible* and, therefore, we would not let panic chase us back to town. Instead, as in all previous years, we would stay on to the end of the holidays.

Having listened this far, I walked outside, my heart swelling with relief, contentment and gratitude, and gazed with feelings almost of piety at the sun setting over the woods which had been returned to me. The day had been cloudy but had cleared towards evening and the sun, ruddy and gold, floated in the sheerest blue, promising a cloudless new day. Cloudless as, I was sure, would be the entire fourteen-day eternity of those holidays which again lay before me.

When I was awakened next morning, packing was in full swing. At first, I did not understand what had happened. The word 'mobilisation', which they had sought to explain a few days previously, conveyed nothing to me. Anyhow, there was little time to explain anything. We had to clear out, bag and baggage, that very afternoon. It was doubtful if a train would be available any later.

'Today,' said our efficient maid, 'everything's nought point five.' The meaning of this expression remains obscure to me. It seemed to signify that everything was topsy-turvy, and it was a matter of each for himself. Because of that I was able to steal away to the woods unnoticed. There they found me only just before we were due to depart, sitting on a tree stump, my head buried in my hands, weeping inconsolably, and quite unresponsive to the explanation that there was a war on and everyone had to make sacrifices. Somehow they managed to tuck me into the carriage and off we went, drawn at a trot by two brown horses – not Hanne and Wachtel, they were long gone – with clouds of dust rising behind and enveloping everything. I never saw my childhood woods again.

That was the only time I experienced an aspect of the war as reality; and I felt the natural pain of one from whom something is snatched and destroyed. On the journey itself things already began to change; they became more exciting, more adventurous – more glorious. The journey by train lasted twelve hours instead of the usual seven. There were constant stops, and each time a train full of soldiers passed us everyone rushed to the windows, boisterously shouting and waving. Instead of a compartment to ourselves, as had been usual when we travelled, we stood in the corridors, or sat on our bags, tightly squeezed in the crowd who talked and chattered incessantly as though they were not strangers but old acquaintances. They talked mostly of spies. During the journey I learned all about that romantic trade, which I had never heard of before. We crossed every bridge very slowly and each time this gave me a pleasantly creepy sensation. Perhaps a spy had left a bomb underneath. It was midnight when we arrived in Berlin. I had never in my life been up so late. The house was not ready for us, the furniture still buried under dust-sheets, and the beds rolled up. They put me to bed on a sofa in my father's tobacco-scented study. War certainly had its pleasurable side after all.

In the following days I learned an incredible amount in an incredibly short time. I, a seven-year-old boy, who a short while ago hardly knew what war meant, let alone 'ultimatum', 'mobilisation' and 'cavalry reserve', soon knew, as if I had always known, the 'hows' and 'wheres' and 'wherefores' of the war, and I even knew the 'why'. I knew the war was due to France's lust for revenge, England's commercial envy and Russia's barbarism. I could speak these words quite glibly. One day I simply started to read the newspaper and was surprised at how extraordinarily easy it was to understand. I asked to be shown the map of Europe, and saw at a glance that 'we' could handle France and England, but experienced dumb anxiety at the size of Russia. I consoled myself with the thought that the terrifying numbers of Russians were counterbalanced by their unbelievable stupidity, depravity and incessant vodka-swilling. I also learned, as quickly as if I had always known them, the names of the various military chiefs, the strengths of the armies, the types of armaments and displacements of the ships, the positions of the most important fortifications, and the locations of the front lines. In fact I soon realised that a game was being played here that made life more exciting and thrilling than anything before. My enthusiasm for this game, and my interest, held to the bitter end.

Here I must say a word in defence of my family. It was not my close relatives who turned my head. The war oppressed my father from the very start. He looked on the enthusiasm of the first weeks with scepticism, and on the hate propaganda that followed with profound disgust, though as a loyal and patriotic man, he wanted Germany to win. He belonged to the many liberal spirits of his generation who had secretly been convinced that war among Europeans was a thing of the past. The war found him at a loss and, unlike many others, he refused to indulge in wishful thinking. I occasionally heard him utter words full of bitterness and doubt – not just about the Austrians – that offended my newly acquired enthusiastic bellicosity. No, it was not my father's fault, nor any of my other relatives', that within a few days I became a fanatical jingoist and armchair warrior.

You must blame the atmosphere, the general mood, the tug of the masses, which produced unimagined emotions in those who surrendered themselves (even seven-year-old boys), and left those who stayed aloof suffocating in a vacuum of arid emptiness and isolation. For the first time I felt, with naive delight and without a trace of doubt or misgiving, the effect of my people's strange talent for creating mass hysteria (it may be a compensation for their limited talent for individual happiness). I had no idea that one might possibly exclude oneself from this general festive delirium. It did not occur to me that there could be anything bad or dangerous in something which so obviously filled one with joy and provided such delightful intoxication.

For a schoolboy in Berlin, the war was something very unreal; it was like a game. There were no air raids and no bombs. There were the wounded, but you saw them only at a distance, with picturesque bandages. One had relatives at the front, of course, and now and then one heard of a death. But being a child, one quickly got used to their absence, and the fact that this absence sometimes became irrevocable did not seem to matter. As to the real hardships and privations, they were of small account. Naturally, the food was poor. Later there was too little food, and our shoes had clattering wooden soles, our suits were turned, there were school collections for bones and cherry stones, and surprisingly frequent illnesses. I must admit, all that made little impression. Not that I bore it all 'like a little hero'. It was just that there was nothing very special to bear. I thought as little about food as a football enthusiast at a cup final. The army bulletins interested me far more than the menu.

The analogy with the football fan can be carried further. In those childhood days, I was a war fan just as one is a football fan. I would be making myself out to be worse than I was if I were to claim to have been caught up by the hate propaganda, which, from 1915 to 1918, sought to whip up the flagging enthusiasm of the first few months of the war. I hated the French, the English and the Russians as little as the Portsmouth supporters detest Wolverhampton fans. Of course, I prayed for their defeat and humiliation, but only because these were the necessary counterparts of my side's victory and triumph.

What counted was the fascination of the game of war, in which, according to certain mysterious rules, the numbers of prisoners taken, miles advanced, fortifications seized and ships sunk, played almost the same role as goals in football and points in boxing. I never wearied of keeping internal score-cards. I was a zealous reader of the army bulletins, which I would proceed to recalculate in my own fashion, according to my own mysterious, irrational rules: thus, for instance, ten Russian prisoners were equivalent to one English or French prisoner, and fifty aeroplanes to one cruiser. If there had been statistics of those killed, I would certainly not have hesitated to 'recalculate' the dead. I would not have stopped to think what the objects of my arithmetic looked like in reality. It was a dark, mysterious game and its never-ending, wicked lure eclipsed everything else, making daily life seem trite. It was addictive, like roulette and opium. My friends and I played it all through the war: four long years, unpunished and undisturbed. It is this game, and not the harmless battle games we organised in streets and playgrounds nearby, that has left its dangerous mark on all of us.

Four

It may not seem worth while to describe the obviously inadequate reactions of a child to the Great War at such great length. That would certainly be true if mine were an isolated case, but it was not. This, more or less, was the way an entire generation of Germans experienced the war in childhood or adolescence; and one should note that this is precisely the generation that is today preparing its repetition.

The force and influence of these experiences are not diminished by the fact that they were lived through by children or young boys. On the contrary, in its reactions the mass psyche greatly resembles the child psyche. One cannot overstate the childishness of the ideas that feed and stir the masses. Real ideas must as a rule be simplified to the level of a child's understanding if they are to arouse the masses to historic actions. A childish illusion, fixed in the minds of all children born in a certain decade and hammered home for four years, can easily reappear as a deadly serious political ideology twenty years later.

From 1914 to 1918 a generation of German schoolboys daily experienced war as a great, thrilling, enthralling game between nations, which provided far more excitement and emotional satisfaction than anything peace could offer; and that has now become the underlying vision of Nazism. That is where it draws its allure from: its simplicity, its appeal to the imagination, and its zest for action; but also its intolerance and its cruelty towards internal opponents. Anyone who does not join in the game is regarded not as an adversary but as a spoilsport. Ultimately that is also the source of Nazism's belligerent attitude towards neighbouring states. Other countries are not regarded as neighbours, but must be opponents, whether they like it or not. Otherwise the match would have to be called off!

Many things later bolstered Nazism and modified its character, but its roots lie here: in the experience of war – not by German soldiers at the front, but by German schoolboys at home. Indeed, the front-line generation has produced relatively few genuine Nazis and is better known for its 'critics and carpers'. That is easy to understand. Men who have experienced the reality of war tend to view it differently. Granted, there are exceptions: the eternal warriors, who found their vocation in war, with all its terrors, and continue to do so; and the eternal failures, who welcome its horrors and its destruction as a revenge on a life that has proved too much for them. Göring perhaps belongs to the former type; Hitler certainly to the latter. The truly Nazi generation was formed by those born in the decade from 1900 to 1910, who experienced war as a great game and were untouched by its realities.

Quite untouched? At least, you may protest, they suffered starvation. True enough; but hunger interfered with the game little. It may even have enhanced it. Well-fed, satisfied men are not given to visions and imaginings. At any rate, hunger alone did not bring disillusion. It was, one could say, digested. Its final result has merely been a certain indifference to undernourishment – one of the more admirable traits of this generation.

We were early accustomed to make do with a minimum of food. Most Germans alive today have lived through three periods of malnutrition: first during the Great War, then during the peak of the inflation in 1923 and now, for the third time, under the slogan of 'guns before butter'. The German people have been well trained in this respect, and are not very demanding.

I think the widespread opinion that the Germans lost the war because of hunger is quite mistaken. By 1918 they had already gone hungry for three years, and food had been scarcer in 1917 than in 1918. In my opinion, the Germans abandoned their war effort not because they were starving, but because they thought the war militarily lost and politically without prospect. Be that as it may, the Germans will scarcely give up Nazism or a second world war out of hunger. Today they consider hunger almost as a moral duty and anyhow, it is not so hard to bear. They have become rather ashamed of their natural needs. Paradoxically, the Nazis have acquired a new, indirect propaganda weapon by giving the people too little to eat.

Anyone who grumbles is alleged to be doing so because they cannot get butter or coffee. There is, of course, a great deal of grumbling in Germany, but most people complain for very different, and generally far more honourable, reasons than food shortages. They would be ashamed of complaining because of those. People grumble far less about the scarcity of food than one would assume from the Nazi newspapers; but these journals know perfectly well what they are doing when they imply the contrary. For rather than be thought to be complaining out of mere greed, most Germans prefer to suffer in silence.

As I said above, that is one of their more likeable traits.

Five

In the course of the four war years from 1914 to 1918 I gradually lost all sense of what peace might be like. The memory of pre-war times slowly paled. I could not imagine a day without the army bulletins. Such a day would have been without its chief attraction. What else did life have to offer? One went to school, learned reading, writing and arithmetic, and later Latin and history; one played with friends, one went out with one's parents – but was that a life? Life gained its thrill, the day its colour, from the current military events. If a great offensive was on, with the number of prisoners running to five figures, fortifications captured and 'immeasurable gains of war material', it felt like the holiday season. There was an endless supply of food for the imagination, and life was grand; just as later when one was in love. If there were only tedious defensive operations, 'All quiet on the Western front' or 'a strategic retreat, carried out according to plan', then life was all grey, the battle games with one's friends lacked excitement and schoolwork became twice as boring.

Every day I went to a police station a few blocks from our house. There the army bulletin was posted several hours before it appeared in the newspapers: a narrow sheet of white paper on a noticeboard, sometimes long, sometimes short, covered with dancing capital letters, obviously produced by a very worn duplicating machine. I had to stand on tiptoe and strain my neck to decipher it. I did that every day, patiently and reverently.

As I said, I no longer had any clear conception of peace, though I had some idea of the 'Final Victory'. The Final

Victory – the grand total that would one day be the inevitable result of all the many partial victories mentioned in the military bulletins – was for me what the Last Day and the Resurrection is for a pious Christian, or the coming of the Messiah for a religious Jew. It was the stupendous climax of all those triumphant bulletins in which the numbers of prisoners, size of territory gained, and quantity of booty outdid each other. What would follow was beyond imagining. I waited for the Final Victory with eager but timorous trepidation. That it would come was inevitable. The only question was what life could possibly offer afterwards.

Even in the months from July to October 1918 I still confidently expected victory, although I was not so stupid as to fail to notice that the army bulletins were getting gloomier and gloomier, and that my expectation defied reason. Well, had not Russia been defeated? Did 'we' not possess the Ukraine, which would provide all that was needed to win the war? Were our armies not still deep in France?

I could not fail to notice also that many, very many, people and indeed finally almost everyone began to take a different view of the war from mine. Yet mine had originally been the common view. Indeed, it had only become mine because it was the common view. It was most exasperating that almost everyone seemed to have lost their taste for the war just then – when only a little extra effort was all that was needed to raise the army bulletins out of the mournful depression of the 'enemy attempt to overrun our lines defeated' and 'orderly withdrawal into prepared positions', and bring them into the brilliant sunshine of '30 mile advance', 'break through enemy lines', and '30,000 prisoners'!

Outside the shops where I queued up for artificial honey or skimmed milk (my mother and the maid could not always spare the time, and I sometimes had to help out) I used to hear the women grumble and utter ugly words that showed their total lack of comprehension. I was not always content to listen. Sometimes I would speak out fearlessly in my rather high-pitched voice and lecture them on the need to 'hold out'. The women would laugh at first, then begin to wonder, and sometimes become touchingly diffident and subdued. I would leave the field of verbal battle victorious, unselfconsciously swinging a quarter-litre of skimmed milk ... But the army bulletins refused to improve.

From October onwards the revolution drew near. Like the war, it approached with a flurry of new words and ideas; and yet, like it, too, it finally came almost as a surprise. There the comparison ceases. The war, whatever one might say about it, was something complete in itself, something that came off, a success in its way – at least at first. One cannot say that of the revolution.*

It has been of ominous significance for the later history of Germany that in spite of all the terrible misfortunes that the war brought, its outbreak was associated in almost everyone's memories with a number of unforgettable days of great exaltation and intensity, while the revolution of 1918, though it finally produced peace and freedom, only awakens dark memories in the minds of most Germans. The very fact that the war began in brilliant summer weather and the revolution in cold, wet November fog was a severe handicap for the revolution. That may sound ridiculous, but it is nevertheless true. The republicans felt it later themselves. They never really wished to be reminded of the 9th of November and have never celebrated it. The Nazis who countered November 1918 with August 1914 always had an easy victory. Though November 1918 meant the end of the war, husbands restored to wives, and life restored to men, it recalls no sense of joy, only a bad mood, defeat, anxiety, senseless gunfights, confusion and bad weather.

I myself saw little of the actual revolution. On Saturday the papers announced that the Kaiser had abdicated. I felt somehow

---

* The German 'revolution' started with a naval mutiny in the final week of October 1918. It spread across Germany and by 9 November had forced the abdication of the Kaiser. In the spring of 1919 it was bloodily put down by the right-wing mercenaries (the so-called Freikorps – Free Corps) brought in by the Social Democrat Government, usually led by ex-army officers and often supplied with army weapons.

surprised that there was so little fuss. It was just another newspaper headline, and I had seen bolder ones during the war. Incidentally he had not yet abdicated when the headlines appeared, but as he soon did so that was not very important.

The fact that the very next day, on Sunday the 10th, our newspaper was suddenly called *Die Rote Fahne* (The Red Flag) instead of *Tägliche Rundschau* (Daily Review) gave me a much greater shock than the headline 'Kaiser abdicates'. A group of revolutionary printers had apparently demanded the new name. The contents were, however, little changed. A few days later, it reverted to *Tägliche Rundschau*. This small detail is emblematic of the revolution of 1918 as a whole.

That Sunday I heard shots fired for the first time. During the whole of the war I had not heard a single shot. Yet now, when it was over, they began shooting in Berlin. We stood by the open windows in one of our back rooms and heard the faint but distinct sounds of spasmodic machine-gun fire. I felt uneasy. Someone explained the difference between the sounds of heavy and light machine-guns. We tried to guess where the fighting was taking place. The shooting sounded as if it came from the neighbourhood of the Palace. Was the Berlin garrison defending itself after all? Was the revolution perhaps not going so smoothly?

If I had indulged in such hopes – for it will scarcely surprise the reader to hear that I was wholeheartedly against the revolution – they were disappointed the next day. It turned out to have been a rather pointless brawl between rival revolutionary groups, each claiming possession of the royal stables. There was no sign of resistance. The revolution had clearly triumphed.

What did that mean? Glorious mayhem perhaps, everything topsy-turvy, adventure and colourful anarchy? Nothing of the sort. That same Monday morning, our most feared master, a choleric tyrant with wicked, rolling little eyes, declared that at least 'here', at school, no revolution had taken place, and discipline would continue to prevail. Doubtless in pursuance of this edict, those boys who had especially distinguished themselves playing revolution during the break were made to bend over and receive a demonstrative beating. All of us who witnessed the punishment felt it as an evil omen. There was something not quite right about a revolution when the next day schoolboys were beaten for playing at it. Nothing could come of such a revolution. Nothing did.

Meanwhile the war was still not quite over. It was clear to me, as to everyone, that the revolution was synonymous with the end of the war; an end that was obviously not the Final Victory because the necessary little extra effort had inexplicably not been made. I had no idea what the end without victory would look like. I would have to see it to comprehend it.

As the war took place somewhere in distant France, in an unreal world, from which the army bulletins appeared like messages from 'the beyond', its end also had no reality for me. Nothing changed in my immediate, physical surroundings. The event belonged exclusively to the dream world of the great game, in which I had lived the last four years; a world that had become far more important to me than the real one.

On the 9th and 10th of November army bulletins of the usual kind still appeared: 'enemy breakthrough attempts repulsed', 'after courageous resistance, our troops withdrew into previously prepared positions'. On the 11th there was no army bulletin on the noticeboard at my local police station when I appeared there at the usual time. Empty and black, the board yawned at me. Horror overcame me to think that the board, which had sustained my spirit and nourished my dreams every day for years, would remain empty and black for evermore. I walked on. There must be some news from the front somewhere. If the war was over (and one had to reckon with that possibility) there must at least have been some sort of end worth reporting, something like the final whistle at a football match. A few streets away there was another police station. Perhaps there was a bulletin there.

There was none there either. The police had obviously also been infected by the revolution, and the old order had collapsed. I could not come to terms with it. I wandered on through the streets in the fine November drizzle, looking for news. The neighbourhood became less familiar.

Somewhere, I saw a bunch of people gazing into the window of a newsagent's shop. I joined them and carefully edged my way to the front. There I could read what they were all reading in silence and gloom. It was an early edition of a newspaper and it bore the headline: 'Armistice signed'. Underneath were the terms, a long list. I read them. As I read, I turned to stone.

How shall I describe my feelings – the feelings of an eleven-year-old boy whose entire inner world has collapsed? However much I try, I find it difficult to find an equivalent in ordinary, everyday life. Certain fantastic catastrophes are only possible in dream worlds. Maybe one could imagine someone who year after year has deposited large sums of money in his bank, and when one day he asks for a statement, discovers a gigantic overdraft instead of a fortune; but that only happens in dreams.

The terms no longer spoke the careful language of the army bulletins. They spoke the merciless language of defeat; as merciless as the bulletins had been, when they spoke of *enemy* defeats. The fact that such a thing could happen to 'us', not as an isolated incident, but as the final result of victory upon victory, just would not fit in my head.

I read the terms again and again, craning my neck, as I had done for the last four years. At length I withdrew from the crowd and wandered off, not knowing where. My search for news had brought me into a neighbourhood that was almost unknown to me, and soon I found myself in one even less familiar. I drifted through streets I had never seen before. The thin November rain was still falling.

Like these streets, the whole world had become strange and unsettling. Apart from the fascinating rules I knew, the great game had clearly had other secret rules that I had failed to grasp. There must have been something deceitful and false about it. Where could one find stability and security, faith and confidence, if world events could be so deceptive? If triumph upon triumph led to ultimate disaster, and the true rules of history were only revealed retrospectively in a shattering outcome? I stared into the abyss. I felt a horror for life.

I do not think the German defeat could have come as a greater shock to anyone than to the eleven-year-old boy wandering through those unfamiliar, wet November streets, not seeing where he went, or feeling the drizzle gradually drenching him. I certainly do not think it was a greater shock to Corporal Hitler, who at about the same time could not bear to listen to the announcement of the defeat at the military hospital in Pasewalk. He reacted far more dramatically than I. 'It became impossible for me', he writes, 'to stay on and listen. While all went black again about my eyes, I groped and tumbled my way back to the dormitory, flung myself on my bed, and buried my burning head in the sheets and pillows.' Whereupon he decided to become a politician.

His gesture was far more childish and self-willed than mine, and not only on the surface. When I compare the deeper conclusions that Hitler and I drew from the same painful experience – the one fury, defiance and the resolve to become a politician, the other doubt as to the validity of the rules of the game, and a horrified foreboding of the unpredictability of life – then I cannot help thinking that the reaction of the eleven-year-old child was more mature than that of the twenty-nine-year-old adult.

Undoubtedly, at that moment it was written in the stars that I could never be on friendly terms with Hitler's Reich.

Six

For the moment, however, I did not have to deal with Hitler's Reich, but with the revolution of 1918, and the German Republic.

The effect of the revolution on me and my contemporaries was exactly the reverse of that of the war. The war had left our actual everyday lives unaltered, often to the point of boredom, while it supplied an inexhaustible fund of raw material for our imaginations. The revolution brought many changes to our daily lives, and the novelty was vivid and exciting enough – I shall soon be going into that – yet it failed to engage our imaginations. Unlike the war, it did not provide a simple, plausible narrative to explain events. Its crises, strikes, gunfights, coups and demonstrations remained contradictory and confusing. It never became clear what was going on. We felt no enthusiasm for it. We did not even understand it.

The revolution of 1918 was not planned or premeditated. It was a by-product of the military collapse. Feeling betrayed by their military and political leaders, the people themselves – there was virtually no leadership – chased them away. Rather, they shooed them away. At the first threatening, alarming gesture all those in authority, from the Kaiser downwards, disappeared without a squeak and without a trace; just as the leaders of the Republic disappeared in 1932–3. German politicians, from the Right to the Left, have no skill in the art of losing.

Power lay in the streets. Among those who seized it there were very few true revolutionaries; and even they seem in retrospect to have had no clear conception of what they wanted and how they were going to get it. It was not just bad luck, but a sign of lack of talent, that they were almost all disposed of within six months.

Most of the new leaders were embarrassed, respectable men, grown old and comfortable in the habit of loyal opposition, quite overcome to find power suddenly thrust into their hands and anxious to be rid of it as soon as decently possible. Among them there were a number of saboteurs who were resolved to 'tame' the revolution, that is to say, betray it. The most notorious of these was the monstrous Noske.*

The game was soon under way. While the real revolution-aries attempted a number of badly organised and amateurish coups, the saboteurs organised the counter-revolution, with the help of the Free Corps who, in the guise of government troops, proceeded to mop up the revolution with bloody thoroughness.

With the best will in the world one could find nothing inspiring in the spectacle. As middle-class boys, who moreover had only just been roughly jolted out of a four-year-long patriotic intoxication with war, we were naturally against the Red revolutionaries; against Karl Liebknecht, Rosa Luxemburg and their Spartacus League.† Although we only vaguely knew that they would 'rob us of everything', probably liquidate those of our parents who were well-off, and altogether make life frightful and 'Russian', we had thus to be in favour of Ebert‡ and Noske and their Free Corps. But, alas, it was impossible to work up any enthusiasm for these figures. The spectacle they offered was too obviously repellent, the stench of treachery that clung to them was too pervasive; it was plain even to the nose of an eleven-year-old boy. (I reiterate that we should take note of

* Gustav Noske, a leading Social Democrat, was responsible for organising the Free Corps to fight against the revolution in 1918–19. He was Minister of Defence at the time of the Kapp Putsch in 1920.
† The Spartacus League was a left-wing faction of the socialists, which later became the German Communist Party. Its leaders, Karl Liebknecht and Rosa Luxemburg, were murdered while under arrest in January 1919.
‡ Friedrich Ebert had been the leader of the mainstream Social Democrats since before the First World War. He became Chancellor in November 1918 and was the first President of the Weimar Republic until his death in 1925.

the political reactions of children. What 'every child knows' is generally the last irrefutable quintessence of a political development.) There was something loathsome about the way the brutal, martial Free Corps – whom we would perhaps have liked to restore the Kaiser and Hindenburg* – fought so emphatically for 'the Government'; that is, for Ebert and Noske, people who had obviously betrayed their own cause and who, incidentally, even looked like traitors.

What is more, as events impinged on us more closely, they became much more obscure and less intelligible than before, when they had taken place in distant France and had been placed in their proper perspective by the daily army bulletin. At times one heard shots fired every day, but one rarely found out why.

Some days there was no electricity, on others no trams, but it was never clear whether it was because of the Spartacists or the Government that we had to use oil lamps or go on foot. Leaflets were thrust into one's hands or one saw posters proclaiming 'The Hour of Reckoning is Near'. But to find out whether expressions like 'traitors', 'murderers of the workers' or 'unscrupulous demagogues' meant Ebert and Scheidemann† or Liebknecht and Eichhorn‡ one had to wade through paragraphs of vituperation and tangled denunciations. Demonstrations were a daily event. A slogan would be shouted by one of the demonstrators, and the rest would yell 'Hoch' ('Up') or 'Nieder' ('Down') as the case may be. From afar one could only hear the chorus of 'Hoch' or 'Nieder'; the solo voice that had provided the cue was inaudible, so one did not know what it was about.

---

* Paul von Hindenburg was born in 1847. In the first year of the First World War he returned from retirement to lead the German army in the East and later became Commander-in-Chief. After the war he came to symbolise the aristocratic pre-war world and was elected President after the death of Ebert in 1925. He remained in office until he died in 1934.
† Philip Scheidemann was deputy leader of the Social Democrats. He proclaimed the German Republic on 9 November 1918.
‡ Emil Eichhorn was a member of the USPD (a party to the left of the Social Democrats and to the right of the Spartacus League), and Berlin Police President during the revolution.

This went on, at intervals, for six months. Then it began to die down. By then it had long lost all meaning. For the fate of the revolution had been sealed – though naturally I did not know this at the time – when on the 24th of December 1918, after a victorious street battle in front of the Palace, the workers and sailors dispersed and went home to celebrate Christmas. After the holidays, they were on the warpath again, but in the meantime the Government had amassed their Free Corps in sufficient numbers. For two weeks there were no newspapers in Berlin, only gunfights near and far – and rumours. Then the newspapers appeared again. The Government had won. Next day came the news that Karl Liebknecht and Rosa Luxemburg had been shot, both 'while attempting to escape'. As far as I know, that was the origin of 'shooting while attempting to escape', which has since become the conventional manner of dealing with political opponents east of the Rhine. At that time people were so unused to it that the words were taken literally and believed. Civilised times indeed!

After that the revolution was doomed, but there was no respite. On the contrary, the fiercest street battles did not take place in Berlin till March 1919 (and April in Munich), when it was only a matter of, so to speak, burying the corpse of the revolution. In Berlin they broke out when Noske disbanded the 'People's Naval Division', the original regiment of the revolution, formally and without ceremony. They refused to be disbanded and put up resistance, joined by the workers from the north-east of Berlin. For a week, the 'misguided masses', who could not understand how their own government could lead their enemies against them, engaged in a desperate, hopeless and bitter struggle. The outcome was certain from the start and the vengeance of the victors was frightful. It is interesting to note that, even then, in the spring of 1919, when the revolution of the Left tried in vain to establish itself, the Nazi revolution was already fully formed and potent. It only lacked Hitler. The Free Corps, who had rescued Noske and Ebert, resembled the later Nazi storm troops which most of them later joined. They certainly had the same outlook, behaviour and fighting methods. They had already invented the device of 'shooting while attempting to escape', and had made significant advances in the science of torture. They also anticipated the events of the 30th of June 1934,* with their bold habit of lining less important opponents up against a wall, without many questions or distinctions. All that was lacking was the theory to justify the practice. That would be provided by Hitler.

* On 30 June 1934, 'the Night of the Long Knives', Hitler, having summoned the leaders of the SA to a meeting in Bavaria, had them arrested and executed. On the same day many nationalist conservative leaders, among them the ex-chancellor Kurt von Schleicher, were also rounded up and killed. Ernst Röhm was shot the following day.

Seven

When I think about it, I have to say that by 1919 even the Hitler Youth had almost been formed. For example, in our school class we had started a club called the Rennbund Altpreussen (Old Prussia Athletics Club), and took as its motto 'Anti-Spartacus, for Sport and Politics'. The politics consisted in occasionally beating up a few unfortunates, who were in favour of the revolution, on the way to school. Sports were the main occupation. We organised athletic championships in the school grounds or public stadia. These gave us the pleasurable sensation of being decidedly anti-Spartacist. We felt very important and patriotic, and ran races for the fatherland. What was that, if not an embryonic Hitler Youth? In truth, certain characteristics later added by Hitler's personal idiosyncrasies were lacking, anti-Semitism for one. Our Jewish schoolmates ran with the same anti-Spartacist and patriotic zeal as everyone else. Indeed, our best runner was Jewish. I can testify that they did nothing to undermine national unity.

During the fighting in March 1919, the Rennbund's activities were temporarily interrupted while our sports grounds were used as battlefields. Our neighbourhood became the main area of street fighting. Our school was the headquarters of the government troops, and the adjacent primary school was used as a base by the 'Reds'. The German name for primary school is *Volksschule*, people's school. How apt! For days the battle raged for possession of these two buildings. Our headmaster, who had remained in his school quarters, was shot dead. When we saw it again, the façade of the building was pockmarked with bullet holes. A large bloodstain that could not be removed, remained under my desk for many weeks. We had unscheduled holidays for weeks on end, and experienced our baptism of fire. Whenever we could, we stole away and headed for the fighting in order 'to see something'.

There was not much to be seen. Even the street fighting demonstrated 'the emptiness of the modern battlefield'. There was all the more to be heard. We were soon quite hardened to the sound of ordinary machine-guns, light artillery and even trench fire and only got excited by mortars or heavy artillery.

It became a sport to enter blockaded streets. We would steal through houses, yards and basements and suddenly appear behind the blockading troops, well beyond the notices saying 'Halt! Anyone found beyond this point will be shot.' We were not shot.

The barricades did not always function very well. Normal civilian life often mingled grotesquely with military operations. I remember a particular beautiful Sunday, one of the first warm Sundays of the year, with crowds of people strolling down a broad tree-lined street. It was utterly peaceful, not a shot to be heard anywhere. Suddenly the people dived left and right into the doorways of the houses. Armoured cars came rattling by. We heard ear-splitting detonations frighteningly close by. Machine-guns sprang to life. All hell was let loose for five minutes. Then the armoured cars rattled off and disappeared. The machine-guns subsided. We boys were the first to emerge. We saw a strange sight. The long avenue was deserted, but piled in front of each house were heaps of broken glass of varying sizes: all the windows had been blown out by the explosions. Then, as nothing more seemed to be happening, the strollers timidly reappeared. A few minutes later the street was again bathed in the atmosphere of a spring Sunday, as though nothing had happened.

It was all eerily unreal, and the details remained unexplained. I never found out, for instance, what this gunfight had actually been about. The newspapers did not mention it. They did reveal, however, that on this very Sunday, while we were strolling under the blue spring sky, a few kilometres away, in the suburb of Lichtenberg, several hundred (perhaps several thousand – the figure fluctuated)* captured workers had been rounded up and 'disposed of' in batches by firing squads. That frightened us. It was so much closer and more real than anything that had happened far away in France.

However, nothing followed after the massacre. None of us knew any of the dead. The newspapers ran other news the next day. So the fright soon passed. The year advanced, spring merged into a beautiful summer. School began again, and the Rennbund Altpreussen resumed its beneficent, patriotic activities.

---

* Noske estimated the number of workers killed by his Free Corps in Lichtenberg between 11 and 13 March 1919 at 1,200. Other sources give slightly lower estimates.

Eight

Oddly enough, the Republic held up. Oddly – seeing that, from the spring of 1919 at the latest, its defence was placed exclusively in the hands of its enemies. All the militant revolutionary organisations had been destroyed, their leaders killed, their rank and file decimated. Only the Free Corps carried arms – the Free Corps, who were already good Nazis in all but name. Why did they not overthrow their weak masters and set up the Third Reich there and then? It would hardly have been difficult.

What stopped them? Why did they disappoint the hopes of so many, not only us members of the Rennbund Altpreussen? Probably for the same highly irrational reason that later led the army to disappoint the many who, during the first years of the Third Reich, thought it would soon put an end to Hitler's monstrous corruption of its ideals and aspirations. It was because the German military lacked the moral courage to make its own decisions and take responsibility for them.

As Bismarck once remarked in a famous speech, moral courage is, in any case, a rare virtue in Germany, but it deserts a German completely the moment he puts on a uniform. As soldier and officer, he is indisputably and outstandingly courageous on the field of battle. He is usually even prepared to open fire on his own compatriots if ordered to do so. Yet he is as timid as a lamb at the thought of opposing authority. The suggestion of such a confrontation always conjures up the nightmare of a firing squad and he is immediately paralysed. It is not death he fears, but this particular death, which scares him out of his wits. That makes any idea of insubordination or a *coup d'état* altogether impossible for the German military – whoever happens to be in power.

The only apparent counter-example actually corroborates my assertion. It is the Kapp Putsch of March 1920, an attempted *coup d'état* by anti-republican political outsiders. Though they had the wholehearted support of half the republican army leadership, and the sympathy of the rest; though the Government immediately revealed its weakness, and offered no resistance; though men with the military magnetism of Ludendorff belonged to its party, only a single body of soldiers, the so-called Ehrhardt Brigade, finally joined the undertaking. All the other Free Corps remained 'loyal to the Government' – but they afterwards saw to it that this attempted putsch of the Right ended with reprisals against the Left.

It is a dismal story, quickly told. One Saturday morning, the Ehrhardt Brigade marched through the Brandenburg Gate. The Government fled and sought safety, having quickly proclaimed a general strike and called out the workers.

Kapp, the leader of the putsch, announced the National Republic under the black, white and red flag of the old Reich. The workers went on strike. The army remained 'loyal to the Government'. The new administration never got started, and five days later Kapp abdicated.

The Government returned and ordered the workers back to work. Now they demanded their reward. At least some of the most obviously compromised ministers should be dismissed, first and foremost the notorious Noske. Thereupon the Government marched its loyal troops against the workers. These once more carried out their bold and bloody deeds, particularly in western Germany where veritable battles were fought.

Many years later, I heard a former member of the Free Corps, who had been there, talk about it. He spoke, not without a certain good-natured sympathy, of the victims who had fallen or been 'shot while attempting to escape' in their hundreds. 'That was the cream of the working-class youth,' he observed thoughtfully and sadly. This was simply how his mind had filed away these memories. 'Brave lads, some of them,' he declared, continuing, 'Not like 1919 in Munich. Those were ne'er-do-wells, loafers and Jews. I didn't have a spark of sympathy for them. But 1920, in the Ruhr, that was really the cream of the working-class youth. I felt really sorry for many of them. But they were so pig-headed. They left us no choice but to shoot them. When we wanted to give them a chance, and during the interrogation kept asking them, "So you've only been led astray, haven't you?" they would yell, "No!" and "Down with the murderers of the working class and the traitors to the people!" Well, there was nothing for it but to shoot them, a dozen at a time. In the evening our colonel said he had never felt so sad at heart in all his life. Yes, that was the cream of the working-class youth that fell there in the Ruhr in 1920.'*

Of course, I knew nothing of this at the time. The Ruhr was far away. In Berlin, life was less dramatic. There was not much bloodshed or barbarity. After the savage affrays of 1919, this March of 1920 seemed eerily quiet. It was uncanny because nothing happened. Everything just came to a complete halt. A peculiar revolution.

This is how I experienced it. It started one Saturday. At midday at the grocer's, people were saying that now 'the Kaiser would come back'. In the afternoon there were no lessons at school – we often used to have school only during the afternoons. Half the school building had been closed on account of the coal shortage and two schools shared the same building, one in the morning, the other in the afternoon. In the playground we played 'Nationalists and Reds' in the fine weather, though this was difficult because no one wanted to be a Red. It was all quite satisfactory, just a little unbelievable. It had happened so suddenly, and no one knew any details.

---

* The Kapp Putsch, an attempt to institute a military dictatorship, took place on Saturday 13 March, 1920. It was answered by a general strike throughout Germany on Monday 15 March. In the Ruhr it turned into an armed revolt. After Kapp resigned at the end of the week, the reinstated Government used the very troops who had supported him to put down the revolt. The exact number of dead never came out.

These were not forthcoming, for by that evening there were no newspapers and, as we soon discovered, no electricity. Next morning, for the first time, there was no water. The post did not arrive. There was no public transport. The shops were closed. There was, in a word, nothing.

At certain street corners in our neighbourhood there were some old wells, independent of the waterworks. They now came into their own. People queued up in hundreds, carrying cans and jugs to fetch their ration of water. A couple of strong young men operated the hand pump. On the way back, the full jugs were carefully balanced to avoid spilling a drop of the precious liquid.

Otherwise, as I said, nothing happened. Indeed, in a way, less than nothing. Even the usual everyday occurrences ceased. There were no shots, no demonstrations and processions, no mob gatherings and no street debates. Nothing.

On Monday there was no school. An air of satisfaction still prevailed there, mingled with a slight anxiety because things seemed to be proceeding oddly. Our sports teacher, who was a great nationalist (all our masters were nationalists, but none more than he), declared several times with conviction, 'You can tell at once there's another hand at the helm.' In truth one could tell no such thing. He spoke that way to console himself for the absence of anything observable.

From school we went off to Unter den Linden, the broad avenue in central Berlin. We felt darkly that one ought to be in Unter den Linden on such momentous days in the fatherland's history, and we also hoped we might see or find out something. There was nothing to see or find out. Here and there a few bored soldiers stood behind superfluously posted machine-guns. No one came to attack them. It felt strangely like a Sunday, quiet and peaceful. That was the effect of the general strike.

The following days were merely boring. Queuing for water at the wells, which had at first had the charm of novelty, soon became as great a nuisance as did the refusal of the WC to function, the lack of news of any kind and even of letters, the difficulty of procuring food, the total blackout every night, and the fact that every day seemed like Sunday. Besides, there was nothing to arouse our nationalist enthusiasm, no parades, no appeals 'To my people'. Nothing. If only there had been the wireless then! Just once there were posters on the walls: 'The outside world will not intervene.' So there was not even going to be that!

Then suddenly one day we learned that Kapp had stood down. There were no more particulars to be had, but as we heard occasional shots next day, we realised that the good old Government was back. Soon the water pipes began to wheeze and gurgle. A little later school reopened. The atmosphere there was somewhat dampened. Then even the newspapers reappeared.

After the Kapp Putsch, interest in politics flagged among us boys. All parties had been compromised and the entire topic lost its attraction. The Rennbund Altpreussen was dissolved. Many of us sought new interests: stamp-collecting, for example, piano-playing, or the theatre. Only a few remained true to politics, and it struck me for the first time that, strangely enough, those were the more stupid, coarse and unpleasant among my schoolfellows. They proceeded to enter the 'right sort' of leagues: the German National Youth Association or the Bismarck League (there was still no Hitler Youth), and soon they showed off knuckledusters, truncheons and even coshes in school. They boasted of dangerous nocturnal poster-pasting or poster-removing expeditions and began to speak a certain jargon which distinguished them from the rest of us. They also began to behave in an unfriendly way towards the Jewish boys.

About this time, not long after the Kapp Putsch, I saw one of them scribble a strange design in his notebook during a tedious lesson. Again and again the same pattern was repeated. A few strokes combined in an unexpected, pleasing way to form a symmetrical, box-like ornament. I was immediately tempted to copy him. 'What is that?' I asked in a whisper as it was during a lesson, boring though that was. 'Anti-Semitic sign,' he whispered back in telegraphic staccato. 'The Ehrhardt Brigade wore it on their helmets. Means "Out with the Jews". You ought to know it.' And he went on scribbling.

It was my first acquaintance with the swastika. It was the only legacy of the Kapp Putsch. One saw it quite frequently in the following months.

Nine

*I*t was another two years before politics became interesting
again, and that was due to the appearance of one man –
Walther Rathenau.

Never before or afterwards did the German Republic produce
a politician who so deeply stirred the imagination of young
people and the masses. Gustav Stresemann and Heinrich Brüning, who enjoyed longer periods of power and whose policies
could be said to have moulded two brief periods of history, never
radiated the same personal charisma. Hitler alone can be
compared to Rathenau, and that also with a reservation: so much
publicly has been deliberately focused on him that it is impossible
to distinguish the genuine appeal of the man from the fabrication.

Political stardom was unknown in Rathenau's day, and he
never did anything to attract the limelight. He is the most
striking example I have experienced of the mysterious developments that mark a 'great' man's appearance in public life:
the immediate contact with the masses across all barriers; the
general sense of something in the air; the excitement, and
the way even boring events become interesting; the impression
that there is 'no getting away from the man'; the inevitable
passionate partisanship; the sudden growth of legends and a
personality cult; love and hate; all this involuntarily and
unavoidably, almost subconsciously. It is like the effect of a
magnet on a heap of iron filings – just as irrational, just as
inevitable, just as inexplicable.

Rathenau* became minister of reconstruction, then foreign

* Walter Rathenau, one of the most successful industrialists before the First

minister – and immediately one sensed that politics were on the move again. When he attended an international conference, one felt for the first time that Germany was being properly represented. He concluded an agreement for reparation deliveries in kind with Loucheur, and a treaty of friendship with Russia with Chicherin.

Though scarcely anyone had previously had any idea what 'deliveries in kind' meant, and the text of the Treaty of Rapallo, with its formal, diplomatic phraseology, conveyed nothing to the non-expert, both achievements were animatedly discussed at the grocer's and the baker's, and at the newspaper kiosks; while we of the fifth form exchanged blows because some called the treaties 'a work of genius', while the others spoke of a 'Jewish betrayal of the nation'.

It was not just politics. Rathenau's face appeared in the illustrated papers, like that of all the other politicians. The others were soon forgotten, but his face seemed to look straight at you and was difficult to forget, with its dark eyes full of intelligence and sadness. One read his speeches and behind the words one heard an unmistakable tone of reproach, challenge, and promise: the tone of a prophet. Many sought his books (I, for one). In them, one again sensed that dark emotional appeal, something both compelling and persuasive, challenging and seductive. This mixture was their greatest charm. They were at once restrained and fantastic, sobering and stirring, sceptical and enthusiastic. They spoke the bravest words in the most hesitant and gentle voice.

Strange to say, Rathenau has not yet found the great biography he deserves. He belongs, without doubt, to the five or six great personalities of this century. He was an aristocratic

World War, was made responsible for organising the supply of raw materials in 1914 and his brilliant planning ensured that Germany suffered no shortages of war materials throughout the war. In 1921, as minister of reconstruction, he negotiated a treaty for payment of reparations in kind. In 1922, as foreign minister, he concluded the Treaty of Rapallo with Russia. He was assassinated on 24 June 1922.

revolutionary, an idealistic economic planner, a Jew who was a German patriot, a German patriot who was a liberal citizen of the world, and a citizen of the world who was a believer in a coming Messiah and a strict observer of the Law (that is, a Jew in the only true sense of the word). He was cultured enough to be above culture, rich enough to be above riches, man of the world enough to be above the world. One felt that if he had not been the German foreign minister in 1922, he might equally well have been a German philosopher in 1800, an international monarch of finance in 1850, a great rabbi or an anchorite. He combined within himself qualities that in another person would have been dangerously incompatible. In him, the synthesis of a whole sheaf of cultures and philosophies became – not thought, not deed – but a person.

Can such a man, you ask, be a leader of the masses? Surprisingly, the answer is Yes. The masses – by which I mean not the proletariat, but the anonymous collective body into which all of us, high and low, amalgamate at certain moments – react most strongly to someone who least resembles them. Normality coupled with talent may make a politician popular. But to provoke extremes of love and hate, to be worshipped like a god or loathed like the devil, is given only to a truly exceptional person who is poles apart from the masses, be it far above or far below them. If my experience of Germany has taught me anything, it is this. Rathenau and Hitler are the two men who excited the imagination of the German masses to the utmost; the one by his ineffable culture, the other by his ineffable vileness. Both, and this is decisive, came from inaccessible regions, from some sort of 'beyond'. The one from a sphere of sublime spirituality where the cultures of three millennia and two continents hold a symposium; the other from a jungle far below the depths plumbed by the basest penny dreadfuls, from an underworld where demons rise from a brewed-up stench of petty-bourgeois back rooms, doss-houses, barrack latrines and the hangman's yard. From their different 'beyonds' they both drew a spell-binding power, quite irrespective of their politics.

It is difficult to say where Rathenau's policy would have led Germany and Europe if he had been granted time to carry it out. He was not. He was murdered after just six months in office.

I have mentioned that he provoked love or hate. Both were genuine. The hate was savage, irrational, elemental and brooked no discussion. Only one other German politician has since aroused such feeling: Hitler.

The Rathenau-haters differed from the Hitler-haters as widely as the one leader differed from the other. 'The swine should be bumped off!' was the language of Rathenau's opponents. Nevertheless, it came as a surprise when one day the lunch-time editions carried the blunt, stark headline: 'Foreign minister Rathenau murdered'. One felt the ground shift under one's feet, and the feeling intensified when one read of the simplicity and straightforwardness with which the crime had been committed.

Every morning, at a fixed hour, Rathenau drove in an open car from his house in Grunewald to the Wilhelmstrasse. One morning another car stood waiting in the quiet street lined with villas. It followed the minister's car and overtook it. At that moment, its three occupants simultaneously fired their revolvers point-blank at their victim's head and chest. Then they sped off at full throttle (today a monument marks the spot and celebrates their deed).

How surprisingly easy! It happened here, in Berlin's Grunewald, not in Caracas or Montevideo, in a suburban street like any other. One could go and look at the spot. The perpetrators, as we soon learned, were young fellows like ourselves, one of them an upper-fifth-form boy. Could it not just as easily have been one of my school-mates who only the other day had declared that Rathenau should be 'bumped off'? Aside from the indignation, the fury and the grief, there was something almost laughable about this impudent coup that had been pulled off. It was so simple, too simple for anyone to have anticipated: it was a truly uncanny way of making history. Obviously the future belonged not to the Rathenaus who took infinite pains to become exceptional personages, but to the Techows and Fischers who learned to drive a car and shoot a pistol.

For the moment this uneasy feeling was washed away by an overwhelming flood of wrath and mourning. Even the massacre of the thousand workers in Lichtenberg in 1919 had not inflamed the masses as much as the murder of this one man, capitalist though he was. The wizardry of his personality survived his death. For some days there prevailed what I have never since experienced – a genuine atmosphere of revolution. Without threat or compulsion, people attended his funeral in hundreds of thousands. Afterwards they did not disperse, but paraded for hours through the streets, in endless processions, silent, wrathful and challenging. One felt that if they had been invited to finish off those who still passed for 'reactionaries' but were in fact Nazis, they would have done the job with swift and energetic thoroughness.

The invitation was not forthcoming. Instead, they were told to maintain discipline and order. For weeks, the Government deliberated about a 'Bill for the Defence of the Republic', which imposed light sentences of imprisonment on those who insulted ministers, and soon incurred general ridicule. A few months later the Government sadly and silently collapsed, and was replaced by a ministry of the Right.

What the short-lived Rathenau epoch left behind was the confirmation of the lesson already learned in the years 1918 and 1919: nothing the Left did ever came off.

Ten

*T*hen came 1923. That extraordinary year is probably what has marked today's Germans with those characteristics that are so strange and incomprehensible in the eyes of the world, and so different from what used to be thought of as the German character: the uncurbed, cynical imagination, the nihilistic pleasure in the impossible for its own sake, and the energy that has become an end in itself. In that year an entire generation of Germans had a spiritual organ removed: the organ which gives men steadfastness and balance, but also a certain inertia and stolidity. It may variously appear as conscience, reason, experience, respect for the law, morality, or the fear of God. A whole generation learned then – or thought it learned – to do without such ballast. The preceding years served as a novitiate in nihilism, but in 1923 its high priests were ordained.

No other nation has experienced anything comparable to the events of 1923 in Germany. All nations went through the Great War, and most of them have also experienced revolutions, social crises, strikes, redistribution of wealth and currency devaluation. None but Germany has undergone the fantastic, grotesque extreme of all these together; none has experienced the gigantic, carnival dance of death, the unending, bloody Saturnalia, in which not only money but all standards lost their value. The year 1923 prepared Germany, not specifically for Nazism, but for any fantastic adventure. The psychological and political roots of Nazism reach further back, as we have seen, but that year gave birth to its lunatic aspects: the cool madness, the arrogant, unscrupulous, blind resolve to achieve the impossible, the principle that 'Might is right' and ' "Impossible" is not in our vocabulary'. Nations, it seems, cannot go through such experiences without spiritual damage. I shudder to think that after the next war the whole of Europe will probably experience a magnified 1923 – that is, unless very wise men make the peace.

The year began with an atmosphere of patriotic fervour. It was almost a repeat of 1914. The French under Poincaré occupied the Ruhr, the Government announced passive resistance, and among the German masses the feeling of national humiliation and danger (probably more genuine and more serious than in 1914) once more overcame their weariness and disappointment. They 'rose up', and with strenuous emotion declared their readiness – but for what? For sacrifice? For struggle? It was not clear. Nothing was demanded of them. The 'Ruhr war' was not a war. No one was called up. There were no bulletins. With no outlet, the fury subsided, but for days crowds solemnly intoned the Rütli oath from *Wilhelm Tell*:* 'We shall be a united nation of brothers.'

Gradually the gesture became slightly ridiculous and absurd because it was being made in such a void. Outside the Ruhr, nothing at all happened. In the Ruhr itself, there was a sort of subsidised strike. Not only were the workers paid, but also the manufacturers – and these only too well, as soon became widely known. Was this patriotism – or compensation for lost profit? Some months later, the Ruhr war, which had begun so well with the Rütli oath, began to smell unmistakably of corruption. Soon the public lost all interest. Far stranger things were happening nearer home.

That year newspaper readers could again play a variation of the exciting numbers game they had enjoyed during the war, when counts of prisoners and size of booty had dominated the headlines. This time the figures did not refer to military events, in spite of the warlike way the year had begun, but to an otherwise quite uninteresting, everyday item in the financial pages: the exchange rate of the dollar. The fluctuation of the

* A play by Friedrich Schiller about the founding of Switzerland by William Tell.

dollar was the barometer by which, with a mixture of anxiety and excitement, we measured the fall of the mark. The higher the dollar went, the more extravagant became our flights into the realms of fancy.

There was nothing really new in the devaluation of the mark. Even in 1920, the first cigarette I had secretly smoked had already cost fifty pfennigs. By the end of 1922, prices had gradually risen to between ten and a hundred times the pre-war peacetime level, and the dollar stood at about five hundred marks. This, however, had happened gradually. Wages, salaries, and prices in general had risen at the same pace. It was a bit inconvenient to work with the large numbers, but not overly difficult. Many people still spoke of it as a 'rise in prices'. There were more exciting things to think about.

But the mark now went on the rampage. Soon after the beginning of the Ruhr war, the dollar shot to 20,000 marks, rested there for a time, jumped to 40,000, paused again and then, with small periodic fluctuations, coursed through the ten thousands and then the hundred thousands. No one quite knew how it happened. Rubbing our eyes, we followed its progress like some astonishing natural phenomenon. It became the topic of the day. Then suddenly, looking around, we discovered that this phenomenon had devastated the fabric of our daily lives.

Anyone who had savings in a bank, bonds or gilts, saw their value disappear overnight. Soon it did not matter whether it was a penny put away for a rainy day or a vast fortune. Everything was obliterated. Many people quickly moved their investments only to find that it made no difference. Very soon it became clear that something had happened that forced everyone to forget about their savings and attend to a far more urgent matter.

The cost of living had begun to spiral out of control. Traders followed hard on the heels of the dollar. A pound of potatoes which yesterday had cost fifty thousand marks now cost a hundred thousand. The salary of sixty-five thousand marks brought home the previous Friday was no longer sufficient to buy a packet of cigarettes on Tuesday.

What was to be done? Casting around, people found a life-raft: shares. They were the only form of investment which kept pace – not all the time, and not all shares, yet on the whole they managed to keep up. So everyone dealt in shares. Every minor official, every employee, every shift-worker became a share-holder. Day-to-day purchases were paid for by selling shares. On wage days there was a general stampede to the banks, and share prices shot up like rockets. The banks were bloated with wealth. Obscure new ones sprouted up like mushrooms and did a roaring trade. Every day the entire population studied the stock-market listings. Sometimes some shares collapsed and thousands of people hurtled towards the abyss. In every shop, every factory, every school, share tips were whispered in one's ear.

The old and unworldly had the worst of it. Many were driven to begging, many to suicide. The young and quick-witted did well. Overnight they became free, rich and independent. It was a situation in which mental inertia and reliance on past experience was punished by starvation and death, but rapid appraisal of new situations and speed of reaction was rewarded with sudden, vast riches. The twenty-one-year-old bank direc-tor appeared on the scene, and also the sixth-former who earned his living from the stock-market tips of his slightly older friends. He wore Oscar Wilde ties, organised champagne parties, and supported his embarrassed father.

Amid all the misery, despair and poverty there was an air of light-headed youthfulness, licentiousness and a carnival atmos-phere. Now, for once, the young had money and the old did not. Moreover, its nature had changed. Its value lasted only a few hours. It was spent as never before or since; and not on the things old people spend their money on.

Bars and nightclubs opened in large numbers. Young couples whirled about the streets of the amusement quarters. It was like a Hollywood movie. Everyone was hectically, feverishly search-ing for love and seizing it without a second thought. Indeed, even love had assumed an inflationary character.

Unromantic love was the fashion: carefree, restless, light-hearted promiscuity. Typically, love affairs followed an extremely rapid course, without detours. The young who learned to love in those years eschewed romance and embraced cynicism. I myself and those of my age were not among them. At fifteen or sixteen we were a few years too young. In later years when we had to entertain our girlfriends with twenty-odd marks' pocket-money, we often secretly envied the older boys who had had their chance at this time. We only caught a glimpse through the keyhole, just enough to preserve a whiff of the perfume of the time for ever in our nostrils. To us, it was thrilling to be taken by chance to a wild party; to experience a precocious, exhausting abandon and a slight hangover next day from too many cocktails; to listen to the older boys with their worn faces showing the traces of their dissolute nights; to experience the sudden transporting kiss of a girl in daring make-up . . .

There was another side to the picture. There were beggars everywhere and many reports of suicides in the papers. The poster columns were full of police 'Wanted' notices for burglars. Robbery and burglary occurred on a grand scale. Once I saw an old woman – perhaps I should say an old lady – seated on a bench in a park looking strangely blank and stiff. A little crowd gathered round her. 'Dead,' said someone. 'Of starvation,' said another. It did not surprise me particularly. At home, we also often went hungry.

Indeed, my father was one of those who did not, or did not wish to, understand the times, just as he had already refused to understand the war. He entrenched himself behind the maxim: 'A Prussian official does not speculate', and bought no shares. At the time I regarded that as extraordinarily narrow-minded and out of character, for he was one of the cleverest men I have known. Today I understand him better. In retrospect, I can sympathise with the disgust with which he rejected the 'monstrous scandal' and with the impatient contempt that lay behind the attitude that 'what ought not to be, cannot be'. Alas, the practical result of such high-mindedness could degenerate into farce, and the farce would have turned to tragedy if it had not been for my mother, who adapted to the situation in her own way.

This is how the family of a high Prussian official lived from day to day. On the 31st or 1st of the month my father would receive his monthly salary, on which we depended for our survival. Bank balances and securities had long since become worthless. What the salary was worth was difficult to estimate; its value changed from month to month. One month a hundred million marks could be quite a substantial sum; a little while later five hundred milliards would be small change.* In any case my father would first try to purchase a monthly pass for the underground as quickly as possible. That would at least enable him to get to his office and back, even though the underground involved considerable detours and waste of time. Then cheques would be written out for the rent and school fees, and in the afternoon the whole family went to the hairdresser's. What was left was handed to my mother. Next day the entire family except for my father, but including the maid, would get up at four or five in the morning and go to the wholesale market by taxi. There, in a giant shopping spree, an *Oberregierungsrat's*† monthly salary would be spent on non-perishable foodstuffs in an hour. Giant cheeses, whole hams, stacks of tinned food and hundredweights of potatoes were piled into our taxi. If there was not enough room, the maid, with one of us to help, would get hold of a hand-cart. At about eight o'clock, before school began, we would return home, more or less provisioned for a month's siege. And that was it. There was no more money for the rest of the month. A friendly baker gave us bread on credit. Otherwise we lived on potatoes, smoked or tinned food and soup cubes. Now and then there might be an unexpected supplementary payment, but it was quite common for us to be as poverty-stricken as the poorest of the poor for four weeks, not even able to afford a tram ride or a newspaper. Putting aside

* This book uses pre-war British number terminology. Milliard = one thousand million; billion = one million million.

† The progression of ranks in the German civil service is: *Referendar*, *Assessor*, *Regierungsrat*, *Oberregierungsrat*.

money for such purposes would have been quite senseless. Within a few days the whole month's salary would not have paid for a single tram ride. I cannot say what would have happened if some misfortune like a serious illness had befallen us.

For my parents it must have been an evil, trying time. For me it was peculiar rather than unpleasant. Privation was balanced by adventure. The fact that my father had to travel to his office by an excessively circuitous route kept him away from the house most of the day and gave me many hours of absolute freedom. I had no pocket-money but my older schoolfriends were literally rich, and one deprived them of nothing by getting oneself invited to their wild parties. I managed to remain indifferent both to the poverty of our home and to the wealth of my friends. I neither regretted the one nor envied the other, but found them both merely strange and remarkable. In fact, in those days only part of me lived in the real world, exciting though it was. More thrilling was the world of books in which I had buried myself and which had captivated the greater part of my being. I read *Buddenbrooks* and *Tonio Kröger*, *Niels Lyhne*, *Malte Laurids Brigge* and the poems of Verlaine, the early Rilke, George and Hofmannsthal, Flaubert's *Novembre*, Wilde's *Dorian Gray* and Heinrich Mann's *Flutes and Daggers*.

I became something like the heroes of these books, a weary, *fin-de-siècle* aesthete in search of beauty, a shabby, rather wild-looking sixteen-year-old who had outgrown his suits and was badly in need of a haircut. I would go through the feverish streets of inflationary Berlin with the manner and feelings of one of Mann's patricians or Wilde's dandies. These fantasies were not seriously impeded by the fact that at five in the morning I might have been packing rounds of cheese and sacks of potatoes into a hand-cart with the maid.

Was this attitude quite unfounded? Was it only the result of reading? Apart from the fact that from autumn to spring young men of sixteen are easily affected by world-weariness, tedium and melancholy, had I and my generation not gone through enough to justify our looking on life with a tired, sceptical, *blasé*, scornful gaze, finding in ourselves something of Thomas Buddenbrook and Tonio Kröger?

We had the great war game behind us and the shock of defeat, the disillusionment of the revolution that had followed, and now the daily spectacle of the failure of all the rules of life and the bankruptcy of age and experience. We had lived through a series of contradictory creeds: pacifism, nationalism and then Marxism. (This last has much in common with sexual infatuation: both are unofficial, slightly illicit; both use shock tactics, both mistake an important, though officially taboo part for the whole, sex in the one case and economics in the other.) Rathenau's murder had taught us that even a great man is merely mortal, the Ruhr war that noble feelings and shady business deals could go hand in hand. Was there anything left to fill us with enthusiasm (for the young need enthusiasm like life's blood)? Only the idea of ageless beauty as it glowed in the poetry of George and Hofmannsthal, or the arrogance of scepticism and, of course, dreams of love.

No girl had yet aroused my passions, but there was a boy with whom I shared my ideals and my taste in books. It was one of those slightly morbid, ethereal, reticently passionate relationships that young boys engage in before girls have fully entered their lives. The capacity for them soon withers. After school, we would wander through the streets for hours, look up the rate of the dollar somewhere or other, agree, with a condescending minimum of thought and words, on the political situation and begin to talk about books. We had agreed to make a thorough analysis of a new book on each walk, and we did. Shyly, anxiously, we felt our way into each other's souls. Meanwhile fever raged around us, society crumbled almost visibly, the German Reich collapsed in ruins – only to provide a background for profound dissertations on, say, the nature of genius and whether it was compatible with moral weakness and decadence.

But what a background! Unimaginable and unforgettable.

In August 1923 the dollar reached a million. We read it with a slight gasp, as if it were the announcement of some spectacular record. A fortnight later, that had become insignificant. For, as if it had drawn new energy at the million mark, the dollar increased its pace ten-fold, and began to mount by a hundred million and milliards at a time. In September, a million marks no longer had any practical value, and a milliard became the unit of payment. At the end of October, it was a billion. By then terrible things had happened. The Reichsbank stopped printing notes. Its notes – 10 million? 100 million? – had not kept up with events. The dollar and price levels in general had anticipated them. There was no longer any usable currency. For some days trade came to a standstill, and in the poorer parts of the city the people resorted to force and plundered the groceries. The atmosphere became revolutionary once again.

In mid-August, the Government fell amid fierce fighting in the streets. A little later, the Ruhr war was abandoned. We gave no more thought to it. How long ago had it been since the Ruhr occupation had made us swear to be a united nation of brothers? Now we began to expect the downfall of the state, even the dissolution of the Reich – some terrible political event corresponding to the events in our private lives. There had never been so many rumours: the Rhineland had seceded; Bavaria had seceded; the Kaiser had come back; the French had marched in. The political 'leagues', both right-wing and left-wing, which had lain dormant for years, suddenly became feverishly active. They held rifle-training sessions in the woods around Berlin; rumours of a 'Black Army' circulated, and a good deal was heard about 'the day of reckoning'.

It was difficult to distinguish the possible from the impossible. A Rhenish republic did in fact come into being for a few days. In Saxony for some weeks there was a Communist government, against which the Reich Government dispatched the army. One morning the newspapers declared that the garrison of Küstrin, a few kilometres away, had begun a 'march on Berlin'.

About this time, too, the phrase 'Traitors will be dealt with summarily' gained currency. The police notices on the poster columns now concerned not just burglaries, but also missing persons and murders. People disappeared in their dozens. Almost always it was people who had something to do with the leagues. Years later, their skeletons might be dug up in some nearby wood. Within the leagues, it had become the practice to dispose of unreliable and suspicious comrades without ceremony.

When we heard rumours of this, it did not seem as incredible as it would have done in normal, civilised days. Indeed, the atmosphere had gradually become apocalyptic. Saviours appeared everywhere, people with long hair and hair shirts, declaring that they had been sent by God to save the world. The most successful in Berlin was a certain Häusser, who used posters and mass meetings and had many followers. His Munich counterpart, according to the press, was a certain Hitler who, however, differed from his Berlin rival by the exciting coarseness of his speeches, which reached new levels of vulgarity in the extravagance of their threats and their unconcealed sadism. While Hitler wanted to bring about the millennium by a massacre of all the Jews, there was a certain Lamberty in Thuringia who wanted to do it by folk dancing, singing and frolicking. Each saviour had a style of his own. No one and nothing was surprising; surprise had become a long-forgotten sensation.

The Munich saviour, Hitler, filled the headlines for two days in November with a ridiculous attempt to stage a revolution in a beer cellar. In fact the revolutionaries had been dispersed by a salvo of police fire as they left the cellar, and that was the end of the matter. Yet for a whole day people seriously thought this was the expected revolution. Our classics master, hearing the news, joyfully informed us that within a few years we would all be soldiers again. His instincts were quite accurate. Indeed, the fact that such an adventure could take place at all was far more interesting than its failure. The saviours obviously had a chance. Nothing was impossible. The dollar stood at a billion. Paradise had just been missed by a hair's breadth.

Then something really unexpected did happen. The incredible fairy story began to circulate that there would soon be stable money again, and a little later, it materialised. Small, ugly, grey-green notes with 'One Rentenmark' written on them. When you offered them in payment for the first time, you waited in suspense to see what would happen. Nothing did. They were actually accepted, and you were handed your goods – goods worth a billion marks. The same thing happened the next day and the day after. Incredible.

The dollar stopped climbing, so did shares. And when one converted them into Rentenmarks, they were reduced to nothing, like everything else. So no one was left with anything. But wages and salaries were paid out in Rentenmarks, and some time later, wonder upon wonder, small change also appeared, solid bright coins. You could jingle them in your pockets and they even kept their value. On Thursday, you could still buy something for the money received on the previous Friday. The world was, after all, full of surprises.

A few weeks earlier, Stresemann had become Chancellor.* Politics became much quieter. No one spoke any more of the decay of the Reich. Grumbling, the leagues returned to their hibernation. Many members deserted. One scarcely heard of any more missing persons. The saviours disappeared from the cities. Politics seemed to consist solely of a dispute among the parties as to who had discovered the Rentenmark. The nationalists said it was Helfferich, a Conservative deputy and former minister of the Kaiser. The Left hotly contradicted this: it was, they claimed, a stalwart democrat and staunch republican, a certain Dr Schacht. This was a time after the Flood. Everything had been lost, but the waters were receding. The older generation did not yet dare to harp upon the value of experience. The young were a bit put out. Twenty-one-year-old bank directors began to look around for clerking jobs again, and sixth-formers had to adjust to having twenty marks' pocket-money. Of course, a few 'victims of stabilisation' committed

---

* Stresemann was Chancellor from 13 August until 2 November 1923 and, thereafter, foreign minister until his death on 3 October 1929. He negotiated the Locarno Treaty and the entry of Germany into the League of Nations.

suicide, but many more people peered timidly out of their holes and asked themselves if life was possible once more.

There was a feeling of 'the morning after' in the air, but also of relief. At Christmas, the whole of Berlin became a vast fair. Everything cost ten pfennigs, and everyone bought rattles, marzipan animals and other such things just to show that one could really buy something for ten pfennigs again, and perhaps also to forget the past year, indeed the past ten years, and feel like a child once more.

All the shops had notices: 'Peacetime prices'. For the first time since the war, it really felt like peace.

Eleven

*S*o it was. The 'Stresemann era' – the only genuine period of peace that my generation in Germany has experienced – had begun: a period of six years, from 1924 to 1929, during which Stresemann directed German policy from the foreign office.

Perhaps one can say the same of policy as of women – the best are the least talked about. If that is right, then Stresemann's policy was outstanding. Politics were hardly discussed during his time. There was still some argument in the first two or three years: clearing up the ravages of inflation, the Dawes Plan, Locarno, Thoiry and the entry into the League of Nations were events that were still talked about, but no more than that. All of a sudden politics ceased to be something worth breaking plates for.

After 1926 or thereabouts there was almost nothing worth discussing any more. The newspapers had to find their headlines in foreign countries.

In Germany all was quiet, all was orderly; events took a tranquil course. There were occasional changes of government. Sometimes the parties of the Right were in power and sometimes those of the Left. It made no great difference. The foreign minister was always Gustav Stresemann. That meant peace, no risk of a crisis and business as usual.

Money came into the country, the currency maintained its value and business was good. The older generation began to retrieve its store of experience from the attic, burnish it bright and show it off, as if it had never been invalidated. The last ten years were forgotten like a bad dream. The Day of Judgement was remote again, and there was no demand for saviours or revolutionaries. The public sector required only competent officials, and the private sector only hard-working businessmen. There was an ample measure of freedom, peace, and order, everywhere the most well-meaning liberal-mindedness, good wages, good food and a little political boredom. Everyone was cordially invited to concentrate on their personal lives, to arrange their affairs according to their own taste and to find their own paths to happiness.

Now something strange happened – and with this I believe I am about to reveal one of the most fundamental political events of our time, something that was not reported in any newspaper: by and large that invitation was declined. It was not what was wanted. A whole generation was, it seemed, at a loss as to how to cope with the offer of an unfettered private life.

A generation of young Germans had become accustomed to having the entire content of their lives delivered gratis, so to speak, by the public sphere, all the raw material for their deeper emotions, for love and hate, joy and sorrow, but also all their sensations and thrills – accompanied though they might be by poverty, hunger, death, chaos and peril. Now that these deliveries suddenly ceased, people were left helpless, impoverished, robbed, and disappointed. They had never learned to live from within themselves, how to make an ordinary private life great, beautiful and worth while, how to enjoy it and make it interesting. So they regarded the end of the political tension and the return of private liberty not as a gift, but as a deprivation. They were bored, their minds strayed to silly thoughts, and they began to sulk. In the end they waited eagerly for the first disturbance, the first setback or incident, so that they could put this period of peace behind them and set out on some new collective adventure.

To be precise (the occasion demands precision, because in my opinion it provides the key to the contemporary period of history): it was not the entire generation of young Germans. Not every single individual reacted in this fashion. There were some who learned during this period, belatedly and a little clumsily, as it were, how to live. They began to enjoy their own lives, weaned themselves from the cheap intoxication of the sports of war and revolution, and started to develop their own personalities. It was at this time that, invisibly and unnoticed, the Germans divided into those who later became Nazis and those who would remain non-Nazis.

I have already remarked in passing that the capacity for individual life and happiness is, in any case, less developed among the Germans than among other peoples. Later, in France and England, I observed with astonishment and envy, but also learned to appreciate, what a wealth of simple joy and what an inexhaustible source of lifelong pleasure the Frenchman finds in eating and drinking, intellectual debate and the artistic pursuit of love; and the Englishman in the cultivation of gardens, the companionship of animals and the sports and hobbies he pursues with such childlike gravity. The average German knows nothing of the sort. Only a certain cultured class – not particularly small, but a minority of course – used to find, and still finds, similar sustenance and pleasure in books and music, in independent thought and the creation of a personal 'philosophy'. For this class the ideals and joys of life were the exchange of ideas, a contemplative conversation over a glass of wine, a few faithfully and rather sentimentally maintained and nurtured friendships and, last but not least, an intense, intimate family life. Almost all of this had fallen into ruin and decay in the decade from 1914 to 1924 and the younger generation had grown up without fixed customs and traditions.

Outside this cultured class, the great danger of life in Germany has always been emptiness and boredom (with the exception perhaps of certain geographical border regions such as Bavaria and the Rhineland, where a whiff of the south, some romance and a sense of humour enter the picture). The menace of monotony hangs, as it has always hung, over the great plains of northern and eastern Germany, with their colourless towns and their all too industrious, efficient and conscientious businesses and organisations. With it comes a *horror vacui* and the yearning for 'salvation': through alcohol, through superstition or, best of all, through a vast, overpowering, cheap mass intoxication.

The basic fact that in Germany only a minority (not necessarily from the aristocracy or the moneyed class) understands anything of life and knows how to lead it – a fact which, incidentally, makes the country inherently unsuitable for democratic government – had been dangerously exacerbated by the events of the years from 1914 to 1924. The older generation had become uncertain and timid in its ideals and convictions and began to focus on 'youth', with thoughts of abdication, flattery and high expectations. Young people themselves were familiar with nothing but political clamour, sensation, anarchy and the dangerous lure of irresponsibile number games. They were only waiting to put what they had witnessed into practice themselves, but on a far larger scale. Meanwhile, they viewed private life as 'boring', 'bourgeois' and 'old-fashioned'. The masses, too, were accustomed to all the varied sensations of disorder. Moreover they had become weak and doubtful about their most recent great superstition: the creed, celebrated with pedantic, orthodox fervour, of the magical powers of the omniscient Saint Marx and the inevitability of the automatic course of history prophesied by him.

Thus, under the surface, all was ready for a vast catastrophe.

Meanwhile, golden peace, serenity, benevolence and goodwill reigned in the tangible world of public affairs. Even the heralds of the coming calamity seemed to fit seamlessly into the peaceable scene.

Twelve

*O*ne of these heralds, quite misunderstood, indeed openly promoted and praised, was the sports craze which took possession of the youth of Germany.

In the years 1924, 1925 and 1926, Germany suddenly blossomed into a great sporting nation. Never before had it been a land of games. Never had it been creative and inventive in sports, like England and America. In fact, the true spirit of sport, the self-effacing playful absorption in a fantasy world with its own rules and regulations is altogether foreign to the German mentality. Nevertheless, in those years the membership of sports clubs and the numbers of spectators at sports meetings multiplied ten-fold at a stroke. Boxers and sprinters became national heroes, and the twenty-year-olds had their heads full of athletics results, the names of winners and all those numerical hieroglyphs into which feats of speed and skill are translated by the press.

It was the last German mass mania to which I myself succumbed. For two years my mental life stood still. I trained doggedly as a medium- and long-distance runner and would have sold my soul to the devil without hesitation if I could once have run 800 metres in under two minutes. I went to every athletics meeting, and I knew every runner and his best times, not to mention the list of German and world records which I would have been able to reel off in my sleep. The sports news played the same role as the army bulletins ten years before, athletic records and race times replacing the numbers of prisoners and quantity of booty. The headline 'Houben Runs 100 Metres in 10.6' evoked the same feelings as, in its day

'20,000 Russians Taken Prisoner'; and 'Peltzer Wins English Championship and Breaks World Record' corresponded to events that the war, alas, had failed to produce: 'Paris Falls', perhaps, or 'England Sues for Peace'. Day and night I dreamed of vying with Peltzer and Houben. I missed no sports meeting. I trained three times a week, stopped smoking and performed exercises before going to bed. I felt the utter joy of being in complete harmony with thousands, tens of thousands of people, yes, even with the entire world. There was no one of my age, however alien, uneducated or unpleasant, with whom I could not at first meeting engage in prolonged, animated conversation – about sports, of course. Everyone had the same figures in their heads. Without the need to say a word, everyone had the same feelings about them. It was almost as grand as the war. It was the same sort of great game again. We all understood each other without the need for words. Our spiritual nourishment was statistics, our souls perpetually aquiver with excitement: Would Peltzer beat Nurmi, too? Would Körnig do it in 10.3? Would one of our German 400-metre runners finally manage 48? We trained and ran our little races, our thoughts always with our 'German champions' at the international athletics meetings, just as we had fought our own little battles with small Tesching rifles and wooden swords in the streets and playgrounds during the war, our thoughts with Hindenburg and Ludendorff. What a simple, exciting life!

Strange to say, politicians from Right to Left outdid themselves in praise of the remarkable fit of imbecility to which the youth of Germany had fallen prey. Not only were we once again able to indulge our old vice, the narcotic of the cold, unreal numbers game. This time we did it with the full attention and the unanimous approval of our mentors. The nationalists, stupid and crass as ever, felt that our healthy instincts had found a practical substitute for military service, which had been abolished. As if any of us were interested in military drill! The Left, over-clever and therefore, as usual, even more stupid than the nationalists, regarded sport as a splendid invention by which we would henceforth be able to vent our warlike instincts harmlessly and peacefully. The peace of the world was, they felt, assured. It did not strike them that the 'German champions', without exception, wore little black, white and red ribbons in their buttonholes, the colours of the pre-war Reich; while the colours of the Republic were black, red and gold. It did not occur to them that, through sport, the lure of the war game, the old thrilling magic of national rivalry, was being exercised and maintained and that this was not some harmless venting of bellicose instincts. They failed to see any connection. They were blind to Germany's relapse.

The only man who seemed to realise that the forces he had released were taking a false and dangerous path was Stresemann himself. He occasionally made hostile references to the 'new aristocracy of the biceps', which added to his unpopularity. He seems to have been aware of what was afoot: that the blind forces and passions, whose entry into politics he had barred, were by no means dead, and were merely seeking an outlet; that the new generation refused to learn to live in an honourable, civilised way and that they would use their freedom only for collective mischief.

In any case, as a mass phenomenon the sports craze lasted just three years. (I, personally, overcame it even earlier.) To last longer, it would have needed something comparable to the concept of the Final Victory in the war: a goal as well as an end. It remained always the same: the same names, the same numbers, the same sensations. It could go on indefinitely, but it could not occupy our imaginations indefinitely. Although Germany had come second at the Amsterdam Olympics in 1928, a marked disillusion and cooling of interest followed immediately. The sports news disappeared from the front pages and returned to its own section of the newspaper. Sports grounds were less full, and it was no longer certain that every twenty-year-old had the latest 'time' of every 100-metres runner at his fingertips. There were even some who did not know the world records by heart.

At the same time, the leagues and parties, that treated politics as a sport and had seemed for a few years to have almost died, returned slowly to life.

Thirteen

*T*he Stresemann era was not a great epoch. It was not a complete success, even while it lasted. Too much trouble rumbled below the surface. Too many evil, diabolic forces stirred perceptibly in the wings, bound and gagged for the moment, but not really destroyed. No great symbol was raised that might exorcise the demons. The period remained one without passion, without greatness, without full conviction in its own cause. The old patriotic, bourgeois, peace-loving, liberal views returned to favour – but they had the unmistakable air of stopgaps, of being there *faute de mieux* and 'until further notice'. It was not a time that could later be recalled as the 'great past' in contrast to a dark present, but as a modest epoch of restoration.

And yet . . .

Talleyrand said that those who had not lived before 1789 had never known the sweetness of life. Elderly Germans have made similar claims for the days before 1914. It would sound a little ridiculous to say anything so extravagant about the Stresemann era. For all that, it was, despite its failings, for us young Germans the best period of our lives. All that we have experienced of the sweetness of life is associated with it. It was the only time when life was set in a major and not a minor key, even though it was a somewhat pale and hesitant major. It was the only time when we were really able to live. Most young Germans, as has already been said, could not cope with it, or were defeated by it. For the rest of us, this is a period from which we still draw sustenance.

It is difficult to speak of things that have never materialised, of beginnings that never got beyond a 'maybe' or an 'almost'. Yet it seems to me that, amid all that dark peril and inhuman evil, something rare and precious did begin to flower in Germany during the Stresemann era. The greater part of the younger generation had been ruined beyond saving, but the remaining minority was perhaps more promising than any generation of the last hundred years. The wild decade of 1914 to 1923 had thrown aside all balance and tradition; but it had also blown away the cobwebs and mental clutter. Most of us emerged as nihilistic cynics. Those who did learn to live again enrolled in an advanced course, as it were – free of the fads and illusions which occupy a sheltered youth. We had not been sheltered, but exposed to raw winds; we were poor, even in traditional spiritual values, but also free from inherited prejudices; we were hard-boiled, and tough. If we did not become callous, we were in no danger of becoming soft. If we avoided cynicism, we were not likely to become dreamy Parsifals. Something very fine and auspicious was silently ripening among the best of German youth from 1925 to 1930: a new idealism beyond doubt and disappointment, a new liberalism broader, more comprehensive and more mature than the political liberalism of the nineteenth century; indeed, perhaps the basis of a new nobility of spirit, a new excellence, a new aesthetic of life. It was as yet a long way from realisation and influence. Hardly had it been thought of and put into words than the quadrupeds arrived and trampled it all underfoot.

Despite everything, one could find a fresh atmosphere in Germany at this time, and there was a remarkable absence of insincere convention. The barriers between the classes had become thin and permeable – perhaps a fortunate by-product of the universal impoverishment. There were many students who were labourers, and many young labourers who were students. Class prejudice and the starched-collar mentality were simply out of fashion. The relations between the sexes were freer and franker than ever – perhaps a fortunate by-product of the lack of discipline of the past years. Instead of a contemptuous superiority, we felt a bewildered sympathy for previous generations who had, in their youth, had the choice between unapproachable virgins for adoration and harlots for relaxation. Finally, a new hope even began to dawn in international relations; there was less prejudice and more understanding of the other side, and an unmistakable pleasure in the vivid variety that the world derives from its many peoples.

Berlin became quite an international city. Admittedly, the sinister Nazi-types already lurked in the wings, as 'we' could not fail to notice with deep disgust. They spoke of 'Eastern vermin' with murder in their eyes and sneeringly of 'Americanisation'. Whereas 'we', a segment of the younger generation difficult to define but instantly and mutually recognisable, were not only friendly towards foreigners, but enthusiastic about them. How much more interesting, more beautiful and richer it made life that the world was not peopled exclusively by Germans! Our guests were all welcome, whether they came voluntarily, like the Americans and the Chinese, or as refugees, like the Russians. Our doors were flung open, the strangers were received with a friendly, curious goodwill, and with a conscious determination to understand and learn to appreciate even what was most foreign to us. In those days many a friendship, many a love linked the far west and far east.

My most treasured and tender memories are associated with just such a local international circle, a bit of the globe in the middle of Berlin. It was a small academic tennis club, in which we Germans were scarcely more strongly represented than the other nations. Strangely enough, Frenchmen and Englishmen were rare, but otherwise the entire universe seemed to have sent its envoys: Americans and Scandinavians, Balts and Russians, Chinese and Japanese, Hungarians and people from the Balkans, even a melancholy wag of a Turk. I never found the same free-and-easy youthful atmosphere again – except perhaps as a casual visitor to the Latin quarter in Paris. Deep nostalgia overcomes me when I recall the summer evenings we spent after matches in our clubhouse, often far into the night, seated in wicker chairs still in our tennis whites, sipping wine and cracking jokes, engaging in long and eager conversations which had nothing in common with the oppressive political discussions of earlier and later years, and which we sometimes interrupted to play a game of Ping-Pong or to put on the gramophone and dance. When I think of those nights today, so full of innocent fun and youthful gravity, of dreams of the future and of universal fellowship and trust, I stop and wonder. I cannot decide whether it is more incredible that all that could have existed in Germany scarcely ten years ago, or that it has been so thoroughly and completely obliterated in just ten years.

It is to this club, too, that I owe my deepest and most enduring love affair. I think it will not be out of place to mention it here, for it has a generic aspect. It is most certainly a romantic lie – yet one which enjoyed the widest popularity in the last century – that one really loves only once in a lifetime. It is rather futile to seek to compare amorous experiences which are in essence incomparable, and try to classify them in some order, and declare, 'I loved this or that woman most of all.' It is true, however, that at a certain stage in life, about the age of twenty, a love affair and the choice of partner affect one's destiny and character more than at others. For the woman one loves stands for more than just herself; a whole view of the world, a notion of life, an ideal, if you will, but one come alive, made flesh and blood. It is the privilege of some youths of twenty to love in a woman what later, as a man, they will look upon as their guiding star.

Today I must cast around for abstract expressions to describe what I love in the world, what I want to see preserved at all costs, and what must never be betrayed on pain of everlasting fire: freedom and human wisdom, courage, grace, wit and music. Even then, I am not sure of being understood. Then all that was needed was a single name, a mere nickname: 'Teddy!', and I could be sure that, at least in our circle, everyone would know what I meant. We all loved her, the bearer of this name, an Austrian girl, slight, honey-blonde, freckled, lithe as a flame. For her sake we learned and unlearned jealousy, acted out comedies and little tragedies, felt like singing hymns and dithyrambs; and we discovered that life is grand when lived with courage and wisdom, with grace and freedom, and with an ear for its humour and its music. Our circle had a goddess in its midst. The woman who was once Teddy may now be older and more earthbound, and none of us may still live life at the same emotional pitch as then; but that there was once a Teddy and that we experienced those raptures cannot be taken from us. It formed us more powerfully and more enduringly than any 'historical event'.

Teddy soon vanished from our midst, as goddesses do. She left for Paris in 1930, already resolved not to return. She was perhaps the first emigrant. More far-seeing and sensitive than us, she sensed the growth of stupidity and evil long before the advent of Hitler. Once, each summer, she would return to pay us a visit, and each time she found the air more stifling. The last time she came was 1933. Never afterwards.

By then 'we' – that indefinite we, with no name, no party, no organisation and no power – had long become a minority; and we knew it. That instinctive feeling of universal comprehension that had accompanied the number games one had indulged in, both of war and sport, had long turned into its opposite. We knew we could not talk with many of our contemporaries because we spoke a different language. We felt the tide of a new 'brown German' rise around us – words like *Einsatz* (strike force), *Garant* (pledge), *fanatisch* (fanatical), *Volksgenosse* (racial comrade), *Scholle* (soil), *Artfremd* (racially alien), *Untermensch* (subhuman) – a revolting jargon, every syllable of which implied a world of violent stupidity. We also had a secret dialect. Among ourselves we summed up people in a word. If they were 'clever' – which did not mean that they were particularly intelligent, but that they had some sense of an individual life – they were one of 'us'. We knew the morons were in the overwhelming majority. But as long as Stresemann was there, we felt more or less sure that they would be held in check. We moved among them with the same unconcern with which visitors to a modern cageless zoo walk past the beasts of prey, confident that its ditches and hedges have been carefully calculated. The beasts for their part probably reciprocated this sentiment. With deep hatred they coined the word 'system' for the impalpable force that held them within bounds while it left them their freedom. For the moment, at least, they were held within bounds.

In all those years, they never once attempted to assassinate Stresemann, though it would have been quite easy. He had no bodyguard, and did not entrench himself behind high walls. We often saw him strolling in Unter den Linden, an unremarkable, stocky man in a Derby hat. 'Isn't that Stresemann over there?' someone would ask, and indeed it was. Sometimes we might see him in the Pariser Platz, standing in front of a flower-bed, nudging a flower with the end of his walking-stick and contemplating it with his protruding eyes. Perhaps he was trying to remember its botanical name.

Remarkable: nowadays Hitler never shows himself except in a speeding car surrounded by ten or twelve cars full of heavily armed SS guards. It is probably just as well. Rathenau in 1922 refused to have armed guards and was consequently promptly murdered. Stresemann, on the other hand, could gaze at the flowers in Pariser Platz unattended and unarmed. Perhaps he was a magician after all, that broad, unprepossessing, unhandsome, unpopular man, with the bull neck and bulging eyes. Or was it just his unpopularity and insignificant looks that saved him?

From afar, we followed him with our eyes as he walked slowly and pensively down Unter den Linden into the Wilhelmstrasse. Many did not even recognise or notice him. Others greeted him and he returned the greeting politely, quietly raising his hat, not shooting out an arm; and to each person in turn, not to a vast concourse. We would ask ourselves whether he, too, was 'clever', and whatever the answer, we felt quietly confident and full of respectful gratitude towards the unprepossessing man. Nothing more. He was not one to kindle a flame.

The strongest feeling he ever roused was by dying: sudden, cold horror. He had been ill for a long time, but it was not known how gravely. Indeed, one later remembered that the last time he had been seen, four weeks previously in Unter den Linden, he had looked paler and more bloated than usual. But he was so unobtrusive, we had not noticed anything special. He died, too, most unobtrusively; in the evening, after a strenuous day, while he was brushing his teeth before going to bed, like the most ordinary citizen. Suddenly, as one read later, he staggered and the glass fell out of his hand. Next day the newspapers carried the headline: 'Stresemann Dead.'

As we read it we were seized with icy terror. Who was there now to tame the beasts? They had, in fact, just begun to stir with their mad 'plebiscite', the first of many its kind: in future it should be a criminal offence for any minister to conclude a treaty 'on the basis of the war-guilt lie'. That was the right stuff for the morons! Placards and processions, mass meetings, marches, and a gunfight here and there. The era of peace was at an end. So long as Stresemann had been there, we had not quite believed it. Now we knew.

October 1929. A vile autumn after a magnificent summer; rain and raw weather, but also something oppressive in the air that had nothing to do with the weather. Angry words on the poster columns; and on the streets for the first time, mud-brown uniforms and unpleasant physiognomies above them; the rat-tat-tat and piping of an unfamiliar, shrill, vulgar, march music. Dismay in bureaucratic circles, violent scenes in the Reichstag, and the newspapers full of a creeping, never-ending government crisis. It was depressingly familiar, had the smell of 1919 or 1920. Was not poor Hermann Müller, who had been Chancellor in that dreary period, once again at the helm? As long as Stresemann had been foreign minister, no one had worried much about the Chancellor. His death was the beginning of the end.

Fourteen

*E*arly in 1930 Müller was succeeded as Chancellor by Heinrich Brüning. For the first time within memory, Germany had a strong master. From 1914 to 1923 all governments had been weak. Stresemann had ruled ably and energetically, but with a gentle hand, not hurting a soul. Brüning constantly hurt a lot of people. It was his way. He was rather proud to be 'unpopular'. He was a hard, bony man, with severe, narrowed eyes peering through rimless spectacles. Anything obliging and polished went against his nature. His successes – and he undoubtedly had some – could always be described by the catch-phrase, 'Operation successful, patient dead', or 'Position held, ranks decimated'. To prove the absurdity of reparation payments, he took them to the extreme and thereby brought Germany's economy to the verge of collapse, causing banks to close their doors and the unemployment figures to reach six million. To keep the budget balanced nevertheless, his grim, steely spirit imposed the precept of the strict *paterfamilias*: 'Tighten your belts'.

In a regular sequence, new 'emergency decrees' appeared every six months, each yet again reducing salaries, pensions, social benefits, and finally even private wages and rates of interest. Each was the logical consequence of the last one, and each time Brüning, clenching his teeth, imposed the painful logic. Many of Hitler's most effective instruments of torture were first introduced by Brüning – such as 'safeguarding foreign reserves', which made travel abroad impossible, and the 'Reich flight tax', which did the same for emigration. Even the beginnings of the restriction of the freedom of the press and the

gagging of parliament can be traced to Brüning. Yet, paradoxically, his actions were rooted in the conviction that he was
defending the Republic. Understandably, the republicans began
to ask themselves whether there was anything left to defend.

To my knowledge, the Brüning regime was the first essay and
model of a form of government that has since been copied in
many European countries: the semi-dictatorship in the name,
and in defence, of democracy against fully-fledged dictatorship.
Anyone who takes the trouble to study Brüning's rule in depth
will find all those factors which make this sort of government
the inevitable forerunner of the very thing it is supposed to
prevent: its discouragement of its own supporters; the way it
undermines its own position; its acceptance of a loss of freedom;
its lack of ideological weapons against enemy propaganda; the
way it surrenders the initiative; and its collapse at the final
moment when the issue is reduced to a simple question of
power.

Brüning had no real following. He was 'tolerated'. He was the
lesser evil: the strict schoolmaster who accompanied the
chastisement of his pupils with the words, 'This will hurt me
more than you', rather than a sadistic torturer. One supported
Brüning because he seemed to be the only bulwark against
Hitler. Knowing that he owed his own political life to the threat
posed by Hitler, Brüning had to fight against him, but at all
costs refrain from destroying him. Hitler must not be allowed
to come to power, but must remain a continual danger. Brüning
kept up this difficult balancing act with a poker face and
clenched teeth for two years. That was his greatest achievement.
The moment would come when he would lose his balance. It
could not be indefinitely postponed. What then? This question
overshadowed the entire Brüning era – a period in which the
gloomy present was lightened only by comparison with the
prospect of a ghastly future.

Brüning had nothing to offer the country but poverty, the
curtailment of liberty and the assurance that there was no
alternative. At best it was a call to austerity. His nature was too
bleak even to make this call in stirring tones. He gave the

country no purpose, no inspiring leadership; he only covered it in joyless shade.

Meanwhile, the forces that had lain low for so long gathered noisily.

On 14 September 1930, there were Reichstag elections. At a bound, the Nazis, hitherto a ridiculous splinter party, became the second largest faction in the house; they jumped from twelve seats to 107. From that day, the central figure of Brüning's period was no longer Brüning but Hitler. The question was no longer whether Brüning would remain in power, but whether Hitler would come to power. The most passionate and embittered political arguments ensued, for and against not Brüning, but Hitler. In the suburbs where the gunfights began again, it was not Brüning's supporters who shot his opponents, but Hitler's supporters who killed Hitler's enemies.

Hitler himself, his past, his character and his speeches were still rather a handicap for the movement that gathered around him. In 1930, he was still widely regarded as a somewhat embarrassing figure with a dismal past: the Munich saviour of 1923, the man of the grotesque beer-cellar putsch. Besides, for ordinary (and not only 'clever') Germans, his personal appearance was thoroughly repellent – the pimp's forelock, the hoodlum's elegance, the Viennese suburban accent, the interminable speechifying, the epileptic behaviour with its wild gesticulations, foam at the mouth, and the alternately shifty and staring eyes. And then there were the contents of those speeches: the delight in threats and in cruelty, the bloodthirsty execution fantasies. Most of those who began to acclaim Hitler at the Sportpalast* in 1930 would probably have avoided asking him for a light if they had met him in the street. That was the strange thing: their fascination with the boggy, dripping cesspool he represented, repulsiveness taken to extremes. No one would have been surprised if a policeman had taken him by the scruff of the neck in the middle of his first speech and

---

* Indoor sports stadium in Berlin, scene of many political speeches, notably by Hitler.

removed him to some place from which he would never have emerged again, and where he doubtless belonged. As nothing of the sort happened and, on the contrary, the man surpassed himself, becoming ever more deranged and monstrous, and also ever more notorious, more impossible to ignore, the effect was reversed. It was then that the real mystery of the Hitler phenomenon began to show itself: the strange befuddlement and numbness of his opponents, who could not cope with his behaviour and found themselves transfixed by the gaze of the basilisk, unable to see that it was hell personified that challenged them.

Summoned as a witness before the highest German court, Hitler bellowed at the judges that he would one day come to power by strictly constitutional means and then heads would roll. Nothing happened. The white-haired president of the supreme court did not think of ordering the witness to be taken into custody for contempt. In the presidential elections against Hindenburg, Hitler declared that victory was his, in any case. His opponent was eighty-five, he was forty-three; he could wait. Nothing happened. When he said it again at his next meeting, the audience tittered, as if it had been tickled. One night, six storm troopers fell on a 'dissident' in his bed and literally trampled him to death, for which they were sentenced to death. Hitler sent them a telegram of praise and acknowledgement. Nothing happened. No, something did happen: the murderers were pardoned.

It was strange to observe how the behaviour of each side reinforced that of the other: the savage impudence which gradually made it possible for the unpleasant, little apostle of hate to assume the proportions of a demon; the bafflement of his tamers, who always realised just too late exactly what it was he was up to – namely, when he capped it with something even more outrageous and monstrous; then also the hypnotic trance into which his public fell, succumbing with less and less resistance to the glamour of depravity and the ecstasy of evil.

Besides, he promised everything to everybody, which naturally brought him a vast, loose army of followers and voters from among the ignorant, the disappointed and the dispossessed. That, however, was not decisive. Beyond demagogy and the details of his election manifesto, he made two promises with obvious honesty: the revival of the great war game of 1914 to 1918 and a repetition of the triumphal anarchic looting of 1923. In other words, his subsequent foreign policy and economic policy. He did not promise these things in so many words. Sometimes he even pretended to deny them (as he did in his later 'peace speeches'). He was understood all the same. It won him his true disciples, the kernel of the Nazi Party. He appealed to the two great experiences which had marked the younger generation. It was a spark that electrified all those who secretly hankered after these experiences. It excluded those who had written them off and mentally marked them with a minus sign; that is to say, 'us'.

'We', however, had no alternative party, no banner to carry, no programme and no battle cry. Whom could we follow? Apart from the Nazis, who were the favourites, there were the civilised bourgeois reactionaries who clustered round the Stahlhelm (Steel Helmets),* people who rather vaguely enthused over 'front-line experiences' and 'German soil', and who may not have had the glaring vulgarity of the Nazis but certainly shared their resentful dimness and their innate hatred of life. Then there were the Social Democrats, beaten even before the battle had started, so frequently had they been discredited. Finally there were the Communists, with their sectarian dogma trailing a comet's tail of defeat. (Strange: whatever they undertook, the Communists were always beaten in the end and 'shot while attempting to escape'. That seemed to be a law of nature.)

Aside from this was the sphinx-like German army, led by a scheming, back-room general;† and also the Prussian police, of whom it was said they were a well-trained, reliable, republican force. We heard it, but after everything we had been through, we did not really believe it.

---

* A semi-military nationalist (non-Nazi) organisation.
† Schleicher (see footnote on page 76).

Those were the forces in play. The game dragged on, tedious and gloomy, without high spots, without drama, without obvious decisive moments. In many respects the atmosphere in Germany resembled that which prevails today in Europe as a whole: a passive waiting for the inevitable, still hoping to avoid it up to the last moment. Today, in Europe, it is the war that has so long threatened. Then, in Germany, it was Hitler's seizure of power, and 'the Night of the Long Knives' of which the Nazis spoke in anticipation. Even the details are similar: the slow approach of the dreaded event; the confusion of the forces opposed to it and their hopeless adherence to the rules of the game which the enemy daily infringes; the one-sidedness of the contest; the sense of hovering between 'peace and stability' and 'civil war' (there were no barricades, but every day meaningless and childish brawls and gunfights, attacks on party offices, and regularly also killings). The mindset of 'appeasement' was also apparent. Powerful groups were in favour of rendering Hitler 'harmless' by giving him 'responsibility'. There were constant political arguments, fruitless and bitter, in cafés and public houses, in shops, schools, and in family homes. I should also not forget to mention a new series of numbers games. More or less important elections were always taking place, and now everyone had election results and numbers of seats in their heads. The Nazis constantly gained ground. What was no longer to be found was pleasure in life, amiability, fun, understanding, goodwill, generosity and a sense of humour. There were few good books being published any more, and certainly no readers. The air in Germany had rapidly become suffocating.

It became more and more suffocating until the summer of 1932. Then Brüning fell, overnight and for no reason, and there was the strange Papen–Schleicher interlude:* a government of unknown aristocrats and six months of a wild political chase.

---

* From June to November 1932 Franz von Papen was Chancellor; he was succeeded in December by Kurt von Schleicher, whose government lasted until 30 January 1933. Both politicians were authoritarian conservatives. Both thought they could tame Hitler by offering him power. Schleicher was one of the right-wing conservatives murdered on 30 June 1934.

The Republic was liquidated, the constitution suspended, the Reichstag dissolved, re-elected, dissolved again, and again re-elected. Newspapers were banned, the Prussian regional government was illegally dismissed, and higher civil servants were replaced – and all this took place in the almost cheerful atmosphere of a final supreme fling. The year 1939, in Europe, has much the same feeling as that German summer of 1932. We really were only a hair's breadth from the end. The worst could happen any day. The Nazis already filled the streets with their uniforms, which they were at last officially permitted to wear, already hurled bombs, already drew up their blacklists.

In August, the Government was already negotiating with Hitler, offering him the vice-chancellorship, and in November, after Papen and Schleicher had quarrelled, the chancellorship itself. All that stood between Hitler and power was the luck of a few aristocratic political gamblers. All serious obstacles had been removed; there was no constitution any more, no legal guarantees, no republic, nothing, not even the Prussian police. Just so today: the League of Nations lies moribund, there is no collective security any longer and treaties and conferences have no value; Spain has fallen, as have Austria and Czechoslovakia. Yet, then as now, at the very last and most dangerous hour, when all was about to be lost, a pathological, unreasonable optimism seized us, a gambler's optimism, a blithe confidence that we would yet escape the catastrophe by the skin of our teeth. Were not Hitler's coffers empty, then as today? Were not his former friends at last resolved to put up a fight, as they are today? Had life not returned to the frozen political scene – just as it has in Europe in 1939?

Then as now, we began to toy with the idea that the worst was over.

Fifteen

We have arrived. The journey has ended. We enter the lists. The duel is about to begin.

THE REVOLUTION

Sixteen

*T*his was me at the beginning of 1933: a young man of twenty-five, well fed, well turned out, well educated, friendly and polite, past the awkward, gangling student phase with some corners already rubbed off, but basically untried – a typical example of the German educated bourgeois class in general but otherwise an unknown quantity. There was nothing particularly interesting or startling to say about my life so far, except that it had been lived against an arrestingly dramatic backdrop. The only experiences that had gone a bit deeper and left some marks, scars and character traits, were the delights and pains of the experiments in love that every young person of this age encounters. At that time they interested me more than anything else; they were the essence of my life. Incidentally – like all young people of my age and class – I still lived at home. I was well looked after and well dressed, but kept short of pocket-money as a matter of principle, by a distinguished, ageing, interesting, uncomfortable father, whom I secretly loved. My father was the most important person in my life, though I was sometimes less than happy about it. If I wanted to undertake something serious or make an important decision, I had no choice but to consult my father. To describe myself as I then was – or, rather, potentially was – I still have no choice but to describe my father.

He was by conviction a liberal and by stance and disposition a Prussian puritan.

There is a specifically Prussian variant of puritanism that was one of the most important spiritual forces in German life before 1933 and still plays a certain role beneath the surface. It is related to classical English puritanism but has some characteristic differences. Its prophet is Kant rather than Calvin; its greatest standard-bearer, Frederick the Great rather than Cromwell. Like English puritanism it demands severity, dignity, abstinence from the pleasures of life, attention to one's duty, loyalty, honesty, indeed self-denial, and a sombre scorn for the world. Just like his English counterpart, the Prussian puritan keeps his sons short of pocket-money and frowns at their youthful experiments with love. Prussian puritanism is, however, secular. It serves and owes allegiance to, not Jehovah, but the *roi de Prusse*. Its distinctions and earthly rewards are not private wealth, but promotion in the civil service. Perhaps the most important difference is that Prussian puritanism has a back door into unsupervised freedom. It is marked 'private'.

It is well known that in private the dark, ascetic King Frederick the Great, the exemplar of Prussian puritanism, played the flute, wrote verses, was a free thinker and friend of Voltaire. Through two centuries the majority of his disciples, senior Prussian civil servants and officers, with their severe, pinched faces, followed similar inclinations in private. Prussian puritanism echoes the motto: 'Hard outside, soft inside'. The Prussian puritan is the inventor of the curious construct that says, 'As a human being I tell you . . . , but as an official I say . . .' This accounts for the fact, so difficult for foreigners to understand, that while Prussia as a whole – and also Prussian Germany – always seems and acts like an inhuman, cruelly voracious machine, when you visit it and get to know Prussians and Germans as 'private' individuals they make an altogether attractive, humane, harmless and amiable impression. As a nation, Germany leads a double life because almost every German leads a double life.

In 'private' my father was a passionate lover of literature. He had a library of some 10,000 volumes that he added to right up until his death. What is more, he did not just own all these books, he had actually read them. The great names of nineteenth-century European literature – Dickens and Thackeray, Balzac and Hugo, Turgenev and Tolstoy, Raabe and

Keller, to mention only his favourites – were not just names to him, but intimate friends, with whom he had held long, silent, passionate discussions. His conversation blossomed when he met someone with whom he could continue these discussions out loud.

Now literature is an awkward hobby. You can keep a love of collecting or cultivating flowers 'private', and that may also go for a love of art or music, but the daily occupation with the living spirit cannot be kept entirely 'private'. One can easily imagine that a man who for years had surveyed all the heights and depths of European thought and literature would one day find it impossible to be a narrow, pedantic, dutiful Prussian civil servant. Not so my father. He remained just that. However, without ever breaking the mould, he developed a sceptically wise, liberal attitude within himself, that reduced the civil servant's persona to a mere mask. The glue by which he held both together was a secret, silent, sublime irony. That seems to me the only means to ennoble and legitimise the highly problematical figure of the bureaucrat in human terms; never for a moment to forget that the powerful dignitary behind the desk and the puny supplicant in front of it are both just humans and nothing more. They both have their parts in the play, and that of the official requires strictness and coolness but also sensitivity, benevolence and care. Writing an order in a critical matter in the coldest formal terms may require more delicacy of touch than a lyric poem, more wisdom and fairness than the dénouement of a novel. During the walks that my father liked to take with me at this time he gently tried to introduce me to these mysteries of the higher civil service.

It was important for him that I should become a civil servant. He had observed, not without a certain disquiet, that what in him had been confined to reading and discussion, showed a tendency in me to degenerate into writing. He had not particularly encouraged this tendency. Of course he had not used clumsy prohibitions; certainly not. That was out of the question. I could write as many novels, short stories and essays in my free time as I liked. If they contributed to my income, so much the better, but I should first study something 'sensible' and pass my exams. At bottom, his puritanical soul mistrusted a life that consisted of visiting cafés and scribbling at irregular hours. His liberal spirit was, moreover, disinclined to leave the administration of the state in the hands of philistines, lovers of power and chicanery, who would squander the precious capital of state authority in meaningless decrees and regulations. There were, in his opinion, too many of these already. He did his best to make me into what he had been: a civilised administrator. He probably thought that that way he was doing the best for me and the German state.

So I had studied law and become a *Referendar*. In contrast to the Anglo-Saxon countries, a future judge or administrator is introduced to the exercise of power immediately after graduation at the age of twenty-two or twenty-three. As a *Referendar* (roughly like an articled clerk, the word literally means someone who reports to a mentor) he participates in the work of the courts or the civil service like a judge or administrator, but without responsibility or the power to take decisions (and also without pay). Even so, many judgements are written by *Referendars*, though they are signed by judges, and in the deliberations of the courts the *Referendar* has the right to be heard even though he has no vote. This sometimes gives him real influence. At two of the courts where I worked, the judge even let me run the proceedings. This sudden power has a profound effect on a young man who is still living with his parents, and it inevitably influences him deeply. It had two principal effects on me. The first was composure, an attitude of cool, calm, benevolent dryness, perhaps only to be learned behind an official's desk. The second was a certain facility in following official thought processes and legal abstractions. As things turned out, I had little opportunity to exercise either as they were intended. However, the second facility was literally to save the life of my wife, and my own a few years later. My father could not have foreseen that when he ensured that I undertook a course of study preparing me to be a civil servant.

Apart from that, I can only smile ruefully when I consider

how prepared I was for the adventure that awaited me. I was not prepared at all. I had no skills in boxing or ju-jitsu, not to mention smuggling, crossing borders illegally, using secret codes and so on; skills that would have stood me in good stead in the coming years. My spiritual preparation for what was ahead was almost equally inadequate. Is it not said that in peacetime the chiefs of staff always prepare their armies as well as possible – for the previous war? I cannot judge the truth of that, but it is certainly true that conscientious parents always educate their sons for the era that is just over. I had all the intellectual endowments to play a decent part in the bourgeois world of the period before 1914. I had an uneasy feeling, based on what I had experienced, that it would not be much help to me. That was all. At best I smelled a warning whiff of what was about to confront me, but I did not have an intellectual system that would help me deal with it.

True, that was not just my situation but that of my whole generation, and even more the situation of the older generation. (It is still the situation of most foreigners, who only know about Nazism from the newspapers and newsreels.) Our thinking is usually constrained by a certain civilisation in our outlook, in which the basics are unquestioned – and so implicit that they are almost forgotten. When we argued about certain opposites – freedom and slavery, for example, or nationalism and human- ism, or individualism and socialism – the discussion always respected certain Christian, humanistic, civilised principles as axiomatic. Even some of those who became Nazis at this time did not fully realise what they were doing. They might think that they stood for nationalism and socialism, were against the Jews and for the pre-1914–18 *status quo*, and many of them secretly looked forward to a new public adventure, a repeat of 1923. Still, they expected all that to take the humane forms usual in a civilised nation. Most of them would have been deeply shocked if one had suggested that what they really stood for were torture chambers and officially decreed *pogroms* (to name but two of the most obvious things, and these are certainly not yet the final horrific culmination). Even today there are Nazis who are shocked and alarmed if this is pointed out to them.

At that time I had no strong political views. I even found it difficult to decide whether I was 'Right' or 'Left', to use the most general political categories. When I was asked this once in 1932, I answered, hesitantly, 'Well, probably Right . . .' In day-to-day politics I formed my views according to the circumstances; sometimes I had no view at all. None of the existing political parties seemed particularly attractive to me, despite the abundant choice. Anyway, belonging to any of them would not have saved me from becoming a Nazi, *ut exempla docent*.

What saved me was – my nose. I have a fairly well-developed figurative sense of smell, or to put it differently, a sense of the worth (or worthlessness!) of human, moral, political views and attitudes. Most Germans unfortunately lack this sense almost completely. The cleverest of them are capable of discussing themselves stupid with their abstractions and deductions, when just using their noses would tell them that something stinks. I had already acquired the habit of using my nose to test the few opinions I held firmly.

As for the Nazis, my nose left me with no doubts. It was just tiresome to talk about which of their alleged goals and intentions were still acceptable or even 'historically justified' when all of it stank. How it stank! That the Nazis were enemies, my enemies and the enemies of all I held dear, was crystal clear to me from the outset. What was not at all clear to me, was what terrible enemies they would turn out to be. I was inclined not to take them very seriously – a common attitude among their inexperienced opponents, which helped them a lot, and still helps them.

There are few things as comic as the calm, superior indifference with which I and those like me watched the beginnings of the Nazi revolution in Germany, as if from a box at the theatre. It was, after all, a movement with the declared intention of doing away with us. Perhaps the only comparably comic thing is the way that now, years later, Europe is permitting itself exactly the same indifferent attitude, as though it were a superior, amused onlooker, while the Nazis are already setting it alight at all four corners.

Seventeen

*A*t first the revolution only gave the impression of being a 'historical event' like any other: a matter for the press that might just possibly have some effect on the public mood.

The Nazis celebrate the 30th of January as their day of revolution. They are wrong. There was no revolution on the 30th of January 1933, just a change of government. Hitler became Chancellor, by no means the Führer of a Nazi regime (the cabinet contained only two Nazis apart from him). He swore an oath of allegiance to the Weimar constitution. The general opinion was that it was not the Nazis who had won, but the bourgeois parties of the Right, who had 'captured' the Nazis and held all the key positions in the Government. In constitutional terms, events had taken a much more conventional, unrevolutionary course than most of what had happened during the previous six months. Outwardly also, the day had no revolutionary aspects, unless one considers a Nazi torchlight procession through the Wilhelmstrasse or a minor gunfight in the suburbs that night as signs of a revolution.

For most of us outsiders, the experience of the 30th of January was that of reading the papers – and the emotions we felt while we were doing so.

The morning headline was 'Hitler called to President'. That produced a certain nervous, impotent irritation. Hitler had been called to the President in August and November. He had been offered the vice-chancellorship and then the chancellorship. Both times he had set impossible conditions, and both times there had been solemn declarations: 'Never again . . .' Each time 'never again' had lasted exactly three months. Hitler's opponents in Germany at that time suffered from a compulsive urge to offer him everything he wanted, indefatigably and at an ever cheaper price, indeed to press it upon him. It is the same now with his opponents outside Germany. Again and again this 'appeasement' was formally renounced, and again and again it gaily reappeared at the crucial moment; just so today. Then as now, one's only hope was Hitler's own unreasonableness. Would it not sooner or later exhaust the patience of his opponents? Then as now, it became apparent that their patience knew no bounds . . .

At midday the headline said: 'Hitler makes impossible demands'. We nodded, half reassured. It was only too credible. It would have gone against his nature to ask for less than too much. Perhaps the cup had once more passed from us. Hitler – the last defence against Hitler.

At about five o'clock the evening papers arrived: 'Cabinet of National Unity formed – Hitler Reichschancellor'.

I do not know what the general reaction was. For about a minute, mine was completely correct: icy horror. Certainly this had been a possibility for a long time. You had to reckon with it. Nevertheless it was so bizarre, so incredible, to read it now in black and white. Hitler Reichschancellor . . . for a moment I physically sensed the man's odour of blood and filth, the nauseating approach of a man-eating animal – its foul, sharp claws in my face.

Then I shook the sensation off, tried to smile, started to consider and found many reasons for reassurance. That evening I discussed the prospects of the new Government with my father. We agreed that it had a good chance of doing a lot of damage, but not much chance of surviving very long: a deeply reactionary government, with Hitler as its mouthpiece. Apart from this, it did not really differ much from the two governments that had succeeded Brüning's. Even with the Nazis it would not have a majority in the Reichstag. Of course that could always be dissolved, but the Government had a clear majority of the population against it, in particular the working class, which would probably go Communist, now that the Social Democrats had completely discredited themselves. One could prohibit the Communists, but that would only make them more dangerous. In the meantime the Government would be likely to implement reactionary social and cultural measures, with some anti-Semitic additions to please Hitler. That would not attract any of its opponents to its side. Foreign policy would probably be a matter of banging the table. There might be an attempt to rearm. That would automatically add the outside world to the 60 per cent of the home population who were against the Government. Besides, who were the people who had suddenly started voting Nazi in the last three years? Misguided ignoramuses for the most part, victims of propaganda, a fluctuating mass that would fall apart at the first disappointment. No, all things considered, this government was not a cause for alarm. The only question was what would come after it. It was possible that they would drive the country to civil war. The Communists were capable of going on the attack before a prohibition against them came into force.

The next day this turned out to be the general opinion of the intelligent press. It is curious how plausible an argument it is, even today, when we know what came next. How could things turn out so completely differently? Perhaps it was just because we were all so certain that they could not do so – and relied on that with far too much confidence. So we neglected to consider that it might, if the worst came to the worst, be necessary to *prevent* the disaster from happening.

Through the whole of February 1933 everything that happened remained a matter for the press, in other words, it took place in an arena which would lose all reality for 99 per cent of the population the moment there were no newspapers. Admittedly, enough occurred in that arena: the Reichstag was dissolved; then, in a flagrant breach of the constitution, Hindenburg also dissolved the Prussian regional parliament. There were fast and furious changes of personnel in the higher civil service, and the election campaign was accompanied by ferocious acts of terror. The Nazis no longer felt any restraint;

with their gangs, they regularly broke up the election meetings of other parties. They shot one or two political opponents every day. In a Berlin suburb they even burned down the house of a Social Democrat family. The new Prussian regional interior minister (a Nazi: a certain Captain Göring) promulgated an incredible decree. It ordered the police to intervene in any brawl on the side of the Nazis, without investigating the rights and wrongs of the matter, and furthermore to shoot at the other side without prior warning. A little later an 'auxiliary police force' was formed from the ranks of the SA.

All this was still something one only read about in the press. You did not see or hear anything that was any different from what had gone on before. There were brown SA uniforms on the streets, demonstrations, shouts of 'Heil', but otherwise it was 'business as usual'. In the *Kammergericht*, the highest court in Prussia, where I worked as *Referendar* at that time, the process of the law was not changed at all by the fact that the interior minister enacted ridiculous edicts. The newspapers might report that the constitution was in ruins. Here every paragraph of the Civil Code was still valid and was mulled over and analysed as carefully as ever. Which was the true reality? The Chancellor could daily utter the vilest abuse against the Jews; there was none the less still a Jewish *Kammergerichtsrat* (*Kammergericht* judge) and member of our senate who continued to give his astute and careful judgements, and these judgements had the full weight of the law and could set the entire apparatus of the state in motion for their enforcement – even if the highest office-holder of that state daily called their author a 'parasite', a 'subhuman' or a 'plague'. Who cut the worse figure? Who was the butt of the irony of the situation?

I must admit that I was inclined to view the undisturbed functioning of the law, and indeed the continued normal course of daily life, as a triumph over the Nazis. They could behave as raucously and wildly as they wished. They could still only stir up the political surface. The depths of the ocean of life remained unaffected.

Entirely unaffected? Did not some of the surface waves send

out vibrations, as evidenced by a new jittery tension, a new intolerance and heated readiness to hate, which began to infect private political discussions, and even more by the unrelenting pressure to think about politics all the time? Was it not a remarkable effect of politics on private life that we suddenly considered any normal daily private event as a political demonstration?

Be that as it may, I still clung to this normal unpolitical life. There was no angle from which I could attack the Nazis. Well then, at least I would not let them interfere with my personal life. It was partly this feeling of defiance that made me decide to go to one of the great carnival balls. I was not particularly in the mood for that kind of thing; but let's see if the Nazis can stop me enjoying the carnival . . .

Eighteen

Carnival in Berlin is, like so many of the city's customs, a somewhat artificial, stage-managed affair. There are no droll rituals sanctified by long usage as there are in the Catholic areas of Germany. It does not have the spontaneous warm-heartedness that carries one along in the Munich carnival. Its major characteristics are the very Berlinish ones of 'bustle' and 'organisation'. A carnival ball in Berlin is like a large, colourful, well-organised love tombola, with winning tickets and duds. You take your chance, join up with a girl, kiss and cuddle her, and go through all the preparatory stages of a love affair in a single night. The usual end is a taxi drive at daybreak and the exchange of phone numbers. By then you usually know whether it is the start of something that you would like to take further, or whether you have just earned yourself a hangover. It all takes place in a wild, garish environment (the 'bustle'), with the clashing noise of several dance bands, in a building decorated with coloured paper-chains and lanterns, accompanied by as much alcohol as you can afford. You are packed in like sardines with several thousand other young couples all doing the same thing, not bothering about anyone else.

The ball I went to was for some reason called 'Dachkahn' – 'Roof Punt' – and was organised by an art academy. It was big, loud, colourful and full, like all Berlin carnival balls. It took place on the 25th of February, a Saturday. I arrived fairly late and it was already in full swing, a teeming crowd, glimpses of silk, naked shoulders and female legs, a crush in which one could hardly move, the cloakrooms full, no room at the bars. The crush was part of the obligatory 'bustle'.

I found it difficult to get into the mood. On the contrary, I arrived feeling rather depressed. I had had some worrying news that afternoon. The election campaign was not going the way the Nazis wanted. They were planning a coup, with massive arrests and a regime of terror. We should be prepared for the worst in the next few weeks. It made me uneasy, but of course it was still only a matter for the press. This was the true reality, wasn't it: the overheard scraps of conversation, laughter, music, the freely given smiles?

I stood there on a step, distracted and undecided, watching the revellers around me – the hot, shiny, glowing, eager, smiling faces; so many, so innocent, all just hoping to meet a nice boyfriend or girlfriend for a night, or a season, a whiff of the sweetness of life, a little adventure, something to be fondly remembered. All at once I had a strange, dizzy feeling. I felt as though I was inescapably imprisoned with all these young people in a giant ship that was rolling and pitching. We were dancing on its lowest, narrowest deck, while on the bridge it was being decided to flood that deck and drown every last one of us.

An arm pushed itself through mine from behind. I recognised a familiar voice and surfaced back to reality (if that was what it was). It was an old acquaintance from happy tennis-club days, a girl called Lisl, whom I had lost sight of for some time, almost forgotten. Now she stood there comforting and friendly, ready for some fun. She interposed herself firmly between me and my black thoughts. Her small solid body screened out the world and the Nazis, and brought me back to the path of carnival duty. Within an hour I had been found a partner. I had my tombola prize, a small black-haired girl, in a Turkish pageboy's costume, very dainty to look at, with large brown eyes. At first glance she resembled the actress Elizabeth Bergner. That was her intention – many Berlin girls wanted to look like Elizabeth Bergner at that time. One could not ask for better.

Lisl gave me a wink and disappeared into the throng and Miss 'Bergner' became my girlfriend for the night; and not just for that night but for a whole desolate period to come. It was not to be an entirely happy friendship, but I did not know that yet. She was light as a feather, lay easily in my arms when we danced, spoke precociously in a small high-pitched voice, making cheeky little jokes with a certain brittle, dry, Berlin charm. As she did so her large eyes, so much older than her face, lit up. She was very attractive and I was satisfied with my tombola prize. We danced a while and then had some drinks. After that we strolled about a bit and came to a small room where the music could only be heard faintly from a distance. We settled down and tried to guess one another's names. After a little while we gave up and decided to invent new ones. She called me 'Peter'. I called her 'Charlie'. Good names for lovers in a Vicki Baum novel. You could not ask for better. In giving ourselves these names we were preparing to become a pair of lovers *à la mode*. The few other couples on either side of us were occupied only with themselves. They did not bother us. However an elderly actor, commanding and lonely as he stood in the centre of the room, gave us his whimsical blessing, calling us his children and ordering cocktails for all of us. It was almost like a little family. After a while I felt like dancing again. I had promised Lisl to look her up later, but events took a different turn.

I do not know how the rumour first spread that the police were in the building. From time to time people had come into the room and tipsily tried to attract our attention by cracking more or less successful jokes as well as they could. Someone may have shouted, 'Get up, the police are here!' I did not think that was a particularly good joke. Then the rumour intensified. A few girls started to become nervous, jumped up and left, followed by their cavaliers. Suddenly there was a young man dressed completely in black, with black hair and black eyes, in the middle of the room. He declared in a fierce, rough voice that we would all do well to get out unless we wanted to spend the night at the Alexanderplatz (that was where the police headquarters were, and the police cells). He behaved rather as if he were a policeman himself, but on closer inspection I remembered that he had been in the room, kissing a girl, for quite a while. The girl had disappeared. Now I noticed that he was wearing a badge on his cap that represented the *fasces* bundle of a Roman *lictor* and, my God, his black costume was a fascist uniform! Strange costume! Strange behaviour! The old actor rose from his chair and, swaying a little, left the room. It felt like a dream.

Somewhere in one of the rooms which gave ours its dim illumination the lights went out. There were loud screams. All of a sudden we all looked pale as ghosts. It made a very theatrical effect. 'Is that true about the police?' I asked the black-clad young man. 'It is true, my son!' he bawled out. 'But why? What's up?' 'Work it out for yourself. There are people who don't like this sort of thing,' and he slapped a nearby girl loudly on her naked thigh. I was not quite sure whether he was on the side of the police, or whether this was some kind of wild gesture of defiance. I shrugged. 'Let's see for ourselves, eh Charlie?' She nodded and followed me trustingly.

There was tumult everywhere, turmoil, unease and an edge of panic. Something was definitely up. Perhaps something unpleasant had happened, maybe an accident, or a fight. Could it be that even here some people had shot at each other, Nazis or Communists? It did not seem altogether impossible. We pushed our way through several rooms. There! The police really were there in their helmets and their blue uniforms. They stood there amid the turbulent flow of alarmed brightly costumed figures, like rocks in the breaking waves. Now we would find out. I approached one of them, a little deprecatingly, smiling, and confident, as one approaches a policeman to ask for directions. 'Do we really have to leave?'

'You have *permission* to leave,' was the reply, and I flinched, so threateningly had it been said: slowly, icily and maliciously. I looked at him – and flinched again. What kind of face was that? Not the usual, familiar, friendly, honest face of an ordinary policeman. This face seemed to consist entirely of teeth. The man had literally snarled at me, baring both rows of teeth, an unusual grimace for a human being. His teeth showed, small, pointed and evil like a shark's. The whole pale, blond face was fish-like and shark-like under the helmet, with watery colourless eyes and a pike's pointed nose above the teeth. Very Nordic, one had to admit, but then again not really human, rather more like the face of a crocodile. I shuddered. I had seen the face of the SS.

Nineteen

Two days later there was the Reichstag fire.

There have been few contemporary events that I missed so completely. While it was taking place I was visiting a friend in the suburbs. He was also a *Referendar*. We spoke of politics. Today he has a high position in the military administration. He is 'strictly apolitical', dutifully and conscientiously working on the technical aspects of attacks on foreign countries. Then he was a *Referendar* like me, a good companion, chagrined by his somewhat dry character, the product of an all too sheltered upbringing. As the only child of parents whose great hope he represented, he had been unable to escape the loving incarceration of their home. His great regret was that it seemed impossible for him ever to have a real love affair. He was certainly not a Nazi, but a 'nationalist' and for 'law and order'. He could not find his way out of this dilemma. He had always voted for the Deutsche Volkspartei (German People's Party), but he sensed that this was futile now. Perhaps he would not vote at all.

His visiting friends were wrestling for his political soul. 'You can't fail to see,' said one, 'that we now have a clear nationalist policy. How can you still dither? You have to decide one way or the other. So what if a few clauses go by the board?' A second friend countered that at least the Social Democrats had the merit of having 'integrated the working class into the state'. The present Government placed this hard-won achievement at risk. I provoked general mild disapproval with the 'frivolous' comment that it seemed to me a matter of good taste to vote against the Nazis, independently of where one stood politically.

'Well, then at least vote black, white and red' (meaning nationalist), the champion of the Nazis remarked carelessly.

While we were arguing rather pointlessly and drinking Moselle wine the Reichstag was burning. Poor Marinus van der Lubbe was found in the building, equipped with every conceivable piece of identification. Outside, against a flaming backdrop, like a Wagnerian Wotan, Hitler uttered the memorable words, 'If this is the work of the Communists, *which I do not doubt*, may God have mercy on them!' We had no inkling of all that. The radio was switched off. Around midnight we sleepily took the night buses to our various homes. At that very moment the raiding parties were already on their way to get their victims out of bed, in the first great wave of concentration-camp arrests: left-wing deputies and literary figures, unpopular doctors, officials and lawyers.

It was only next morning that I read about the fire, and not until midday that I read about the arrests. Around the same time a decree of Hindenburg's was promulgated. It abolished freedom of speech and confidentiality of the mail and telephone for all private individuals, while giving the police unrestricted rights of search and access, confiscation and arrest. That afternoon men with ladders went around, honest workmen, covering campaign posters with plain white paper. All parties of the Left had been prohibited from any further election publicity. Those newspapers that still appeared reported all this in a fawning, fervently patriotic, jubilant tone. We had been saved! What good luck! Germany was free! Next Saturday all Germans would come together in a festival of national exaltation, their hearts swelling with gratitude! Get the torches and flags out!

Thus the press. The streets were exactly the same as always. The cinemas were open. The law courts sat and heard cases. No sign of a revolution. At home people were a little confused, a little anxious, and tried to understand what was happening. That was difficult, very difficult, in such a short time.

So the Communists had burned down the Reichstag. Well, well. That could well be so, it was even to be expected. Funny, though, why they should choose the Reichstag, an empty building, where no one would profit from a fire. Well, perhaps it really had been intended as the 'signal' for the uprising, which had been prevented by the 'decisive measures' taken by the Government. That was what the papers said, and it sounded plausible. Funny also that the Nazis got so worked up about the Reichstag. Up till then they had contemptuously called it a 'hot air factory'. Now it was suddenly the holy of holies that had been burned down. Well, what suits their book, don't you agree, my friend, that's politics, isn't it? Thank God we don't understand it. The main thing is: the danger of a Communist uprising has been averted and we can sleep easy. Good night.

More seriously: perhaps the most interesting thing about the Reichstag fire is that the claim that it was the work of the Communists was so widely believed. Even the sceptics did not regard it as entirely incredible. That was the Communists' own fault. They had become a strong party in recent years, and had again and again trumpeted their 'readiness'. Nobody believed they would allow themselves to be 'prohibited' and slaughtered without putting up a fight. During the whole of February we had been permanently at 'eyes left', waiting for the Communist counter-strike. Not a Social Democrat counter-strike. Nobody expected anything from them any more, after the events of the 20th of July 1932.* On that day Severing and Grzesinski, protected by 80,000 heavily armed policemen and by the full support of the law, had backed down in the face of the 'superior might' of a single company of the army. A Communist attack was what we expected. The Communists were determined people, with fierce expressions. They raised their fists in salute, and had weapons – at least they used guns often enough in the everyday pub brawls. They boasted continually about the strength of their organisation, and they had probably learned how to do 'these things' in Russia. The Nazis had left no one in doubt that they wanted to destroy them. It was natural, indeed

---

* This is a reference to the illegal dismissal of the Prussian regional government, of which they were ministers, by the Chancellor of the time, Franz von Papen.

obvious, that the Communists would retaliate. It was only surprising that there had been nothing of the kind so far.

It took a long time for the Germans to realise that the Communists had been sheep in wolves' clothing. The Nazi myth of the Communist putsch that had been averted fell on fertile ground which had been prepared by the Communists themselves. Who would have believed that there was nothing behind the façade of raised fists? There are still some people in Germany who fall for the Communist scare, and that is the Communists' own doing. The number who do so is not very large any more; the poor showing of the German Communists is becoming common knowledge. Even the Nazis tend to avoid this particular tune, except with distinguished foreign visitors. They still fall for anything.

After all that, I do not see that one can blame the majority of Germans who, in 1933, believed that the Reichstag fire was the work of the Communists. What one can blame them for, and what shows their terrible collective weakness of character clearly for the first time during the Nazi period, is that this settled the matter. With sheepish submissiveness the German people accepted that, as a result of the fire, each one of them lost what little personal freedom and dignity was guaranteed by the constitution; as though it followed as a necessary consequence. If the Communists had burned down the Reichstag, it was perfectly in order that the Government took 'decisive measures'!

Next morning I discussed these matters with a few other *Referendars*. All of them were very interested in the question of who had committed the crime, and more than one of them hinted that they had doubts about the official version; but none of them saw anything out of the ordinary in the fact that, from now on, one's telephone would be tapped, one's letters opened and one's desk might be broken into. 'I consider it a personal insult,' I said, 'that *I* should be prevented from reading whichever newspaper I wish, because allegedly a Communist set light to the Reichstag. Don't you?' One of them cheerfully and harmlessly said, 'No. Why should I? Did you read *Forwards* and *The Red Flag* up to now?'

On the evening of this eventful Tuesday I made three telephone calls. The first was to my girlfriend Charlie, to arrange a rendezvous. I was a little in love with her, but it was largely out of defiance. I did not want my affairs interfered with, especially not now. Besides, Charlie was Jewish.

Then I phoned a ju-jitsu club and asked about their terms and ordered a prospectus. I had the feeling that the time had come when I ought to learn ju-jitsu. (However, I soon realised that the time had passed when ju-jitsu might have helped. A form of mental ju-jitsu was what was needed now.)

Finally, I phoned my faithful friend Lisl. Not for a rendez-vous, just to apologise for not seeing her since the ball and to ask how she had been, a more serious question than usual under the current circumstances.

On the phone Lisl's voice was tearful. She said: 'You are involved with the law, aren't you?' Did I know anything about what had happened to those detained yesterday? Her voice failed her. Then, with a hard edge to it, she asked, were they at least still alive? She had not yet adjusted to the phones being tapped.

Her partner had been arrested. This was not just a carnival boyfriend, but the man she loved. He was a well-known left-wing doctor. He was famous for organising a magnificent social/medical service in his borough – a working-class area. He had published articles in which he advocated legalising abortion on social grounds. So he was on the Nazis' first list.

I spoke to Lisl a few times during the next few weeks. There was no way of helping her, and it became ever harder to find anything comforting to say.

Twenty

W hat is a revolution?
Constitutional lawyers define it as a change of constitution by means not foreseen therein. By this definition the Nazi revolution of March 1933 was not a revolution. Everything went strictly 'by the book', using means that were permitted by the constitution. At first there were 'emergency decrees' by the President of the Reich, and later a bill was passed by a two-thirds majority of the Reichstag giving the Government unlimited legislative powers, perfectly in accordance with the rules for changing the constitution.

Now, that is obviously shadow-boxing, but even if we look at things as they really were, there is still room for doubt whether what happened that March really deserves the name of a revolution. From a simple common-sense point of view, one would say that the essential characteristic of a revolution is that people violently attack the established order and its representatives, police, army, etc., and overcome them. It need not always be thrilling and glorious. It can be accompanied by atrocities, brutality, plunder, murder and arson. At all events, we expect revolutionaries to be on the attack, to show courage, risk their lives. Barricades may be out of date, but some form of spontaneity, uprising, commitment and insurrection seem to be an essential part of a genuine revolution.

None of that was to be found in March 1933. The events were a combination of the most disparate ingredients. What was completely absent was any act of courage or spirit by any of the participants. The month of March demonstrated that the Nazis had achieved an unassailable position of power: through terror, celebration and rhetoric, treachery and finally a collective breakdown – a million individuals simultaneously suffered a nervous collapse. More bloodshed has accompanied the birth of many European states, but none came into being in a more loathsome way.

European history knows two forms of terror. The first is the uncontrollable explosion of bloodlust in a victorious mass uprising. The other is cold, calculated cruelty committed by a victorious state as a demonstration of power and intimidation. The two forms of terror normally correspond to revolution and repression. The first is revolutionary. It justifies itself by the rage and fever of the moment, a temporary madness. The second is repressive. It justifies itself by the preceding revolutionary atrocities.

It was left to the Nazis to combine both forms of terror in a manner that invalidates both justifications. In 1933 the terror was practised by a real bloodthirsty mass (namely the SA – the SS did not play a part until later) – but this mass acted as 'auxiliary police', without any emotion or spontaneity, and without any risk to themselves. Rather, they acted from a position of complete security, under orders and with strict discipline. The external picture was one of revolutionary terror: a wild unkempt mob breaking into homes at night and dragging defenceless victims to the torture chambers. The internal process was repressive terror: cold, calculated, official orders, directed by the state and carried out under the full protection of the police and the armed forces. It did not take place in the excitement following a victorious battle or danger successfully overcome – nothing of the kind had happened. Nor was it an act of revenge for atrocities committed by the other side – there had been none. What happened was a nightmarish reversal of normal circumstances: robbers and murderers acting as the police force, enjoying the full panoply of state power, their victims treated as criminals, proscribed and condemned to death in advance.

An example that became public knowledge because of its scale occurred some months later in the Cöpenick area of Berlin, where a Social Democratic trade unionist defended himself, with the help of his sons, against an SA patrol that broke into his home at night to 'arrest' him. In obvious self-defence he shot two SA men. As a result, he and his sons were overcome by a larger troop of SA men and hanged in a shed in the yard that same night. Next day the SA patrols appeared in Cöpenick, in disciplined order, entered the homes of every known Social Democrat and killed them on the spot. The exact number of deaths was never made public.

This form of terror had the advantage that, according to the circumstances, one could either shrug one's shoulders and speak of 'the unavoidable, if regrettable, side effects of any revolution' – using the justification for revolutionary terror – or point to the strict discipline and explain that public law and order were being maintained and that these actions were required to prevent revolutionary disorder overwhelming Germany – the justification for repressive terror. Both excuses were used in turn, depending on the audience being addressed.

Certainly, this kind of publicity made, and still makes, the terror under the Nazis more repulsive than under any other regime in European history. Even cruelty can have a magnificent aspect, if it is practised with open commitment and idealism; when those who are cruel stand by their deeds with fervour – as happened in the French Revolution and the Russian and Spanish civil wars. In contrast, the Nazis never showed anything but the sly, pale, cowardly face of a murderer denying his crime. While they were systematically torturing and murdering their defenceless victims, they daily declared in fine, noble words that not a single hair of anyone's head would be harmed, and that never before had a revolution shed less blood or been conducted more humanely. Indeed, only a few weeks after the atrocities began, a law was passed that forbade anyone, under pain of severe penalties, to claim, even in the privacy of their own home, that atrocities were taking place.

Of course, it was not the intention to keep the atrocities secret. In that case they would not have served their purpose, which was to induce general fear, alarm and submission. On the contrary, the purpose was to intensify the terror by cloaking it in secrecy and making even talking about it dangerous. An open declaration of what was happening in SA cellars and concentration camps – in a public speech or in the press – might still have led to desperate resistance, even in Germany. The secret whispered rumours, 'Be careful, my friend! Do you know what happened to X?' were much more effective in breaking people's backbones.

The effect was intensified by the way one was permanently occupied and distracted by an unending sequence of celebrations, ceremonies, and national festivities. It started with a huge victory celebration before the elections on the 4th of March – 'Tag der nationalen Erhebung' (day of national rising). There were mass parades, fireworks, drums, bands and flags all over Germany, Hitler's voice over thousands of loudspeakers, oaths and vows – and all before it was even certain that the elections might not be a setback for the Nazis, which indeed they were. These elections, the last that were ever held in pre-war Germany, brought the Nazis only 44 per cent of the votes (in the previous elections they had achieved 37 per cent). The majority was still against the Nazis. If you consider that terror was in full swing, that the parties of the Left had been prohibited from all public activity in the decisive final week before the elections, you have to admit that the German people as a whole had behaved quite decently. However, it made no difference at all. The defeat was celebrated like a victory, the terror intensified, the celebrations multiplied. Flags never left the windows for a whole fortnight.

A week later Hindenburg abolished the Weimar national flag, which was replaced by the swastika banner and a black, white and red 'temporary national flag'. There were daily parades, mass meetings, declarations of gratitude for the liberation of the nation, military music from dawn to dusk, award ceremonies for heroes, the dedication of flags and, as a final climax, the tasteless display of the 'Day of Potsdam' – with the traitor Hindenburg visiting the grave of Frederick the Great, Hitler swearing loyalty to something or other for the n-th time, bells tolling, a solemn procession to church of the members of the Reichstag, a military parade, swords lowered in salute, children waving flags and a torchlight parade.

The colossal emptiness and lack of meaning of these never-ending events was by no means unintentional. The population should become used to cheering and jubilation, even when there was no visible reason for it. It was reason enough that people who distanced themselves too obviously – sshh! – were daily and nightly tortured to death with steel whips and electric drills. Better to celebrate, howl with the wolves, 'Heil, Heil!' Besides, people began to enjoy doing so. The weather in March 1933 was glorious. Was it not wonderful to celebrate in the spring sunshine, in squares decked with flags? To merge with the festive crowds and listen to high-sounding patriotic speeches, about freedom, and fatherland, exaltation and holy vows? (It was certainly better than having one's belly pumped up with a water hose in some hidden SA cellar.)

People began to join in – at first mostly from fear. After they had participated, they no longer wanted to do so just from fear. That would have been mean and contemptible. So the necessary ideology was supplied. That was the spiritual basis of the victory of the National Socialist revolution.

True, something further was necessary to achieve all this. That was the cowardly treachery of all party and organisational leaders, to whom the 56 per cent of the population who had voted against the Nazis on the 5th of March had entrusted themselves. This terrible and decisive event was not much noticed by the outside world. Naturally, the Nazis had no interest in drawing attention to it, since it would considerably devalue their 'victory', and as for the traitors themselves: well, of course, they did not want attention drawn to it. Nevertheless, it is finally only this betrayal that explains the almost inexplicable fact that a great nation, which cannot have consisted entirely of cowards, fell into ignominy without a fight.

The betrayal was complete, extending from Left to Right. I have already described how, behind their façade of being 'ready' and prepared for civil war, the Communists were only preparing for the emigration of their leading members.

What of the Social Democratic leadership? Their betrayal of their faithful and blindly loyal millions of followers, for the most part decent, unimportant individuals, had begun on the 20th of July 1932, when Severing and Grzesinski 'yielded to greater force'. They had fought the election campaign of 1933 in a dreadfully humiliating way, chasing after the Nazi slogans and emphasising that they were 'also nationalist'. On the 4th of March, a day before the elections, their 'strong man', the Prussian prime minister Otto Braun, drove across the Swiss frontier. He had prudently bought a small house in Ticino. In May, a month before they were finally dissolved, the Social Democratic faction in the Reichstag had unanimously expressed their confidence in Hitler and joined in the singing of the Horst Wessel Song, the Nazi anthem. (The official parliamentary report noted: 'Unending applause and cheers, in the house and the galleries. The Reichschancellor turns to the Social Democratic faction and applauds.')

The great middle-class, Catholic party, Zentrum, which in the last few years had attracted the backing of more and more middle-class Protestants, had already fallen in March. It was this party that supplied the votes necessary for the two-thirds majority that 'legalised' Hitler's dictatorship. In this it followed its leader, the ex-Reichschancellor Brüning. This is frequently forgotten abroad, and Brüning is still considered as a possible replacement for Hitler. Believe me, it is not forgotten in Germany. A man who, even on the 23rd of March 1933, thought it tactically justifiable to procure for Hitler the votes of his party on a decisive issue has ruled himself out for ever there.

Finally, the German nationalists, the right-wing conservatives, who venerated 'honour' and 'heroism' as the central characteristics of their programme. Oh God, what an infinitely dishonourable and cowardly spectacle their leaders made in 1933 and continued to make afterwards! One might at least have expected that, once their claim in January proved illusory – that they had 'tamed' the Nazis and 'rendered them harmless' –

they would act as a 'brake' and 'prevent the worst'. Not a bit of it. They went along with everything: the terror, the persecution of the Jews, the persecution of Christians. They were not even bothered when their own party was prohibited, and their own members arrested. Socialist officials who abandon their party members and voters are a dismal enough sight; but what is one to say of aristocratic officers – like Herr von Papen – who stand by when their nearest friends and associates are shot, and who remain in office and shout 'Heil Hitler!'?*

As the parties, so the leagues. There was a 'League of Communist Front-Line Veterans' and a centrist association called Reichsbanner with a black, red and gold flag, the colours of the Weimar Republic. It was organised on military lines by a coalition of centrist parties including the Social Democrats, had arms and millions of members and was explicitly intended to hold the SA in check. During the whole period this association remained completely invisible, not a glimmer. It disappeared without trace, as though it had never existed. Resistance in Germany only took the form of individual acts of desperation – as in the case of the trade union official in Cöpenick. The officers of the Reichsbanner showed not the slightest opposition when their facilities were 'taken over' by the SA. The Stahlhelm, the army of the German nationalists, permitted itself to be absorbed and then dissolved bit by bit. They grumbled, but offered no resistance. There was not one single example of energetic defence, of courage or principle. There was only panic, flight, and desertion. In March 1933 millions were ready to fight the Nazis. Overnight they found themselves without leaders. Some tried to join the Stahlhelm and the German nationalists, when it became clear that none of the others were going to fight. For a few weeks their membership numbers showed an exceptional rise, then the organisation was disbanded – and it, too, capitulated without a fight.

This terrible moral bankruptcy of the opposition leadership is

* This is a reference to the murder of Kurt von Schleicher on 30 June 1934 (see page 29).

a fundamental characteristic of the March 'revolution' of 1933. It made the Nazi victory exceedingly easy. On the other hand, it also sheds doubt on the strength and durability of that victory. The swastika has not been stamped on the Germans as though they were a firm, resistant but malleable mass, but as though they were a formless, yielding pulp that can equally easily take a different form. Admittedly, March 1933 has left open the question as to whether it is worth the effort to try and reshape it. The moral inadequacy of the German character shown in that month is too monstrous to suppose that history will not one day call them to account for it.

With other nations, every revolution has ultimately led to an enormous increase in the moral energy of both sides, however much blood might initially have been shed, however much they had at first been weakened. In the long run, revolutions have thus always strengthened the nations concerned. Just consider the vast quantity of heroism, death-defying courage and human greatness exhibited by the Jacobins and the Royalists in the French Revolution – admittedly against a backdrop of cruelty and violence. It is the same with the Republicans and Franco supporters in Spain. Whatever the outcome, the courage of the fighters remains a source of strength in the mind of the nation. Instead of that source of strength, today's Germans have the memory of shame, cowardice and weakness. That will inevitably have consequences one day, perhaps even lead to the dissolution of the German state.

It was out of this treachery of its opponents, and the feeling of helplessness, weakness and disgust that it aroused, that the Third Reich was born. In the elections of the 5th of March the Nazis had remained a minority. If there had been elections three weeks later, the German people would almost certainly have given them a true majority. This was not just a result of the terror, or intoxication resulting from the constant festivities (though the Germans like being intoxicated by patriotic celebrations). The decisive cause was anger and disgust with the cowardly treachery of their own leadership. That had become for a moment stronger than the rage and hate against the real enemy. Hundreds of thousands, who had up till then been opponents, joined the Nazi Party in March 1933. The Nazis called them the 'casualties of March' and treated them with suspicion and contempt. The workers also left their Social Democratic and Communist unions in equally large numbers and joined Nazi Betriebszellen (factory cells) or the SA. They did it for many reasons, often for a whole tangled web of them; but however hard one looks, one will not find a single solid, positive, durable reason among them – not one that can pass muster. In each individual case the process of becoming a Nazi showed the unmistakable symptoms of nervous collapse.

The simplest and, if you looked deeper, nearly always the most basic reason was fear. Join the thugs to avoid being beaten up. Less clear was a kind of exhilaration, the intoxication of unity, the magnetism of the masses. Many also felt a need for revenge against those who had abandoned them. Then there was a peculiarly German line of thought: 'All the predictions of the opponents of the Nazis have not come true. They said the Nazis could not win. Now they have won. Therefore the opponents were wrong. So the Nazis must be right.' There was also (particularly among intellectuals) the belief that they could change the face of the Nazi Party by becoming a member, even now shift its direction. Then of course many just jumped on the bandwagon, wanted to be part of a perceived success. Finally, among the more primitive, inarticulate, simpler souls there was a process that might have taken place in mythical times when a beaten tribe abandoned its faithless god and accepted the god of the victorious tribe as its patron. Saint Marx, in whom one had always believed, had not helped. Saint Hitler was obviously more powerful. So let's destroy the images of Saint Marx on the altars and replace them with images of Saint Hitler. Let us learn to pray: 'It is the Jews' fault' rather than 'It is the capitalists' fault'. Perhaps that will redeem us.

The sequence of events is, as you see, not so unnatural. It is wholly within the normal range of psychology, and it helps to explain the almost inexplicable. The only thing that is missing is what in animals is called 'breeding'. This is a solid inner kernel that cannot be shaken by external pressures and forces, something noble and steely, a reserve of pride, principle and dignity to be drawn on in the hour of trial. It is missing in the Germans. As a nation they are soft, unreliable and without backbone. That was shown in March 1933. At the moment of truth, when other nations rise spontaneously to the occasion, the Germans collectively and limply collapsed. They yielded and capitulated, and suffered a nervous breakdown.

The result of this million-fold nervous breakdown is the unified nation, ready for anything, that is today the nightmare of the rest of the world.

Twenty-One

*T*hat was the sequence of events as it presents itself with the clarity and certainty of hindsight today. At the time, while I experienced them, it was not possible to gauge their significance. I felt, intensely, the choking, nauseous character of it all, but I was unable to grasp its constituent parts and place them in an overall order. Each attempt was frustrated and veiled by those endless, useless, vain discussions in which we attempted again and again to fit the events into an obsolete, unsuitable scheme of political ideas. How eerie these discussions now seem, when an accident of memory throws up a scrap of one of them. In spite of all our historical and cultural education, how completely helpless we were to deal with something that just did not feature in anything we had learned! How meaningless our explanations, how infinitely stupid the attempts at justification, how hopelessly superficial the jury-rigged constructions with which the intellect tried to cover up the proper feeling of dread and disgust. How stale all the 'isms' we brought up. I shudder to think of it.

Daily life also made it difficult to see the situation clearly. Life went on as before, though it had now definitely become ghostly and unreal, and was daily mocked by the events that served as its background. I still went to the *Kammergericht*, the law was still practised there, as though it still meant something, and the Jewish judge still presided in his robes, quite unmolested. However his colleagues now treated him with a certain tactful delicacy, like one does somebody suffering from a serious disease. I still phoned my girlfriend Charlie. We went to the cinema, had a meal in a small wine bar, drank Chianti, and went dancing together. I still saw my friends, had discussions with acquaintances. Family birthdays were still celebrated as they always had been. But while in February we could still question whether all this did not represent a triumph of indestructible reality over the Nazis' carryings-on, now it was no longer possible to deny that daily life itself had become hollow and mechanical. Every minute merely confirmed the victory of the enemy forces flooding in from all sides.

Strangely enough, it was just this automatic continuation of ordinary life that hindered any lively, forceful reaction against the horror. I have described how the treachery and cowardice of the leaders of the opposition prevented their organisations from being used against the Nazis or offering any resistance. That still leaves the question why no individuals ever spontaneously opposed some particular injustice or iniquity they experienced, even if they did not act against the whole. (I am not blind to the fact that this charge applies to me as much as to anyone else.)

It was hindered by the mechanical continuation of normal daily life. How different history would be if men were still independent, standing on their own two feet, as in ancient Athens. Today they are yoked to the details of their work and daily timetable, dependent on a thousand little details, cogs in a mechanism they do not control, running steadily on rails and helpless if they become derailed. Only the daily routine provides security and continuity. Just beyond lies a dark jungle. Every European of the twentieth century feels this in his bones and fears it. It is the cause of his reluctance to do anything that could 'derail' his life – something audacious or out of the ordinary. It is this lack of self-reliance that opens the possibility of immense catastrophes of civilisation like the rule of the Nazis in Germany.

Yes, I roared and raged during that March of 1933. Yes, I frightened my parents with wild proposals: I would leave the law courts; I would emigrate and demonstratively convert to Judaism. But it went no further than the expression of these intentions. Though it was not really relevant to current events, my father's immense experience of the period from 1870 to

1933 was deployed to calm me down and sober me up. He treated my heated emotions with gentle irony. I must admit that calm scepticism has always had a stronger influence on me than emotionally proclaimed convictions. It took me quite a while to realise that my youthful excitability was right and my father's wealth of experience was wrong; that there are things that cannot be dealt with by calm scepticism. I lacked the self-confidence to draw active conclusions from my feelings.

Perhaps, after all, I was exaggerating events. Perhaps it was best to hold steady and let things just pass over me. The only place where I felt confident and sure of myself was at the courts, where I was protected by the paragraphs of the Civil Code and legal procedure. Though for the moment the activities of the courts seemed to lack meaning, nothing had changed there. Maybe they would turn out to be durable and strong.

In this way, unsure of myself, temporising, I performed my routine daily duties. At home I gave way to fruitless and ridiculous outbursts at the dinner table. Excluded from events and passive like millions of others, I let events come at me.

And they did.

Twenty-Two

*A*t the end of March the Nazis felt strong enough to initiate the first act of their real revolution, a revolution not against some constitution or other, but against the basis of human society on earth, a revolution that, if nothing is done, will stop at nothing. The first diffident move was the boycott of the Jews on the 1st of April 1933.

It had been thought up by Hitler and Goebbels over tea and biscuits at the Obersalzberg in Bavaria the Sunday before. On Monday the papers carried the peculiarly ironic headlines, 'Mass Demonstrations Announced'. From Saturday the 1st of April, they said, all Jewish shops would be boycotted. SA troops would stand guard in front of them and prevent anyone from going in. All Jewish doctors and lawyers were also to be boycotted. SA patrols would check their consulting rooms to ensure that the ruling was obeyed.

One could see the advances that the Nazis had made in just one month by considering the justification for the boycott. The myth of a Communist coup that had been used to override the constitution and remove civil liberties had been carefully and plausibly constructed. They had even felt the need to supply some direct evidence in the form of the Reichstag fire. The justification for this new affront was a barefaced insult and mockery of those who were expected to act as though they believed it. The boycott was to be carried out as a defence and reaction against the totally unfounded horror stories about the new Germany that the German Jews were alleged to have cleverly spread abroad. Yes, just so.

Further measures were added in the next few days (some of

them later temporarily rescinded). All 'Aryan' shops had to sack their Jewish employees. Then all Jewish shops had to do so too. Jewish shops had to pay their 'Aryan' employees in full during the period they were closed by the boycott. Jewish owners had to withdraw from their businesses and install 'Aryan' managers. And so on.

At the same time a great 'education campaign' against the Jews was set in motion. The Germans were informed through pamphlets, posters and meetings that it had been a mistake to consider the Jews as human beings. In reality they were a kind of 'subhuman' animal, but with the characteristics of a devil. The consequences that would be drawn from this were not spelt out for the moment. Still, the campaign slogan was given out as *'Juda verrecke'* (Perish Judah). A man who had hitherto been unknown to most Germans was appointed as leader of the boycott: Julius Streicher.

All this aroused in the German people something one might not have expected after the previous four weeks: widespread alarm. A murmur of dissent, suppressed but audible, spread through the land. The Nazis sensed that they had gone too far for the moment, and withdrew some of their measures after the 1st of April. Not, however, without first allowing these to unleash the full force of their terror. By now everyone knows to what extent the Nazis have changed their true intentions.

Apart from the terror, the unsettling and depressing aspect of this first murderous declaration of intent was that it triggered off a flood of argument and discussions all over Germany, not about anti-Semitism but about the 'Jewish question'. This is a trick the Nazis have since successfully repeated many times on other 'questions' and in international affairs. By publicly threatening a person, an ethnic group, a nation, or a region, with death and destruction, they provoke a general discussion not about their own existence, but about the right of their victims to exist. In this way that right is put in question.

Suddenly everyone felt justified, and indeed required, to have an opinion about the Jews, and to state it publicly. Distinctions were made between 'decent' Jews and the others. If some pointed to the achievements of Jewish scientists, artists and doctors to justify the Jews (justify? what for? against what?), others would counter that they were a detrimental 'foreign influence' in these spheres. Indeed, it soon became customary to count it against the Jews if they had a respectable or intellectually valuable profession. This was treated as a crime or, at the very least, a lack of tact. The defenders of the Jews were frowningly told that it was reprehensible of the Jews to have such-and-such a percentage of doctors, lawyers, journalists, etc. Indeed, per cent calculations were a popular ingredient of the 'Jewish question'. People discussed whether the percentage of Jews among the members of the Communist Party was not too high, and among the casualties of the Great War perhaps too low. (This is the literal truth. I heard this argument in the mouth of an educated man with a Ph.D., who reckoned himself a member of the cultured class. He argued quite seriously that the 12,000 Jewish dead in the Great War was too small a proportion of the Jewish population in comparison with the corresponding number of 'Aryans' killed, and derived from this a certain justification for Nazi anti-Semitism.)

Today it is quite clear that Nazi anti-Semitism has nothing to do with the virtues or vices of the Jews. The interesting thing about the Nazis' intention to train the Germans to be persecutors of the Jews throughout the world, and if possible exterminate them, an intention they made no secret of, is not the justification they give. That is such utter nonsense that it is demeaning even to take it seriously enough to argue against it. It is the intention itself that is significant. It is something new in the history of the world: an attempt to deny humans the solidarity of every species that enables it to survive; to turn human predatory instincts, that are normally directed against animals, against members of their own species, and to make a whole nation into a pack of hunting hounds. Once the violence and readiness to kill that lies beneath the surface of human nature has been awakened and turned against other humans, and even made into a duty, it is a simple matter to change the target. That can be clearly seen today; instead of 'Jews', one can just as easily say 'Czechs' or 'Poles' or anyone else.

We have here the systematic infection of a whole nation, Germany, with a germ that causes its people to treat their victims like wolves; or, to put it differently, the freeing and revitalisation of precisely those sadistic instincts whose chaining and restraint has been the work of a thousand years of civilisation. In a later chapter I intend to show how, in spite of its general weakness and dishonour, large parts of the German nation still find the strength to resist, perhaps from a dark feeling for what is at issue. Were it different, and should the central core of the Nazis' programme become a reality, it would amount to a major crisis for humanity, and would place the survival of the species *Homo sapiens* at risk. It might only be possible to save the species by destroying the part infected by the 'wolf virus' completely.

This brief discourse shows that it is precisely the Nazis' anti-Semitism that raises the most basic questions of existence, not just for the Jews. That is not true to the same extent of any of their other election pledges. It shows how ridiculous the attitude is, still found widely in Germany, that the anti-Semitism of the Nazis is a small side issue, at worst a minor blemish on the movement, which one can regret or accept, according to one's personal feelings for the Jews, and of 'little significance compared to the great national issues'. In reality these 'great national issues' are unimportant day-to-day matters, the ephemeral business of a transitional period in European history – while the Nazis' anti-Semitism is a fundamental danger and raises the spectre of the downfall of humanity.

Again, these are all things that nobody saw with any clarity in March 1933. In this case, however, I can pride myself in having had a sense of what was in the air. I felt distinctly that what had happened so far was merely disgusting and no more. But what was in the offing had something apocalyptic about it. In rarely visited corners of my mind I felt that we were facing ultimate questions, though I did not yet know quite what they were.

At the same time, coupled with the feeling of dread, I had an almost joyful sense that events were closing in on me. I am what the Nazis call an 'Aryan'. Of course I know as little as anyone else which races go to make up my genetic heritage, but Jewish blood has not been in the family during the two or three hundred years that it can be traced. Nevertheless I feel a stronger instinctive affinity to the world of the German Jews than to the ordinary northern Germans among whom I grew up. My relationships with Jews go back a long way and have been very close. My oldest and closest friend was Jewish. My new little girlfriend Charlie was Jewish. I had really not taken this affair very seriously, but now that the hand of doom was reaching for her, I felt that I loved her a little more fiercely and passionately.

I phoned her on the evening of the day of the first announcements in the papers. That week I saw her almost every day, and our relationship began to take on the shape of a true love affair. Of course, in everyday life Charlie was not a little Turkish pageboy, as she had been at the ball. She was a girl from a lower-middle-class family with a confusing background and with many relatives. But she was a small, fragile, friendly person, and calamity threatened her. During these weeks I truly loved her.

I remember a bizarre scene with Charlie in that last week of March, amid the distant thunder of the approaching boycott. We had gone for a walk in the Grunewald, the woods to the west of Berlin. It was beautiful, unusually warm spring weather, as it had been throughout that March. We sat on the grass among the fir trees inhaling the scent of resin, under an indescribably clear sky with little clouds, like a couple in a film. The world was full of the peace of springtime. We sat there for about two hours and every ten minutes or so a group of young people would go past. It seemed to be a day for school outings. They were all fresh-faced adolescents accompanied and super-vised by their teachers, who often wore a pince-nez or a little beard, as one expects of a teacher faithfully watching over his little flock. Every one of these classes, as they passed, shouted '*Juda verrecke!*' to us in their bright young voices, as though it was a sort of hiker's greeting. It may not have been aimed at us in particular. I do not look at all Jewish, and Charlie (who was Jewish) did not look very Jewish either. Perhaps it was just a friendly greeting. Perhaps, though, it was intended for us and was a challenge.

So there I sat 'on the springtime hill' with a small, graceful, vivacious girl in my arms. We kissed and caressed each other, and every so often a group of boys went past and cheerfully told us to perish. Well, we did not oblige, and they went on their way, unconcerned by our failure to comply.

A surreal image.

Twenty-Three

*F*riday the 31st of March. Tomorrow things would get serious. I still could not quite believe it. I scanned the papers, looking for signs of any mitigation, perhaps some movement towards a more reasonable, acceptable position. There was nothing. Just the intensification of some measure or other and pedantic instructions about the details of the action and the manner in which it was to be executed.

Otherwise it was business as usual. Looking at the steady bustle and traffic on the streets, one had no sense that anything special was about to take place. Jewish shops were still open and trading as usual. Today one was still permitted to shop there. It would not be prohibited until tomorrow, at 8 a.m. precisely.

I went to the *Kammergericht*. It stood there, cool and grey as always, set back from the street in a distinguished setting of lawns and trees. Its halls were filled with the hushed fluttering of barristers in their bat-like, black silk gowns, carrying briefcases under their arms, with concentrated, serious expressions on their faces. Jewish barristers were pleading in court as though this were a day like any other.

Not being due in court, I went to the library (as though this were a day like any other), settled down at one of the long work tables, and started reading a document about which I had to give an opinion. Some complicated affair with intricate points of law. I carried the heavy legal tomes to my place and surrounded myself with them. I looked up decisions of the high courts of the Reich and made notes. As always, the high-ceilinged, spacious room was filled with the inaudible electricity of many minds hard at work. In making pencil marks on paper, I was setting the instruments of the law to work on the details of my case, summarising, comparing, weighing the importance of this or that word in a contract, investigating what bearing this or that clause would have on the matter, according to the precedents. When I scribbled a few words something happened, like the first cut in a surgical operation: a question was clarified, a component of a judicial decision put in place. Not the final decision, naturally: 'It is thus irrelevant whether the plaintiff . . . so it remains to investigate whether . . .' Careful, precise, silent work. Everybody in the room was similarly immersed in their own cases. Even the ushers, somewhere between beadles and policemen, moved more quietly here in the library, and seemed to try and make themselves invisible. The room was full of extreme silence, a silence filled with the high tension of deeply concentrated work. It was like a silent concert. I loved this atmosphere. At home I would have been unable to work today, here it was perfectly easy. Your thoughts just could not stray. It was like being in a fortress, or better, a test-tube. No breath came in from the outside world; here there was no revolution.

What was the first noticeable noise? A door banging? A distant sound like an order being given? Suddenly everybody raised their heads, and strained to hear what it was. The room was still utterly quiet: but the quality of the silence had changed. It was no longer the silence of concentrated work. It was filled with alarm and agitation. There was a clatter of footsteps outside in the corridor, the sound of rough boots on the stairs, then a distant indistinct din, shouts, doors banging. A few people got up and went to the door, looked out, and came back. One or two approached the ushers and spoke quietly with them – in here no one ever raised their voice. The noise from outside grew stronger. Somebody spoke into the silence: 'SA.' Then, not particularly loudly, somebody else said, 'They're throwing out the Jews,' and a few others laughed. At that moment this laughter alarmed me more than what was actually happening. With a start I realised that there were Nazis working in this room. How strange.

Gradually the disturbance took shape – at first it had been

intangible. Readers got up, tried to say something to one another, paced about slowly to no great purpose. One man, obviously a Jew, closed his books, packed his documents and left. Shortly afterwards somebody, perhaps a superintendent, appeared in the doorway and announced clearly but calmly, 'The SA are in the building. The Jewish gentlemen would do well to leave.' Almost at once we heard shouts from outside: 'Out with the Jews!' A voice answered, 'They've already gone,' and again I heard two or three merry giggles, just as before. I could see them now. They were *Referendars* just like me.

The premature end to the carnival ball four weeks ago came unpleasantly to mind. Things were breaking down now, as then. Several readers packed their cases and left. I was reminded of the phrase, 'You have *permission* to leave.' Did they still have permission? Today it was no longer so certain. Others left their things on the tables and went out of the library to see what was going on. More than ever, the ushers tried to be invisible. Of those of us who stayed behind, one or two lit cigarettes – in the library of the *Kammergericht*! The ushers took no action. That itself was something of a revolution.

The scouts later explained what had happened in the main part of the building. No atrocities, why, certainly not! Everything went extremely smoothly. The courts had, for the most part, adjourned. The judges had removed their robes and left the building quietly and civilly, going down the staircase lined with SA men. The only place where there had been trouble was the barristers' room. A Jewish barrister had 'caused a fuss' and been beaten up. Later I heard who it was. He had been wounded five times in the last war, had lost an eye, and even been promoted to captain. It had probably been his misfortune that he still remembered the tone to use with mutineers.

In the meantime, the intruders had arrived at the library. The door was thrust open and a flood of brown uniforms surged in. In a booming voice, one of them, clearly the leader, shouted, 'Non-Aryans must leave the premises immediately.' It struck me that he used the careful expression 'non-Aryans', but also a rather colloquial expression for 'premises'. Someone, probably the same person as before, answered, 'They've already left.' Our ushers stood there as though they were about to salute. My heart beat heavily. What should I do, how keep my poise? Just ignore them, do not let them disturb me. I put my head down over my work. I read a few sentences mechanically: 'The defendant's claim that . . . is untrue, but irrelevant . . .' Just take no notice!

Meanwhile a brown shirt approached me and took up position in front of my work table. 'Are you Aryan?' Before I had a chance to think, I had said, 'Yes.' He took a close look at my nose – and retired. The blood shot to my face. A moment too late I felt the shame, the defeat. I had said, 'Yes'! Well, in God's name, I was indeed an 'Aryan'. I had not lied, I had allowed something much worse to happen. What a humiliation, to have answered the unjustified question as to whether I was 'Aryan' so easily, even if the fact was of no importance to me! What a disgrace to buy, with a reply, the right to stay with my documents in peace! I had been caught unawares, even now. I had failed my very first test. I could have slapped myself.

As I left the *Kammergericht* it stood there, grey, cool and calm as ever, set back from the street in its distinguished setting. There was nothing to show that, as an institution, it had just collapsed. There was also nothing about my appearance to show that I had just suffered a terrible reverse, a defeat that would be almost impossible to make good. A well-dressed young man walked down the Potsdamer Strasse. There was nothing untoward about the scene. Business as usual, but in the air the approaching thunder of events to come . . .

Twenty-Four

*T*hat evening I had two more noteworthy experiences. The first was that for about an hour I feared for the life of my little friend Charlie. The fear turned out to be unfounded – but not unjustified.

The cause was ridiculous enough. We missed each other. We had agreed to meet outside the department store where she earned 100 marks a month in the typing pool. She was not, after all, a Turkish pageboy, but a young girl from a hard-working family, with plenty to worry about. When I arrived at 7 p.m. the store was already closed. It lay dark and silent with the roller shutters all drawn. It was a Jewish business, there was no one there. Perhaps the SA had been there today already.

I took the underground to Charlie's home and climbed the stairs of the large apartment building. I rang the doorbell, twice, three times. There was no sound from the flat. I went down to the street and phoned from a telephone box. No reply. I went and waited rather futilely at the entrance to the underground, where she would have arrived if she had come home from work. Crowds flowed in and out, undisturbed and unchecked, as they did every day. Charlie was not among them. Every now and then I tried to phone again, without success.

All this while I felt a weakness in my knees, a feeling of utter helplessness. Had she been 'picked up' in her flat or 'taken away' from work? Perhaps she was already in the police cells at the Alexanderplatz or on her way to Oranienburg, where the first concentration camp had been opened? There was no knowing. Anything was possible. The boycott could be just a demonstration, but it could also be the excuse – '*Juda verrecke!*' – for deliberate, general, disciplined murder and slaughter. The uncertainty was one of the most subtle effects of the terror. To fear for the life of a Jewish girl on the 31st of March 1933 was not unreasonable – even if the fear turned out to be groundless.

This time it was groundless. After about an hour, when I again made my phone call, I unexpectedly heard Charlie's voice at the other end of the line. The employees of the store had left together and sat around trying to decide what to do, since they had obviously just lost their jobs. They had not had any ideas. No, the SA had not been in the store today. 'I'm so sorry. It took so long. I was on tenterhooks the whole time . . .' Her parents? They had gone to the hospital to visit an aunt who had had a baby today of all days, impertinently disobeying the order '*Juda verrecke!*' However, it was difficult to imagine what would happen tomorrow, when the hospital and the doctor had to be boycotted. The possibility that the patients would be driven out – as indeed happened five years later – was already in the air then. We felt it darkly, but we could not quite bring it into the open. The coming events remained, for the moment, unreal.

At that instant I felt mainly relief, and also perhaps that in my anxiety I had made myself ridiculous. Five minutes later Charlie appeared, very chic, with a little feather cap cocked on one side of her head, a young city girl ready for a night out. Indeed, our current problem was where to go. It was past nine, too late for the cinema, but we wanted to go somewhere; after all we had a date. At last I thought of something that only started at half past nine. We took a taxi to the Katakombe.

There was a hint of madness about it all, which you could even sense while it was happening. Now, as I view events from a distance, it is much clearer. Having just experienced real fear for someone's life, and unsure whether the next day might not be genuinely life-threatening for one of us, I nevertheless saw no reason why we should not go to a cabaret.

Incidentally, it is typical of the early years of the Nazi regime that the whole façade of everyday life remained virtually unchanged. The cinemas, theatres and cafés were full. Couples danced in the open air and in the dance halls. People strolled down the streets. The Nazis used this to great effect in their propaganda. 'Come and see our normal, peaceful, quiet country. Come and see how well even the Jews are doing here.' The secret vein of madness, fear and tension, of living by the day, and dancing a dance of death: those one could not see. Just as when you see the smiling face on a poster for razor blades in today's underground stations, you do not see that it belongs to a man whose head was cut off in Plötzensee prison four years ago, for 'high treason', or what goes by that name today.

The fact that this was possible also speaks against us. Our reaction to the experience of fearing for one's life, and being totally at the mercy of events, was only to try and ignore the situation and not allow it to disturb our fun. I think a couple of a hundred years ago would have known better how to deal with such an experience – if only by celebrating a great night of love, spiced by danger and the sense of loss. Charlie and I did not think of doing anything special, and just went to the cabaret because nobody stopped us: firstly because we would have gone anyway, and secondly, in order to think about unpleasant things as little as possible. That may seem cold-blooded and daring, but it really only indicates a weakness of the emotions. We were not equal to the situation, even as victims. If you will allow me this generalisation, it is one of the uncanny aspects of events in Germany that the deeds have no doers and the suffering has no martyrs. Everything takes place under a kind of anaesthesia. Objectively dreadful deeds produce a thin, puny emotional response. Murders are committed like schoolboy pranks. Humiliation and moral decay are accepted like minor incidents. Even death under torture only produces the response: 'Bad luck'.

That evening, however, we were recompensed for our inadequacy beyond our deserts. Chance had led us to the Katakombe, and this was the second remarkable experience of the evening. We arrived at the only place in Germany where a kind of public, courageous, witty and elegant resistance was taking place. That morning I had witnessed how the Prussian *Kammergericht*, with a tradition of hundreds of years, had ignobly capitulated before the Nazis. In the evening I experienced how a small troop of artistes, with no tradition to back them up, saved our honour with grace and glory. The *Kammergericht* had fallen but the Katakombe stood upright.

The man who led this small group of actors to victory – standing firm in the face of overwhelming, murderous odds must be counted as a victory – was called Werner Fink.* This minor cabaret master of ceremonies has his place in the annals of the Third Reich, indeed one of the very few places of honour there. He did not look like a hero, and if he finally became something like one, it was in spite of himself. He was not a revolutionary actor, had no biting satire; he was not David with a sling. His character was at bottom harmless and amiable, his wit gentle, light and capricious. His jokes were based on double entendre and puns, which he handled like a virtuoso. He had invented something that could be called the hidden punch-line. Indeed, as time went by it became more and more necessary for him to hide his punch-lines, but he did not conceal his opinions. His act remained full of harmless amiability in a country where these qualities were on the liquidation list. This harmless amiability hid a kernel of real, indomitable courage. He dared to speak openly about the reality of the Nazis, and that in the middle of Germany. His patter contained references to concentration camps, the raids on people's home, the general fear and general lies. He spoke of these things with infinitely quiet mockery, melancholy and sadness. Listening to him was extraordinarily comforting.

This 31st of March was perhaps his greatest evening. The house was full of people staring at the next day as if into an abyss. Fink made them laugh as I have never heard an audience laugh. It was dramatic laughter, the laughter of a newborn defiance, throwing off numbness and desperation, feeding off the present danger. It was a miracle that the SA had not long since arrived to arrest everybody here. On this evening we

* Werner Fink, comic actor and satirical cabaret performer, founded the Katakombe in 1929. It was closed by the Nazis in 1935. Fink survived the war and died in 1978.

would probably have gone on laughing in the police vans. We had been improbably raised above fear and danger. That morning in the *Kammergericht* I had felt weak and indecisive when put to the test. Here I felt strong, brave and resourceful. If they came here – they, not we, would make the worse showing. The proper words had probably already been sharpened.

We felt a strange, morbid ecstasy as we left, at about midnight, still free. We were in high spirits, talked wildly and kissed each other on the street, drunk on something more powerful than alcohol – courage. We felt absurdly invulnerable.

It was already the 1st of April.

Twenty-Five

'If you notice that they are entering people's homes, Charlie, come to me,' I said as we parted; though I must admit I wondered how I could explain it to my parents. That, however must take second place. 'You will be safe with us, I hope. Promise you'll come.' She was touched, and promised to do so.

Thank God she did not need to. She would not have found me at home. For the next day –.

At ten o'clock in the morning, I received a telegram. 'Please come if you can. Frank'. I said goodbye to my parents, almost like someone leaving for war, and took the suburban railway out towards the East to see Frank Landau. I was not unhappy to be called on to do something, instead of passively awaiting the turn of events.

Frank Landau was my oldest and best friend. We had known each other since we started grammar school in the same class, had raced together in the Rennbund Altpreussen and later in proper athletics clubs. We had gone to university together and were now both *Referendars*. We had shared virtually every boyish hobby and enthusiasm. We had read each other our first literary attempts and had continued this with more serious pieces later. We both vaguely considered ourselves to be authors rather than *Referendars*. Some years we had seen each other every day, and we told each other everything – including our love affairs, which we discussed in detail without feeling at all indiscreet, rather as one thinks about them when one is alone. In the seventeen years we had known each other we had never seriously quarrelled. That would have been like quarrelling with yourself. As adolescents we had derived much pleasure from analysing our differences, among which we counted our racial origins the least. They did not separate us.

He was the more brilliant of the two of us. He was very handsome, tall, broad-shouldered, but otherwise lightly built – as a young boy he had been compared to an Apollo; later when his nose had become more prominent, his brow higher and his face more lined, he reminded me more of the young King Saul. His life also, though it was very similar to mine, seemed to be laid out on slightly grander lines. His emotions rose higher and sank deeper, love shook him more than me, and there was more lustre about his adolescence – for which, however, he paid by periods of deep, devouring, desperate despondency, which I was spared.

He was currently in the latest of these depressions, and it had lasted dangerously long. This time it had an external cause. A year before, his girlfriend, Hanni, had been unfaithful – a chance affair, thoughtlessly entered, not really serious. It had completely overwhelmed him. That seems a bit ridiculous by the usual twentieth-century standards in love affairs; but this had been a great passion, of a character quite out of fashion, and, it sometimes seems, no longer possible, like Goethe's *Werther* or *La nouvelle Héloise*, the kind that produced Heine's book of Songs, or Chopin's waltzes. This sort of passion cannot bear light-hearted faithlessness, and what I had witnessed, first with him, and then, when she realised what she had done, with her, was almost a complete inner collapse. The aftermath had been depressing: separation, an incomplete and skewed reconciliation; his attempts at affairs with other women had left him ever more unhappy and at sea. The patched-up friendship with Hanni was merely a caricature of the past; there was a gradual spiritual dwindling and decline, things only got more and more hopeless and tangled. It was the kind of story you read in a novel; it is the toll that is exacted for the bliss of great passion. Recently, another girl had appeared on the scene. Her name was Ellen. She was a cool, intelligent young lady, a student, fairly intellectual in her tastes, who had a not unpleasant air of

SH's family in 1918. He is seated between his parents,
his two brothers and sister stand behind them.

SH's father, c.1932.

SH in the mid-1920s. This was his mother's favourite portrait of him.

SH with his mother in the mid-1930s.

A party in the late 1920s.
SH is on the right.

Carnival in Berlin. SH is
third from the left.

Left: The tennis club at the Heidelberger Platz, *c.*1929. SH with ?Teddy.

Bottom left: SH, ?Teddy and a friend, *c.*1929.

Opposite: Bavaria, September 1923. Hitler and henchmen on the way to a demonstration. Note the swastika on the car door.

Opposite below: A Nazi parade in Berlin in 1930.

Opposite top: Berlin, 22 January 1933. A large Nazi demonstration outside the headquarters of the German Communist Party, in the Bülow Platz, the centre of a working-class area.

Opposite bottom: Berlin, 22 January 1933. A street near the Bülow Platz at the same time. The area in the vicinity of the Platz had been cordoned off and traffic diverted. Thousands of armed police ensured that residents kept their windows shut.

Top: Berlin, 1 April 1933. A Jewish department store.

Right: Berlin, 1 April 1933. Notice in a shoe-shop window. The photo may have been retouched at the time to insert the English text.

Brandenburg Gate, Berlin, 30 January 1933. The night-time parade by the SA, celebrating Hitler's appointment as Chancellor.

upper-middle-class calm and regularity – the personification of a cultured convalescence and rehabilitation after murderous revolutions, turbulence and suffering. I had recently been introduced to her – or rather Frank had presented her to me. Afterwards, he had asked me half jokingly what I would say if he got engaged to her. Then he would take his *Assessor* examinations, marry and become a bourgeois. Was she not the perfect wife for that? I had laughed and called the idea a bit hasty. Frank had also laughed, and we had moved on to other matters.

So now I was travelling to his home. His father, with whom he lived, was a doctor, and so under boycott. I was curious how things would look there.

It looked barbarous but also rather ordinary. The doors of Jewish shops, which were quite common in the Eastern part of Berlin, stood open. SA men stood in front of them with their legs planted apart. Obscenities were smeared on the windows, and the shop owners had for the most part made themselves scarce. Bunches of people stood around, half anxious, half gleeful. The whole business seemed awkward and halting, as though they were all expecting something more, but were not quite sure what. It did not give the impression of imminent bloodshed. I arrived at the Landaus' flat without difficulties. *They* were apparently not coming into people's homes yet, I concluded, with relief for my friend Charlie.

Frank was not there. Instead I was received by his father, a large, jovial old man. We had often had conversations when I was there, and he had generously enquired after my literary work, sung the praises of Maupassant, whom he admired above all others, and pressed me with a certain severity to try quantities of spirits, so to speak testing the fineness of my palate. Today he was offended. Not worried or anxious. Just offended. Many Jews still had this attitude at that time, and I hasten to add that I regard that as a very strong point in their favour. In the meantime the majority have lost the strength for it. They have suffered too many blows. It is the same process that happens, compressed into a few minutes, when an individual in a concentration camp is tied to blocks and flogged to a pulp: the first blow strikes his pride and his spirit rears up wildly; the tenth and twentieth strike only the body and produce little more than a whimper. In the last six years the German Jewish community has collectively gone through a comparable experience.

Old Landau had not yet been beaten to pulp then. He was offended – and the only thing that startled me was that he considered me an emissary of those who had offended him. 'Well, what do *you* say?' he began, and ignoring my stammered explanation that I considered it just as disgusting, he faced up to me and said, 'Do you really think I have invented false horror stories and spread them abroad? Does any one of you believe that?' I was somewhat taken aback to see that he was preparing to plead his cause. 'The Jews would have to be a lot more stupid than we are to send horror stories to foreign countries. As though we had not also seen the newspaper reports that all letters may now be opened! Strangely enough we are still allowed to read the papers. Does anyone really believe this stupid lie, that we are inventing horror stories? And if nobody believes it, then what do they mean by it? Can you tell me that?'

'Of course nobody with any sense believes it,' I said. 'But what does that matter? The fact is that you have fallen into the hands of enemies. We have all fallen into their hands. They have us now, and they can do with us what they will.'

He stared bitterly at the ashtray in front of him and only half listened. 'It's the *lies* that so outrage me,' he said, 'the damned, disgusting lies in all this. Why don't they just kill us, if that's what they want? As far as I'm concerned, I am old enough. But they shouldn't spread these dirty lies as well. You tell me why they're doing that!' Deep inside he could clearly not let go of the idea that somehow I was linked to the Nazis and knew their secrets.

Mrs Landau joined us, greeted me with a sad smile and tried to come to my defence. 'Why are you asking Frank's friend these questions?' she said. 'He knows as little as we do. He's not a National Socialist.' (She said 'National Socialist' formally, politely.) But her husband continued to shake his head as though he were trying to shake off everything we said. 'Tell me please why they are lying,' he insisted. 'Why do they still lie, when they already have the power to do what they like? I want to know that.'

'I think you should look at the boy,' she said. 'He's moaning so.'

'For God's sake,' I said, 'is your son ill?' Frank had a younger brother. They were obviously talking about him.

'It seems so,' said Mrs Landau. 'He was so terribly upset when he was expelled from the university yesterday, and today he's been sick repeatedly and is complaining of stomach pains. It looks a bit like appendicitis, although,' and she made an attempt at a smile, 'although I've never heard of anybody getting appendicitis from being upset.'

'A lot happens nowadays that nobody has ever heard of,' said the old man grimly, and he got up. He went to the door with heavy steps, then turned round once more and said: 'You're a good lawyer, aren't you? Can you tell me this: is my son committing an offence by letting me examine him, instead of boycotting me?'

'Don't be offended,' said Mrs Landau. 'He can't get over it. Frank will be here any minute and we shall have lunch. How are you and your family? Is your father well?'

Frank arrived. He entered the room quickly and spoke very calmly. His calm had an air of great tension and caution, like the calm of generals at a map table or also of certain monomaniacs developing their *idée fixe* with pedantic logic.

'Good of you to come,' he said, 'excuse my lateness. I couldn't help it. Later I want to ask you several favours. I'm leaving.'

'When and where to?' I asked with the same tense calm.

'To Zurich,' he said. 'Tomorrow morning if possible. My father is still opposed, but I will go. You know what happened yesterday at the *Kammergericht*?'

'I was there myself,' I said (oh dear, I remembered that Frank had been in court yesterday!).

'Well, then you know,' he said. 'There's nothing left for me here, so I'm leaving. You must help me get ready. Besides, I have just got engaged.'

'To Ellen?'

'Yes, she's coming with me. I have to talk to her parents today. I'd be grateful if you could come along. She has to talk to them too. I need your help for many things today.'

'And Hanni?'

'I will have to talk to her too, tonight,' he said. For a moment he seemed less calm and collected and there was a strained sound to his voice.

'That's a lot for one day,' I said.

'Yes,' he said, 'and you must help me get through it.'

'Of course,' I said, 'I'm at your disposal.'

Then we were called to lunch.

Mrs Landau tried without success to get a normal conversation going. Her husband kept bursting in; we mostly sat in silence.

'Well, has he told you yet that he wants to leave?' Frank's father asked suddenly. 'What do you think of that?'

'I think it's very sensible,' I said. 'He should leave while he can. What's left for him here?'

'Staying put,' said the old man. 'Just because of the troubles he should stay and not let them chase him away. He has passed his exams, he has the right to become a judge. Let's see if they can –'

'Oh, Papa,' Frank interrupted impatiently.

'I fear,' said I, 'that that right has evaporated since the *Kammergericht* judges allowed the SA into their chambers.' (I remembered what had happened, and I blushed). 'I fear we have no position left to defend. We're all virtually prisoners now, and flight is the only alternative left to us. I want to leave too.'

I really did want to leave, though not quite by tomorrow morning . . .

'You too?' asked Mr Landau. 'Why you?' He could obviously not get rid of the idea that as an 'Aryan' I must have become a Nazi; he had probably experienced that too often recently to consider any other possibility.

'Because I dislike what's happening here,' I said. It sounded rather thin and arrogant, though I had just wanted to say it as simply as possible.

The old man did not reply and sank into silence. 'I shall lose both my sons in one day,' he said after a while.

'Oh Ernst!' cried his wife.

'The little one needs an operation,' he said. The most beautiful acute appendicitis. I can't do it. My hands are not steady enough. And will anybody else do it today? Shall I phone round and beg: oh, dear colleague, or dear ex-colleague, would you operate on my son for God's sake – but he's a Jew?'

'So-and-so will do it,' said Mrs Landau. She mentioned a name that I have forgotten.

'Well he ought to,' said her husband. He laughed and said to me: 'We did amputations in a field hospital together for two years. But can one tell today?'

'I'll phone him,' said Mrs Landau. 'I'm sure he'll do it.' She was quite magnificent that day.

After the meal, we went in to see the sick boy for a few minutes. He smiled awkwardly as though he had done something naughty, suppressing a moan from time to time. 'So you're leaving?' he asked his brother. 'Yes.' 'Well, I can't go today,' the young boy said. 'Will you say goodbye to me later?'

Frank looked dejected as we left the room. 'It's horrible,' I said. 'Yes, it is truly horrible,' he replied. 'I don't know what will become of the boy. He can't stand injustice, and he has no means of coping with it. Do you know what he told me yesterday, after all that has happened? He would like to save Hitler's life; and then say to him, "Right. I'm a Jew. Now let's talk things over for an hour . . ."'

We went into Frank's room. Open suitcases lay around and suits had been laid out. It was about two o'clock. 'At six I have to meet Ellen at *Wannsee* station,' he said, 'so we have to leave at five. There's a lot to do till then.'

'Packing?' I asked.

'That too,' he said, 'but mainly something else. This is where I need your help. I have a pile of stuff – old letters, old pictures, old diaries, poems, souvenirs, and whatever. I don't want to leave it all here, but I can't take it with me. I don't want to destroy it all. Would you look after some of it?'

'Of course.'

'We have to go through it all now. It's fairly untidy, some of it can just be thrown away. Shall we try and go through it quickly?'

He pulled open a drawer. Two great heaps of papers, albums and diaries lay inside: his past life. A large part of it was also mine. Frank took a deep breath and smiled. 'We have to get a move on, we haven't got much time.'

And so we went through the papers, opened old letters, let old photos run through our fingers. Oh, what flowed out towards us there! It was our youth that had been preserved in that drawer, like dried flowers in an album, their perfume made stronger and more concentrated by being dead, belonging irretrievably to the past. Old pictures of us in sporting dress among friends, of a boat trip with some girls ! 'My God, do you remember?' – beach pictures, bathed in the sun of distant days, our faces patches of light and shade; tennis pictures of happy days; where were the friends now, with whom we saw ourselves arm in arm, the cheerful girls chasing tennis balls, for ever suspended by the shutter's click? Frank opened envelopes. Manuscripts that had once been familiar and exciting reappeared and called urgently for our attention. Here was one in my handwriting as it had been a few years ago ...

We are all familiar with the great clear-out. It is a job for rainy Sundays, and we all know the nostalgic titillation of conjuring up the past, the irresistible urge to read everything again, to experience everything again ... also the narcotic stupor that gradually creeps over us with its yielding softness. It always costs one whole day and usually the night as well, and the longer it goes on, the more one yields to these dreams.

We had just three hours and we raced through our dream landscapes with the flickering speed of a cartoon chase. In addition we had to be strict and destructive. The big box only had room for the most valuable items, which would lie there gathering dust for some far-off moment of leisure and smiles – when would I experience that again? The rest went into the wastebasket. A field trial of our own youth. What had value, what was important? We grew ever more silent at our strange work. Time was running. We had to be quick, quick at killing – or burying.

We were interrupted twice. The first time Mrs Landau came in to say that the ambulance was waiting outside. Frank's brother was being taken to the clinic for the operation. She and her husband would go with him. If Frank wanted to say goodbye, now was the time. 'Yes,' said Frank. It was a strange parting; one brother headed for the operating theatre, the other for exile. 'Excuse me a moment,' said Frank and left with his mother.

He stayed away five minutes.

The second interruption came about an hour later. The flat was empty apart from us and the maid. We heard the doorbell, and then the maid knocked and said two SA men were outside.

They were two coarse, plump young men in brown shirts and breeches and marching boots; not SS sharks, just the kind of people who might otherwise be delivering a case of beer, and touch their caps mumbling rough thanks for the tip. They were clearly unused to their new position and task, and they covered up their embarrassment by a certain strident stiffness.

'Heil Hitler,' they chorused at the top of their voices.

Silence. Then the one who was obviously senior asked:

'Are you Dr Landau?'

'No,' answered Frank, 'his son.'

'And you?'

'I'm a friend of Mr Landau,' I said.

'And where is your father?'

'He's gone to the clinic with my brother,' answered Frank. He spoke slowly and measured his words.

'What's he doing there?'

'My brother needs an operation.'

'Well, that's all right then,' said the SA man, with an air of genial satisfaction. 'Show us the consulting room.'

'If you please,' said Frank and opened the door. The two men stomped past us into the consulting room, which lay empty, white and tidy before them, and looked severely at the many shining instruments.

'Any patients today?' asked the spokesman.

'No,' said Frank.

'Well, that's all right then,' he said again. It seemed to be his catch-phrase. 'Show us the other rooms.'

And he stomped through the flat with his companion, casting disapproving, inquisitive glances all around, a bit like a bailiff choosing items to impound. 'So nobody else has been here,' he said at last, and after Frank had confirmed, 'Well, that's all right then,' a third time. We stood at the front door again, and the two men hesitated, as though they felt they ought to do something now. Then out of the general silence they suddenly chorused, 'Heil Hitler!' at the top of their voices again and stomped down the stairs. We shut the door behind them and returned to our work in silence.

Time ran away with us and towards the end we acted more and more summarily. Whole packets of letters were thrown into the bin unread. Perhaps we felt more strongly than an hour ago how completely destroyed and done with our youth had become. What did it matter if its vestiges were obliterated?

Five o'clock. We tied up the box and surveyed our work of destruction. 'I'll pack the other stuff sometime tonight,' said Frank. He still had to phone the clinic, and I had to phone Charlie. Then he told the maid he was leaving.

'Do your parents know about your engagement?'

'No. It would be too much at one go for them. It will all just have to take its course.'

At the kiosk there was a copy of *Angriff!* (Attack!), which had just come off the press, it had the cheering headline, 'Storm Signals.'

We took the suburban railway and rode from the East through the centre of Berlin and out again to the West. In the train we had a chance to talk for the first time that day, but we did not have a real conversation. Too many people got in and out and sat near us. We could not tell whether they were informers, and then there were so many things to organise, with which we had to interrupt ourselves – messages, favours and errands that we had to arrange. His plans? They were vague enough. First he wanted to do a Swiss Ph.D., to survive as a student on 200 marks a month (200 marks a month could still legally be sent abroad). He also had some kind of uncle in Switzerland. Perhaps he could help out … 'The main thing is to get out. I'm worried that soon they won't let us out.'

In truth, that day the whole potion had already been brewed, though it was put on ice again, and only administered five years later. At *Wannsee* station Ellen was waiting for us. Wordlessly she showed us a newspaper. It contained an item 'Exit visas introduced'. The justification was again, I believe, the alleged spreading of horror stories abroad.

'It looks as though we're already trapped,' said Frank. Ellen, a self-controlled and well-brought-up young lady, suddenly punched the sky with clenched fists, a gesture more suited to the stage or pictures in a museum. It was startling, coming from a well-dressed young lady in a leafy suburb.

'Perhaps it won't take effect immediately,' I said.

'Anyway,' said Frank, 'we must hurry all the more now. We may just be lucky. If not – too bad.'

We went through a few streets lined with villas, past gardens. It was quiet here, and there was nothing visible that indicated what was going on today, not even graffiti on shop windows. Ellen had hooked her arm under Frank's and I carried the box with his papers. Dusk was gathering and a warm drizzle began to fall. I felt a certain numbness in my head. Everything was deadened by a deep feeling of unreality. But there was also something threatening in the air. We had fallen too suddenly and too deeply into the impossible for there to be any limits. No one would be really surprised if tomorrow all the Jews were to be arrested or ordered to commit suicide as a punishment for some trumped-up charge. SA men would say, 'Well, that's all right then', genially gratified, when they were told that the Jews had all properly killed themselves. The streets would look the same as always. 'Well, that's all right then.' The villas would be unchanged in their friendly gardens, blustery spring weather and drizzle . . .

I gave a start. We had arrived – and I was disconcerted because I was a stranger and had no reason to be here. I need not have worried. Ellen's family's house was so full that nobody noticed me. From the outside it had appeared quiet, reserved, distinguished; inside it was more like a refugee camp trying vainly to pretend it was a tea party. About twenty guests sat or stood around in the large, elegant reception rooms, apparently younger family friends, used to visiting the house, who had come to find assistance and consolation today, here where they were used to taking tea and listening to music . . . They only found the anxiety and worry of their friends, and the polite, courteous atmosphere was suffused with an air of suppressed panic. Tea was offered, the guests stirred their cups and said 'please' and 'thank you'. It was almost the usual, murmured conversation of a tea party, but the murmuring was so uneasy that one would not have been surprised if there had been a sudden scream.

I knew one of the guests a little. He was a *Referendar* like me, and he had come to ask Ellen for a translation. He had drafted a letter to a lawyer in Brussels in whose office he had worked for a time. 'Here it is,' he said and pulled a scrap of paper from his inside pocket. Perhaps his life depended on this scrap of paper. 'Let me have a look,' said Ellen, and she began to scribble between his lines, but then she was called away. Somebody else wanted her for something. She came back and scribbled a bit more, but then her mother called her again. When she returned she was almost at her wits' end and mumbled to herself, '*Referendar* . . . what's the French for *Referendar*? . . .' Suddenly she burst out, 'Look, I'm sorry, please don't be angry. I simply can't do it today, not now.' 'But of course, not at all,' the poor man said politely, his face falling.

The host, Ellen's father, a portly, friendly man, forced a smile and tried to raise the depressed mood by telling jokes. Ellen's mother drew Frank into a corner to discuss the news about the exit visas with a few others. I joined the group. 'If we only knew when it came into effect!' said somebody. 'Doesn't it say in the paper?' asked another. 'No, not a word. That's the trouble. Have a look,' and Ellen's mother produced another copy of the newspaper, which already looked rather tattered. 'You only have to phone the police,' I suggested. 'But that might just cause us more trouble,' somebody replied. 'You can always give a false name,' I said. 'Anyway, I'd be happy to do it if you wish.'

'Are you really prepared to do it?' exclaimed Ellen's mother. The general relief was as great as if I had offered some momentous service. 'But please, please – not from our phone,' she begged. I realised that her surface poise was thin and crumbling and that, although she was still smiling, she felt more like screaming. 'If you would do us that great favour – there's a telephone box just round the corner. Here wait a minute, I'll get some coins.'

In the meantime Ellen's father had extracted Frank from the group ! 'Ellen's already told me that you wish to speak to me – let's not make it too formal ...' They disappeared, and I went off to the phone box round the corner.

When I got through I gave a false name. After a long wait somebody at the police finally found the information that the exit visa regulation would take effect from the following Tuesday. I said, 'Many thanks,' and hung up, very pleased.

When I came back, the room I had left was almost empty. There was only an old man sitting in a corner – maybe he had been there all along, silent and unnoticed – perhaps he was a grandfather. He looked like one of the old Jews in Rembrandt's paintings. He had a little pointed beard, and wrinkles all over his face. He sat in a large chair and very calmly smoked a pipe, visibly deep in thought. The others must have gone to some other room in this rambling house. I wanted to ask where they were, but before I could put my question, the old man addressed me, his little, deep-seated clear eyes directed straight at me.

'You don't appear to be a Jew,' he said, and when I explained that I had accompanied a Jewish friend, he said with great

authority, 'It is good that you stand by your friend!' I became
rather embarrassed and stammered something, but I was even
more bemused when he continued, 'It is also wise of you. Did
you know that?'

He seemed to enjoy my uneasiness, sucked slowly at his pipe
and then announced with an old, rusty but still strong voice,
'The Jews will survive this. Don't you agree? Oh, you needn't
worry, they will. Many others have sought to eradicate the Jews.
The Jews have outlived them all. They will outlive this as well.
And then they will remember. Have you heard of Nebuchadnezzar?'

'The Nebuchadnezzar in the Bible?' I asked doubtfully.

'Just so,' the grandfather said and regarded me, a spark of
sarcasm in his little eyes. 'He wanted to eradicate the Jews, and
he was a greater man than your Herr Hitler, and his empire was
greater than the German Reich. And the Jews were younger
then, younger and weaker, and they had less experience. He was
a great man, Nebuchadnezzar, a clever man and a cruel man.'

He spoke slowly, as if he were preaching. He relished his
speech, and took solemn, slow puffs at his pipe between the
sentences. I listened politely.

'But the great King Nebuchadnezzar did not succeed,' he
continued. 'In spite of all his greatness and all his cleverness and
all his cruelty. He is so forgotten that you smile when I mention
his name. Only the Jews remember him. And they are still here
and alive. And here comes this Herr Hitler and wants to
eradicate them again. He won't succeed either, this Herr Hitler.
Don't you believe me?'

'I sincerely hope you're right,' I said modestly.

'Let me tell you something,' he said. 'A little trick, one of
God's little tricks, if you wish. Those men that persecute the
Jews always suffer misfortune. Why is that so? How should I
know? I don't know why, but it is a fact.'

As I tried to rack my brain for historical examples and
counter-examples, he continued:

'Consider the great King Nebuchadnezzar. He was a great
man in his time. King of kings, a great, great man. But in old

age he went mad, and he went on all fours in the fields like a cow, and chewed grass with his teeth like a cow.' He broke off for a puff at his pipe, then a little smile appeared on his face, a smile of inner mirth, and his eyes sparkled, as though he had just had a really funny and heart-warming thought. 'Perhaps,' he said, 'perhaps Herr Hitler will one day go on all fours in the fields, eating grass like a cow. You are young, you may experience it yet. I won't.' Suddenly he broke into irresistible laughter at his image. His entire frame shook as he chuckled silently, until he choked a little on the smoke from his pipe, and started coughing.

Just then, Ellen's mother looked in at the door. 'Well?' she asked anxiously, and I gave my good news, for which she thanked me effusively. 'Now you must drink a glass to the health of the young couple,' she said and pulled me away. 'You know all about it?'

I made a bow to the old man as I left and he dismissed me, still amused, with a dignified nod of his head. In another room all the assembled involuntary engagement guests stood around and, with anxious faces, drank wine or held glasses in their hands.

Frank and Ellen stood among them, accepting their congratulations. They looked neither happy nor unhappy. It was a strange engagement party. My news that they had two days free to escape the country was just the right engagement present. However, it made some of the guests uneasy, and they started to talk of leaving.

Half an hour later, I too was on the train again with Frank. Night had fallen and the rain had become steady. Our compartment was empty. Now at last, for the first time that day, we really had a chance to talk. But we were silent.

Suddenly he said: 'What do you think of all this? You haven't said anything yet. Am I doing the right thing?'

'I don't know,' I said. 'It's certainly right for you to leave tomorrow. I only wish I could go too.'

'I had to tie up all the loose ends,' he said, as though I had rebuked him. 'Do you understand? I couldn't go with all these half finished, undecided things left hanging. So now I'm engaged to Ellen, and she's coming with me, and it's all tidy.'

I nodded. 'Are you pleased?' I asked.

'I don't know,' he said. After a while he laughed and said, 'Maybe it's all complete nonsense. I don't know. It happened so quickly.'

'Are you going to see Hanni now?' I said.

'Yes,' he said. And then putting his hand on my arm with sudden warmth, 'Would you do me a real favour? Please stay in touch with Hanni. Phone her in the next few days and comfort her a little, if you can. Tell her – no don't tell her anything. But comfort her a little, if you can, and,' he continued, and he became more eager and warmer than he had been all day, 'try and help her a bit with her passport troubles. She has no passport. It's a dreadful muddle, because she doesn't have a proper nationality. She was born somewhere that was Hungarian at the time, but now belongs to Czechoslovakia. Her father died in 1920. Nobody knows if he opted for a nationality, or which he opted for if he did. Now neither Hungary nor Czechoslovakia will give her a passport. It's dreadfully complicated.'

'Of course,' I said, 'I'll see what I can do. Comforting – well I'll try.'

'Yes,' he said, 'that will be difficult.'

Silence fell again, and the train carried us through the night and rain. Suddenly he said:

'Maybe if Hanni had had a passport it would all be quite different now.'

We arrived at *Zoo* station where we got out. For the first time one saw something of the revolution, in a negative way, to be sure: the usually bright, sparkling streets of the amusement area around the *Zoo* were dead and deserted, as I had never seen them before.

We waited at a phone box. He was already impatient. The time for phoning Hanni had already passed. 'Hanni next,' he said thoughtfully, 'then my father, then packing. Thanks anyway for all your help.'

'Have a safe journey,' I said to him. 'Just get through this night. Tomorrow it will all be behind you and you will be out.' Only at that moment did I fully grasp that this was a parting.

Perhaps there would have been a lot more to say, but it was too late. The telephone box became available, we shook hands and said goodbye.

LEAVE-TAKING

Twenty-Six

Before I continue my story – the private story of just one, not particularly important or interesting, young person in the Germany of 1933 – I interpose here a brief word to the reader; in particular to *that* reader who feels, not without some apparent justification, that I have already over-taxed their interest in my insignificant person.

Am I mistaken, or can I hear some readers, who have so far patiently followed my story, beginning to riffle the pages of the book? A riffling that expresses the feeling, 'What is the point of all this? What concern of ours is the fact that in 1933 in Berlin young Mr XY feared for his girlfriend because she was late for a rendezvous, or that he was gauche in his dealings with the SA – or, for that matter, as the next few chapters will reveal, that he was forced to say farewell to all his friends, his ambitions, and his fairly conventional immature opinions? After all, it seems that things of real historical importance were taking place in Berlin in 1933. If we are to be told anything, then it should be these things: what happened between Hitler and Blomberg or Schleicher or Röhm behind the scenes, who really set fire to the Reichstag, why Braun fled and Oberföhren committed suicide. We should not be fobbed off with the private experiences of a young man who was not much better informed than we are, even if he was closer to the scene of the events, a young man who obviously took no part at all in these events and had no influence on them, who was not even a particularly well-placed witness.'

A weighty accusation; I have to screw up all my courage to confess that I still do not think it justified, and that I do not think I am wasting a serious reader's time by telling my private story. It is all true: I took no direct part in events, and I was not a particularly well-placed witness. Nobody can be more sceptical about my importance than I am myself. Nevertheless – please do not take this as a sign of vanity – I am convinced that by telling my private, unimportant story I am adding an important, unrecognised facet to contemporary German and European history – more significant and more important for the future than if I were to disclose who set fire to the Reichstag, or what Hitler really said to Röhm.

What is history, and where does it take place?

If you read ordinary history books – which, it is often overlooked, contain only the scheme of events, not the events themselves – you get the impression that no more than a few dozen people are involved, who happen to be 'at the helm of the ship of state' and whose deeds and decisions form what is called history. According to this view, the history of the present decade is a kind of chess game between Hitler, Mussolini, Chiang Kai-Shek, Roosevelt, Chamberlain, Daladier and a number of other men whose names are on everybody's lips. We anonymous others seem at best to be the objects of history, pawns in the chess game, who may be pushed forward, or left standing, sacrificed or captured, but whose lives, for what they are worth, take place in a totally different world, unrelated to what is happening on the chess board, of which they are quite unaware.

It may seem a paradox, but it is none the less the simple truth, to say that on the contrary, the decisive historical events take place among us, the anonymous masses. The most powerful dictators, ministers and generals are powerless against the simultaneous mass decisions taken individually and almost unconsciously by the population at large. It is characteristic of these decisions that they do not manifest themselves as mass movements or demonstrations. Mass assemblies are quite incapable of independent action. Decisions that influence the course of history arise out of the individual experiences of thousands or millions of individuals.

This is not an airy abstract construction, but indisputably real and tangible. For instance, what was it that caused Germany to lose the Great War in 1918 and the Allies to win it? An advance in the leadership skills of Foch and Haig, or a decline in Ludendorff's? Not at all. It was the fact that the 'German soldier', that is the majority of an anonymous mass of ten million individuals, was no longer willing, as he had been until then, to risk his life in any attack, or to hold his position to the last man. Where did this change of attitude take place? Certainly not in large, mutinous assemblies of German soldiers, but unnoticed and unchecked in each individual soldier's breast. Most of them would probably not have been able to describe this complicated and historically important internal process and would merely have used the single expletive, 'Shit!' If you had interviewed the more articulate soldiers, you would have found a whole skein of random, private (and probably uninteresting and unimportant) reasons, feelings and experiences, a combination of letters from home, relations with the sergeant, opinions about the quality of the food and thoughts on the prospects and meaning of the war and (since every German is something of a philosopher) about the meaning and value of life. It is not my purpose here to analyse the inner process that brought the Great War to an end, but it would be interesting for those who wish to reconstruct this event, or others like it, to do so.

Mine is a different topic, although the mental processes it involves are similar. They may perhaps be of greater consequence, interest and importance: namely, the psychological developments, reactions and changes that took place simultaneously in the mass of the German population, which made Hitler's Third Reich possible and today form its unseen basis.

There is an unsolved riddle in the history of the creation of the Third Reich. I think it is much more interesting than the question of who set fire to the Reichstag. It is the question: 'What became of the Germans?' Even on the 5th of March 1933 a majority of them voted against Hitler. What happened to that majority? Did they die? Did they disappear from the face of the earth? Did they become Nazis at this late stage? How was it possible that there was not the slightest visible reaction from them?

Most of my readers will have met one or more Germans in the past, and most of them will have looked at their German acquaintances as normal, friendly, civilised people like anyone else – apart from the usual national idiosyncrasies. When they hear the speeches coming from Germany today (and become aware of the foulness of the deeds emanating from there), most of these people will think of their acquaintances and be aghast. They will ask, 'What's wrong with them? Don't they see what's happening to them – and what is happening in their name? Do they approve of it? What kind of people are they? What are we to think of them?'

Indeed, behind these questions there are some very peculiar, very revealing, mental processes and experiences, whose historical significance cannot yet be fully gauged. These are what I want to write about. You cannot get to grips with them if you do not track them down to the place where they happen: the private lives, emotions and thoughts of individual Germans. They happen there all the more since, having cleared the sphere of politics of all opposition, the conquering, ravenous state has moved into formerly private spaces in order to clear these also of any resistance or recalcitrance and to subjugate the individual. There, in private, the fight is taking place in Germany. You will search for it in vain in the political landscape, even with the most powerful telescope. Today the political struggle is expressed by the choice of what a person eats and drinks, whom he loves, what he does in his spare time, whose company he seeks, whether he smiles or frowns, what he reads, what pictures he hangs on his walls. It is here that the battles of the next world war are being decided in advance. That may sound grotesque, but it is the truth.

That is why I think that by telling my seemingly private, insignificant story I am writing real history, perhaps even the history of the future. It actually makes me happy that in my own person I do not have a particularly important, outstanding subject to describe. If I were more important I would be less typical. That is also why I hope my intimate chronicle will find favour in the eyes of the serious reader, who has no time to waste, and reads a book for the information it contains and its usefulness.

On the other hand, I must beg forgiveness of the more casual reader, who lends me his ear less critically and reads the story of an unusual life under unusual circumstances for its interest alone. I have tested his patience with this digression and others, in which I have not resisted the temptation to spin out some of the ideas that seem to me to follow from my story. How better to regain his favour than by quickly getting back to my narrative?

Twenty-Seven

The 1st of April 1933 had been the first climax of the Nazi revolution. In the following weeks, events showed a tendency to revert to being merely matters for the press. Certainly the terror continued, as did the celebrations and parades, but no longer in the *tempo furioso* of March. Concentration camps had become an institution. One was advised to get used to that fact and mind one's tongue. The *Gleichschaltung* – placing Nazis in controlling positions of all ministries, local agencies, boards of large companies, committees of associations – continued, but it now took a pedantic, orderly form with laws and regulations. It no longer had the wild, unpredictable character of the 'individual actions' of the previous months. The revolution became official. It became a fact, something that a German is used to accommodating and putting up with.

It was again permissible to visit Jewish shops. One was still told not to do so, and permanent posters described one as a 'traitor to the race' if one did, but it was permitted. There were no SA guards at the doors. Jewish civil servants, doctors, lawyers and journalists were still dismissed, but now it happened legally and in an orderly fashion, by paragraph such-and-such of the Civil Code, and there were exceptions for veterans and people who had been employed before the war. Could one ask for more? The courts, which had been suspended for a week, were allowed to resume their sessions and pass their verdicts. However, judges could now be removed, quite legally and according to law. The judges, who could now be ousted at a moment's notice, were told that their powers had been immeasurably increased. They had become 'people's judges', 'sovereign judges'. They need no longer anxiously follow the letter of the law. Indeed, it was better if they did not. Understood?

It was strange to sit in the *Kammergericht* again, the same courtroom, the same seats, acting as if nothing had happened. The same ushers stood at the doors and ensured, as ever, that the dignity of the court was not disturbed. Even the judges were for the most part the same people. Of course, the Jewish judge was no longer there. He had not even been dismissed. He was an old gentleman and had served under the Kaiser, so he had been moved to an administrative position in some *Amtsgericht* (lower court). His position on the senate was taken by an open-faced, blond young *Amtsgerichtsrat*, with glowing cheeks, who did not seem to belong among the grave *Kammergerichtsrats*. A *Kammergerichtsrat* is a general, an *Amtsgerichtsrat* a lieutenant colonel.* It was whispered that in private the newcomer was something high up in the SS. He saluted with outstretched arm and a resounding 'Heil Hitler!' The president of the senate and the other old gentlemen thereupon made a vague gesture with their right arm and murmured something inaudible. Previously they had chatted quietly and knowledgeably during the break-fast break in the deliberating room, discussing the events of the day, or professional gossip, the way old gentlemen do. That no longer happened. There was a deep embarrassed silence while they ate their sandwiches.

The deliberations themselves were also often strange. The new member of the senate produced unheard-of points of law in a fresh, confident voice. We *Referendars*, who had just passed our exams, exchanged looks while he expounded. At last the president of the senate remarked with perfect politeness, 'Colleague, could it be that you have overlooked paragraph 816 of the Civil Code?' At which the new high court judge looked embarrassed, like a candidate who has just slipped up in a viva,

---

* The progression of ranks in the German law courts is: *Referendar, Assessor, Amtsgerichtsrat, Kammergerichtsrat*.

leafed through his copy of the Code and then admitted lightly, 'Oh yes. Well, then it's just the other way around.' Those were the triumphs of the older law.

There were, however, other cases – cases in which the newcomer did not back down but held eloquent speeches, in a somewhat over-loud voice, stating that here the paragraph of the law must yield precedence; he would then instruct his co-judges that the meaning was more important than the letter of the law. He would quote Hitler. Then, with the gesture of a romantic stage hero, he would insist on some untenable decision. It was piteous to observe the faces of the old *Kammergerichtsrats* as this went on. They looked at their notes with an expression of indescribable dejection, while their fingers nervously twisted a paper-clip or a piece of blotting paper. They were used to failing candidates for the *Assessor* examination for spouting the kind of nonsense that was now being presented as the pinnacle of wisdom; but now this nonsense was backed by the full power of the state, by the threat of dismissal for lack of national reliability, loss of livelihood, the concentration camp ... They coughed; they said, 'Of course we agree with your opinion, but you will understand ...' They begged for a little understanding for the Civil Code and tried to save what could be saved.

That was the *Kammergericht* in Berlin in April 1933. It was the same *Kammergericht* whose judges had stood up to Frederick the Great 150 years earlier and, faced with a cabinet decree, had preferred jail to changing a judgement they considered correct in the King's favour. In Prussia every schoolchild knows the story of the miller of Potsdam which, whether it is true or not, gives an indication of the court's reputation. The King wanted a windmill removed because it disturbed the view from his new palace of Sans Souci. He offered to buy the mill. The miller refused, he wanted to keep his mill. The King threatened to dispossess the miller, whereupon the miller said, 'Just so, Your Majesty, but there's still the *Kammergericht* in Berlin.' To this day the mill can be seen next to the Palace.

In 1933 the *Kammergericht* toed the line. No Frederick the

Great was needed, not even Hitler himself had to intervene. All that was required was a few *Amtsgerichtsrats* with a deficient knowledge of the law.

I would not remain a witness of the decline of this great, proud, old institution for long. My training period was nearing its end. I only experienced a few short months of the *Kammergericht* of the Third Reich. They were sad months, months of taking leave in more than one sense. I felt as though I were at a deathbed. I was out of place in this building. The spirit that had reigned there was disappearing bit by bit and leaving hardly a trace. I had a chill feeling of homelessness. I had not been a lawyer heart and soul, indeed I had not been particularly enthusiastic about the legal, civil service career my father had planned for me. Nevertheless I had had a sense of belonging in this place. It depressed me to see the dismal, inglorious collapse and destruction of a world in which I had lived, not without some feeling of being at home, of participation, even of pride. It dissolved before my eyes, disintegrated and decayed, and I could do nothing about it. My only option was to shrug my shoulders and to admit the certainty that I had no future here.

Outwardly, though, everything appeared quite different. We *Referendars* rose daily in importance. The Association of National Socialist Lawyers wrote us all (me included) the most flattering letters: we were the generation who would build the new German justice. 'Join us. Help us in the historic task assigned to us by the Führer's will!' I dropped the letters in the wastepaper basket, but not everybody did that. One could sense that the *Referendars* felt their increasing importance. They, not the *Kammergerichtsrats*, were the ones who now knowledgeably discussed court gossip in the breaks. You could hear the invisible field marshal's batons rattling in their bags.

Even those who had hitherto not been Nazis felt their chance. 'Yes, there's a sharp wind blowing, colleague,' they would say and with quiet satisfaction they would report that someone who had only just passed the *Assessor* examination was already employed at the ministry of justice or, on the other hand, of feared, 'sharp' presidents of court senates who had simply been dismissed or sent to some obscure *Amtsgericht* in the provinces: 'He was too close to the Reichsbanner, you know. Now he has to put up with the consequences.' The atmosphere reminded one of the glorious year 1923, when it had suddenly been young people who set the tone, and one could become the director of a bank and possessor of a motor car from one day to the next – while age and cautious reliance on experience had only led to the mortuary.

Yet it was not quite like 1923. The price of admission was somewhat higher. You had to choose your words with care and conceal your thoughts to avoid going to the concentration camp instead of the ministry of justice. Confident and proud though the conversations in the court corridors were, they were hampered by an undertow of fear and mistrust. The opinions that were expressed sounded a bit like exam responses learned by rote. Quite often the speaker broke off suddenly, and looked around to see if someone had perhaps misinterpreted his words.

Jubilant youths, but with butterflies in their stomachs. One day – I do not remember what heresy I had just uttered – one of my co-*Referendars* took me aside, looked closely into my eyes and said, 'A word of warning, colleague. I have your best interests at heart.' Another close look. 'You're a republican, aren't you?' He put a placatory hand on my arm. 'Shh. Don't worry. I am one too at heart. But you must be more careful. Don't underestimate the fascists.' (He used the word 'fascists'.) 'Sceptical comments are no use nowadays. You're only digging your own grave. Don't fancy that there's anything to be done against the fascists now! Certainly not by open opposition, believe me! I think I know the fascists better than you. We republicans must howl with the wolves.'

That was the voice of the republicans.

Twenty-Eight

*I*t was not only the *Kammergericht* that I had to bid adieu to in those days. 'Adieu' had become the motto of the day – a radical leave-taking of everything, without exception. The world I had lived in dissolved and disappeared. Every day another piece vanished quietly, without ado. Every day one looked around and something else had gone and left no trace. I have never since had such a strange experience. It was as if the ground on which one stood was continually trickling away from under one's feet, or rather as if the air one breathed was steadily, inexorably being sucked away.

What was happening openly and clearly in public was almost the least of it. Yes, political parties disappeared or were dissolved; first those of the Left, then also those of the Right; I had not been a member of any of them. The men who had been the focus of attention, whose books one had read, whose speeches one had discussed, disappeared into exile or the concentration camps; occasionally one heard that one or other had 'committed suicide while being arrested' or been 'shot while attempting to escape'. At some point in the summer the newspapers carried a list of thirty or forty names of famous scientists or writers; they had been proscribed, declared to be traitors to the people and deprived of their citizenship.

More unnerving was the disappearance of a number of quite harmless people, who had in one way or another been part of daily life. The radio announcer whose voice one had heard every day, who had almost become an old acquaintance, had been sent to a concentration camp, and woe betide you if you mentioned his name. The familiar actors and actresses who had been a feature of our lives disappeared from one day to the next. Charming Miss Carola Neher was suddenly a traitor to the people; brilliant young Hans Otto who had been the rising star of the previous season, lay crumpled in the yard of an SS barracks – yes, Hans Otto whose name had been on everyone's lips, who had been talked about at every evening party, had been hailed as the 'new Matkowski' that the German stage had so long been waiting for. He had 'thrown himself out of a fourth-floor window in a moment when the guards had been distracted', they said. A famous cartoonist, whose harmless drawings had brought laughter to the whole of Berlin every week, committed suicide, as did the master of ceremonies of a well-known cabaret. Others just vanished. One did not know whether they were dead, incarcerated or had gone abroad – they were just missing.

The symbolic burning of the books in April had been an affair of the press, but the disappearance of books from the bookshops and libraries was uncanny. Contemporary German literature, whatever its merits, had simply been erased. Books of the last season that one had not bought by April became unobtainable. A few authors, tolerated for some unknown reason, remained like individual ninepins in the wreckage. Otherwise you could only get the classics – and a dreadful, embarrassingly bad, literature of blood and soil, which suddenly sprang up. Readers – always a minority in Germany, and as they were daily told, an unimportant one at that – were deprived of their world overnight. Further, since they had quickly learned that those who were robbed might also be punished, they felt intimidated and pushed their copies of Heinrich Mann and Feuchtwanger into the back rows of their bookshelves; and if they dared to talk about the newest Joseph Roth or Jakob Wassermann they put their heads together and whispered like conspirators.

Many journals and newspapers disappeared from the kiosks – but what happened to those that continued in circulation was much more disturbing. You could not quite recognise them any more. In a way a newspaper is like an old acquaintance: you instinctively know how it will react to certain events, what it will say about them and how it will express its views. If it suddenly says the opposite of what it said yesterday, denies its own past, distorting its features, you cannot avoid feeling that you are in a madhouse. That happened. Old-established democratic broadsheets like the *Berliner Tageblatt* or the *Vossische Zeitung* changed into Nazi organs from one day to the next. In their customary, measured, educated style they said exactly the same things that were spewed out by the *Angriff!* or the *Völkischer Beobachter*, newspapers that had always supported the Nazis. Later, one became accustomed to this and picked up occasional hints by reading between the lines of the articles on the arts pages. The political pages always kept strictly to the party line.

To some extent, the editorial staff had been replaced; but frequently this straightforward explanation was not accurate. For instance, there was an intellectual journal called *Die Tat* ('Action'), whose content lived up to its name. In the final years before 1933 it had been widely read. It was edited by a group of intelligent, radical young people. With a certain elegance they indulged in the long historical view of the changing times. It was, of course, far too distinguished, cultured and profound to support any particular political party – least of all the Nazis. As late as February its editorials brushed them off as an obviously ephemeral phenomenon. Its editor-in-chief had gone too far. He lost his job and only just managed to save his neck (today he is allowed to write light novels). The rest of the editorial staff remained in post, but as a matter of course became Nazis without the least detriment to their elegant style and historical perspective – they had always been Nazis, naturally; indeed better, more genuinely and more profoundly so than the Nazis themselves. It was wonderful to behold: the paper had the same typography, the same name – but without batting an eyelid it had become a thoroughgoing, smart Nazi organ. Was it a sudden conversion or just cynicism? Or had Messrs Fried, Eschmann, Wirsing, etc. always been Nazis at heart? Probably they did not know themselves. Anyway I soon abandoned the question. I was nauseated and wearied, and contented myself with taking leave of one more newspaper.

In the event, these leave-takings were not the most painful – taking leave of all the manifestations and elements that make up the atmosphere of an era was harder. They are difficult to describe but should not be underestimated, as they can make life very sombre. It is unpleasant enough when the air over a whole country loses all its freshness and perfume and becomes choking and poisonous. But to a certain extent one can exclude this outside air, shut one's windows tightly, and withdraw into the four walls of one's private life. One can seal oneself off, put flowers in one's room, and close one's eyes and hold one's nose when one goes out. The temptation to do this was great, even for me – and many others gave in to it. Thank God, my attempt to seal myself off failed from the outset. I could not shut the windows. There were leave-takings after leave-takings waiting for me in my most private life.

Twenty-Nine

All the same, the temptation to seal oneself off was a sufficiently important aspect of the period for me to devote some space to it. It has its part to play in the psycho-pathological process that has unfolded in the cases of millions of Germans since 1933. After all, to a normal onlooker most Germans today exhibit the symptoms of lunacy or at the very least severe hysteria. If you want to understand how this came about, you have to take the trouble to place yourself in the peculiar position in which non-Nazi Germans – and that was still the majority – found themselves in 1933, and try to understand the bizarre, perverse conflicts they faced.

The plight of non-Nazi Germans in the summer of 1933 was certainly one of the most difficult a person can find himself in: a condition in which one is hopelessly, utterly overwhelmed, accompanied by the shock of having been caught completely off balance. We were in the Nazis' hands for good or ill. All lines of defence had fallen, any collective resistance had become impossible. Individual resistance was only a form of suicide. We were pursued into the farthest corners of our private lives; in all areas of life there was rout, panic and flight. No one could tell where it would end. At the same time we were called upon, not to surrender, but to renege. Just a little pact with the devil – and you were no longer one of the captured quarry. Instead you were one of the victorious hunters.

That was the simplest and crudest temptation. Many succumbed to it. Later they often found that the price to be paid was higher than they had thought and that they were no match for the real Nazis. There are many thousands of them today in

Germany, Nazis with a bad conscience. People who wear their Nazi badges like Macbeth wore his royal robes, who, in for a penny, in for a pound, now find their consciences shouldering one burden after another, who search in vain for a way out, drink and take sleeping pills, no longer dare to think, and do not know whether they should rather pray for the end of the Nazi era – their own era! – or dread it. When that end comes they will certainly not admit to having been the culprits. In the meantime, however, they are the nightmare of the world. It is impossible to assess what these people might still be capable of in their moral and psychological derangement. Their history has yet to be written.

Our predicament in 1933 held many other temptations apart from this, the crudest; each was a source of madness and mental sickness for those who yielded. The devil has many nets, crude ones for crude souls, finer ones for finer souls.

If you refused to become a Nazi you found yourself in a fiendish situation: it was one of complete and unalleviated hopelessness; you were daily subjected to insults and humiliations, forced to watch unendurable scenes, had nowhere to turn to mitigate your anguish. Such a situation carries its own temptations: apparent remedies that hide the barb of the devil.

One temptation, often favoured by older people, was the withdrawal into an illusion: preferably the illusion of superiority. Those that surrendered to this, clung to the amateurish, dilettantish aspects that Nazi politics undoubtedly exhibited at first. Every day they tried to convince themselves and others that this could not continue for long, and maintained an attitude of amused criticism. They spared themselves the perception of the fiendishness of Nazism, by concentrating on its childishness, and misrepresented their position of complete, powerless subjugation as that of superior, unconcerned onlookers. They found it both comforting and reassuring to be able to quote a new joke or a new article about the Nazis from the London *Times*. They were people who predicted the imminent end of the regime, at first with calm certainty, later, as the months went by, with ever more desperate self-deception. The worst came for them when the Nazi Party visibly consolidated itself and had its first successes: they had no weapons to cope with these.

In the years that followed, this group was the target of a psychologically clever bombardment with boastful statistics. They formed the majority of the late converts to Nazism in the years from 1935 to 1938. Once their strenuously maintained pose of superiority had been rendered untenable, great numbers of these people yielded. Once the successes they had always declared to be impossible became reality, they conceded defeat. 'But he has achieved what no one else achieved!' 'Yes that's just the trouble.' 'Oh, you just love paradoxes, don't you?' (A conversation from 1938.)

A few of them still hold the banner high. Even after all their defeats they still prophesy the inevitable collapse of the regime every month, or at least once a year. Their stand has a certain magnificence, you have to admit, but also a certain eccentricity. The funny thing is that one day, after they have stood fast through all their cruel disappointments, they will be proved right. I can already see them strutting around after the defeat of the Nazis and telling everybody that they had predicted it all along. By then, however, they will have become tragicomic figures. There is a way of being right that is shameful and lends its opponent undeserved glory. Think of Louis XVIII.

The second danger was embitterment – masochistically surrendering oneself to hate, suffering and unrelieved pessimism. This is perhaps the most natural reaction to defeat for the Germans. In their darkest hours (in private or in public life) every German has to fight against this temptation: to give up completely once and for all; to let the world go to the devil with a wan indifference bordering on compliance; to commit sullen, angry suicide.

Oh, I am growing tired of the sun and light,
let creation crumble into empty night!

It looks very heroic: all consolation is utterly rejected – but the sufferer fails to see that this is itself the most poisonous, dangerous, vicious form of consolation. The perverse indulgence in self-sacrifice, a Wagnerian lust for death and destruction – that is the most complete consolation for a defeated man who cannot find the strength and courage to face defeat and bear it. I make bold to prophesy that this will be the basic stance of Germany after it has lost the Nazi war – the wild, headstrong wailing of a child taking the loss of its doll for the end of the world. (There was already a lot of this in the German reaction to the defeat of 1918.) In 1933, little of the inner feelings of the defeated majority was reflected in public attitudes because officially no one had been defeated. Officially there was only celebration, things getting better, 'liberation', 'deliverance', salvation, intoxicating unity. Suffering had to be kept quiet. Yet embitterment was a typical reaction of the defeated after 1933. I encountered it so often myself that I am convinced that the number of those affected in this way must run into millions.

It is difficult to assess the external consequences of such an internal attitude. Occasionally it leads to suicide. Much more commonly, however, people adapt to living with clenched teeth in a manner of speaking. Unfortunately, they form the majority of the representatives of a visible 'opposition' in Germany. So it is no wonder that the opposition has never developed any goals, methods, plans or expectations. Most of its members spend their time bemoaning the atrocities. The dreadful things that are happening have become essential to their spiritual well-being. Their only remaining dark pleasure is to luxuriate in the description of gruesome deeds, and it is impossible to have a conversation with them on any other topic. Indeed, it has gone so far that many of them would feel that something was missing if they did not have atrocities to talk about, and with some of them despair has almost become cosy. Still, it is a way of 'living dangerously': it makes one bilious, and can lead to serious illness and even madness. There is also a narrow side-alley that leads from here to Nazidom: if it makes no difference anyway and everything is lost, then why not be bitterly, angrily cynical and join the devils oneself? Why not take part, secretly cackling with scorn? That attitude is not unheard of.

There is a third temptation I need to mention. It is the one I had to fight against myself, and again I was certainly not the only one. Its starting point is the recognition of the danger of succumbing to the previous temptation. You do not want to let yourself be morally corrupted by hate and suffering, you want to remain good-natured, peaceful, amiable and 'nice'. But how to avoid hate and suffering if you are daily bombarded with things that cause them? You must ignore everything, look away, block your ears, seal yourself off. That leads to a hardening through softness and finally also to a form of madness: the loss of a sense of reality.

For simplicity's sake, let me talk about my own experiences, not forgetting that my case should be multiplied a hundred thousand or a million-fold.

I have no talent for hate. I have always been convinced that involving oneself too deeply in polemics and arguments with incorrigible opponents, hating the despicable too much, destroys something in oneself – something that is worth preserving and is difficult to rebuild. My natural gesture of rejection is to turn away, not to go on the attack.

I also have a strong sense of the honour one does an opponent by deigning to hate him, and I felt that the Nazis in particular were not worthy of this honour. I did not want to be on such close terms with them as to hate them. The worst affront I suffered from them was not their intrusive demands for me to join in – those were beneath thinking or getting upset about – but the fact that, by being impossible to ignore, they daily caused me to feel hate and disgust, feelings that are so much against my nature.

Could I not find an attitude that avoided being forced to feel anything, even hate or disgust? Could I not develop a serene, imperturbable disdain, 'taking one look and then moving on'? What if it cost me half, or if need be all, my external life?

At just this time I read a dangerous, alluringly ambiguous sentence of Stendhal's. He wrote it as a coda after the restoration of 1814, an event that he felt to be a 'descent into the quagmire' just as I viewed the events of 1933. There was only one thing, he wrote, still worth the toil and trouble, namely 'to hold oneself holy and pure'. Holy and pure! That meant not only steering clear of all participation, but also of all devastation through pain, and any distortion through hate – in short, from any reaction at all, even that caused by rejection. Turn away – retreat into the smallest corner if you have to, if you can only keep it free of the polluted air, so that you can save undamaged the only thing worth saving, namely (to use the good old theological word) your soul.

I still think that there is some justification for this attitude; and I do not repudiate it. However, simply ignoring everything and retreating into an ivory tower, the way I imagined it then, was not the right thing to do. I thank God that my attempt to do so failed quickly and thoroughly. Some of my acquaintances' attempts did not fail so quickly, and they had to pay a high price to learn that one can sometimes only save the peace of one's soul by sacrificing and relinquishing it.

In contrast to the first two ways of evading the Nazis, this third way did find a kind of public expression in Germany in the following years. Literary idylls suddenly sprang up and flourished everywhere. In the outside world, even in literary circles, it has gone unnoticed that, as never before, so many recollections of childhood, family novels, books on the countryside, nature poems, so many delicate and tender little baubles were written in Germany in the years 1934–38. Apart from open Nazi propaganda literature, almost everything that was published in Germany belongs to this genre. In the last two years it has declined somewhat, apparently because the effort required to achieve the necessary harmlessness has become too great. Up until then it was uncanny. A whole literature of cow bells and daisies, full of children's summer-holiday happiness, first love and fairy tales, baked apples and Christmas trees, a literature of obtrusive intimacy and timelessness, manufactured as if by arrangement in the midst of marching, concentration camps, armaments factories, and the public displays of *Der Stürmer*.*

---

* A viciously sadistic, pornographic, anti-Semitic propaganda paper, on display in bright red glass cases throughout Nazi Germany.

If you had to read quantities of these books, as I did, you gradually felt that in all their quiet tenderness they were screaming at you, between the lines, 'Don't you see how timeless and intimate we are? Don't you see how nothing can disturb us? Don't you see how unaffected we are? See it please, please, we beg you.'

I knew some of the writers personally. For each of them, very nearly, the moment has since come when it became impossible to go on; some event that could not be blocked out by ear plugs; maybe the arrest of a close acquaintance or something like that. No childhood reminiscences can shield one from that. There were some serious breakdowns. They are sad stories. I will tell one or another when the time comes.*

Those were the conflicts the Germans faced in the summer of 1933. They represented a choice between different forms of spiritual death. People who have lived in normal times may well feel that they are being shown a madhouse, or perhaps a psycho-pathological laboratory. However, there is no avoiding the fact that that is the way it was, and I cannot change it. Incidentally, these were still relatively innocuous times. It gets much worse.

---

* The manuscript breaks off before it can fulfil this promise.

Thirty

My attempt to seclude myself in a small, secure, private domain failed very quickly. The reason was that there was no such domain. Very soon the wind whistled into my private life from all sides and blew it apart. By the autumn there was nothing left of what I had considered my 'circle of friends'.

For instance, there was a small 'working group' of six young intellectuals, all of them *Referendars* approaching the *Assessor* examinations, all from the same social class. I was one of them. We prepared for the exams together, and that was the outward reason the group had been formed. But it had long since become something more than that and formed a small, intimate debating club. We had very different political opinions, but would not have dreamed of hating each other for them. Indeed we were all on very good terms. The opinions were not diametrically opposed, rather – in a manner typical of the range of views held by young intellectual Germans in 1932 – they formed a circle. The extreme ends of the arc almost met.

The most 'left-wing' member was Hessel, a doctor's son with communist sympathies; the most 'right-wing' was Holz, an officer's son who held military, nationalistic views. Yet they often made a common front against the rest of us. They both came from the 'youth movement' and both thought in terms of leagues. They were both anti-bourgeois and anti-individualistic. Both had an ideal of 'community' and 'community spirit'. For both, jazz music, fashion magazines, the Kurfürstendamm,* in

* In pre-war Berlin the city centre was where the Friedrichstrasse and Unter

other words the world of glamour and 'easy come, easy go', were a red rag. Both had a secret liking for terror, in a more humanistic garb for the one, more nationalistic for the other. As similar views make for similar faces, they both had a certain stiff, thin-lipped, humourless expression and, incidentally, the greatest respect for each other. Courtesy was anyway a matter of course between the members of the group.

Two other opponents who understood each other well – and often supported each other against their own confederates – were Brock and I. We were more difficult to locate on the political scale than Hessel and Holz. Brock's opinions were revolutionary and extremely nationalistic, mine rather conservative and extremely individualistic. From the ideas of the Right and the Left we had each picked the exact opposite. Yet there was something that united us: at heart we were both aesthetes, and we both worshipped unpolitical gods. Brock's god was adventure, collective adventure *à la* 1914–18 or 1923; my god was the god of Goethe and Mozart. Forgive me if I do not name him for the moment. So it was inevitable that we were opponents on every topic, but often opponents who gave each other a wink. We could also drink well together. Hessel was a teetotaller and opposed to alcohol on principle. Holz drank in such desperate moderation that it was a shame.

Then there were two natural mediators: Hirsch, the son of a Jewish university professor, and Von Hagen, the son of a very high civil servant. Von Hagen was the only one of us who belonged to a political organisation. He was a member of the Deutsche Demokratische Partei (German Democratic Party) and also of the Reichsbanner. That did not prevent him from mediating. On the contrary, it predestined him for it. He tried to reconcile all opinions and had understanding for every point of view. Further, he was the embodiment of a good upbringing, tact personified and impeccable manners. It was impossible for a discussion to degenerate into altercation if he was present.

den Linden intersected. The Kurfürstendamm to the west was an area of night-life.

Hirsch was his second. His speciality was gentle scepticism and tentative anti-Semitism. Yes, he had a weakness for anti-Semites and always tried to give them a chance; I remember a discussion between us in which he seriously took the anti-Semitic part, and I to redress the balance took the anti-Teutonic part. Such was the chivalry of our debates. Besides, Hirsch and Von Hagen did their very best to bring an occasional tolerant smile to Holz's and Hessel's lips, and to induce Brock and me to make a serious 'avowal' now and then. They did their utmost to prevent Holz and me, or Hessel and Brock, destroying each other's holy of holies (that was only thinkable in these two combinations).

It was a nice group of hopeful young men; if you had seen them in 1932 sitting round a table, smoking and eagerly debating with each other, you could hardly have thought that its members would, within a year, figuratively speaking, be standing on opposing barricades ready to shoot each other. To cut a long story short, today Hirsch, Hessel and I are emigrants, Brock and Holz are high Nazi officials, and von Hagen is a lawyer in Berlin. He is a member of the National Socialist Association of Lawyers and of the National Socialist Drivers' Reserve, and possibly (with regret, but it is necessary) of the Party itself. You can see that he is still faithful to his role of mediator.

From the beginning of March 1933 the atmosphere in our group started to become poisonous. It was no longer as easy as before to hold courteous academic discussions about the Nazis. There was an embarrassing, tense meeting at Hirsch's home shortly before the 1st of April. Brock made no secret of the fact that he greeted the coming events with a pleasantly warm feeling of amusement and he relished the superiority with which he could state that 'there is naturally a certain nervousness among my Jewish friends.' In his view, expressed in the same mode, the organisation seemed to be pretty dreadful, but it was interesting to see how such a mass experiment would turn out. In any case it opened up the most exciting prospects. Thus spoke Brock, and it was difficult to find anything for which he did not have an answer, given with the same brazen smile. Holz responded thoughtfully that there might well be regrettable incidents in such a summary and improvisatory process, but that anyway the Jews ... and so on.

Our host, Hirsch, finding himself thus relieved of the necessity of taking sides with the anti-Semites, sat silently by, biting his lips. Von Hagen pointed out tactfully that on the other hand the Jews ... and so on. It was a beautiful discussion about the Jews, and it dragged on. Hirsch continued to say nothing and occasionally passed round the cigarettes. Hessel tried to attack racism with scientific arguments. Holz defended it with scientific counter-arguments. It was all very pedantic and very sober. 'All right, Hessel,' he said, more or less, taking a slow puff on his cigarette, exhaling and watching the smoke coil upward, 'in a humane state, such as you are tacitly assuming, all these problems may not exist. But you have to admit that when a new form of state is being set up, as is the case at the moment, racial homogeneity ...'

I began to feel nauseated, and decided to say something tactless. 'It seems to me,' I said, 'that the question here is not how a national state should be founded, but quite simply, the personal stance of each one of us. Isn't that so? Apart from that, there is nothing over which we have any power or influence. What I find interesting in your attitude, Mr Holz, is how you reconcile your opinions with your current status as a guest of this house.' At that Hirsch cut me short and emphasised that he had never made his invitation dependent on any particular opinion, etc. 'Of course,' I replied, quite angry now, even with him, 'and it is not your stance that I am criticising, but that of Mr Holz. I would like to know what it feels like to be someone who accepts the invitation of a person whom he intends in principle to do away with, along with all his kind.'

'Who mentioned doing away with?' cried Holz, and everybody started to protest, except Brock who said that he personally saw no contradiction here. 'You may be aware,' he said, 'that in wartime officers are frequently guests in houses that they are going to blow up the next morning.' Holz, on the other hand, soberly proved to me that one could not speak of 'doing away with, when Jewish shops were being boycotted in an orderly and disciplined manner'.

'Why is it not doing away with them?' I cried, outraged. 'If you systematically ruin somebody, and take any possibility of earning a living from them, they must surely finally starve. Is that not so? I call it doing away with someone when you deliberately allow them to starve, don't you?'

'Calm down,' said Holz, 'nobody starves in Germany. If a Jewish shopkeeper is really ruined, they will get social security payments.' The terrible thing was that he said that quite seriously, without the slightest sneer. We parted in a hostile mood.

In the course of April, just before the lists were closed, Brock and Holz became members of the Nazi Party. It would be wrong to say they were jumping on a bandwagon. Both had undoubtedly shared some opinions with the Nazis all along. Up to now the Party had not been strong enough to persuade them to join. The little extra was supplied by the recruiting power of victory.

It became difficult to hold the group together. Von Hagen and Hirsch were kept very busy. Still, it managed to survive for another five or six weeks. Then, at the end of May, there was a meeting at which it broke apart.

It happened just after the mass murders in Cöpenick. Brock and Holz came to our meeting like murderers fresh from the deed. Not that they had taken part in the slaughter themselves, but it was obviously the topic of the day in their new circles. They had clearly convinced themselves that they were in some way accomplices. Into our civilised, middle-class atmosphere of cigarettes and coffee-cups the two of them brought a strange, blood-red cloud of sweaty death.

They started to speak of the matter immediately. It was from their graphic descriptions that we found out what had actually happened. The press had only contained hints and intimations.

'Fantastic, what happened in Cöpenick yesterday, eh?' began Brock, and that was the tone of his narrative. He went into detail, explained how the women and children had been sent into a neighbouring room before the men were shot point-blank with a revolver, bludgeoned with a truncheon, or stabbed with an SA dagger. Surprisingly, most of them had put up no resistance, and made sorry figures in their nightshirts. The bodies had been tipped into the river and many were still being washed ashore in the area today. His whole narrative was delivered with that brazen smile on his face which had recently become a stereotypical feature. He made no attempt to defend the actions, and obviously did not see much need to. He regarded them primarily as sensational.

We found it all dreadful and shook our heads, which seemed to give him some satisfaction.

'And you see no difficulty with your new Party membership because of these things?' I remarked at last.

Immediately he became defensive and his face took on a bold Mussolini expression. 'No, not at all,' he declared. 'Do you feel pity for these people? The man who shot first the day before yesterday knew that it would cost him his life, of course. It would have been bad form not to hang him. Incidentally he has my respect. As for the others – shame on them. Why didn't they put up a fight? They were all long-time Social Democrats and members of the Eiserne Front.* Why should they be lying in their beds in their nightshirts? They should have defended themselves and died decently. But they're a limp lot. I have no sympathy for them.'

'I don't know,' I said slowly, 'whether I feel much pity for them, but what I do feel is an indescribable sense of disgust at people who go around heavily armed and slaughter defenceless victims.'

'They should have defended themselves,' said Brock stubbornly. 'Then they wouldn't have been defenceless. That is a disgusting Marxist trick, being defenceless, when it gets serious.'

At this point Holz intervened. 'I consider the whole thing a regrettable revolutionary excess,' he said, 'and between you and

---

* A left-of-centre semi-military organisation formed by uniting the armed wings of all the left-of-centre parties except the Communists.

me, I expect the responsible officer to be disciplined. But I also think that it should not be overlooked that it was a Social Democrat who shot first. It is understandable, and in a certain sense even justified, that under these circumstances the SA takes, er, very energetic counter-measures.'

It was curious. I could just about stand Brock, but Holz had become a red rag to me. I could not help myself. I felt compelled to insult him.

'It is most interesting for me to hear your new theory of justification,' I said. 'If I am not mistaken, you did once study law?'

He gave me a steely look and elaborately picked up the gauntlet. 'Yes, I have studied law,' he said slowly, 'and I remember that I heard something about state self-defence there. Perhaps you missed that lecture.'

'State self-defence,' I said, 'interesting. You consider that the state is under attack because a few hundred Social Democrat citizens put on nightshirts and go to bed?'

'Of course not,' he said. 'You keep forgetting it was a Social Democrat who first shot two SA men –'

'– who had broken into his home.'

'Who had entered his abode in the course of their official duty.'

'And that allows the state the justification of self-defence against any other citizens? Against me and you?'

'Not against me,' he said, 'but perhaps against you.'

He was now looking at me with really steely eyes and I had a funny feeling in the back of my knees.

'You,' he said, 'are always niggling and wilfully ignoring the monumental developments in the resurgence of the German people that are taking place today.' (I can remember the very word 'resurgence' to this day!) 'You grasp at every little excess and split legal hairs to criticise and find fault. You seem to be unaware, I fear, that today people of your ilk represent a latent danger for the state, and that the state has the right and the duty to react accordingly – at the very least when one of you goes so far as to dare to offer open resistance.'

Those were his words, soberly and slowly spoken in the style of a commentary on the Civil Code. All the while he looked at me with those steely eyes.

'If we are dealing in threats,' I said, 'then why not openly? Do you intend to denounce me to the Gestapo?'

About here Von Hagen and Hirsch began to titter, attempting to turn it all into a joke. This time, however, Holz put a spanner in the works. Quietly and deliberately (and it was only now that I realised, with a certain unexpected satisfaction, how deeply angered he was):

'I admit that for some time I have been wondering whether that is not my duty.'

'Oh,' I said. I needed a few moments to taste all the different flavours on my tongue: a little surprise, a little admiration for how far he was prepared to go; a little sourness from the word 'duty', a little satisfaction at how far I had driven him, and a new cool insight: that is the way life is now, and that is how it has changed – and a little fear. Having made a quick assessment of what he might be able to say about me, if he went through with it, I said, 'I must say that it does not speak for the seriousness of your intentions that you have been thinking about it for some time, only to tell me the result of your thoughts.'

'Don't say that,' he said quietly. Now all the trumps had been played and to raise the stakes further we would have had to become physical. It had all taken place sitting down, while we were smoking. Anyway, the others now intervened and reproachfully tried to calm us both down.

Oddly enough, the political debate continued quietly and bitterly for several hours; but in reality the group had broken up. We made no arrangements for further meetings.

Hirsch took leave of me in September, to go to Paris. I had already lost sight of Brock and Holz. I only heard snippets of gossip about their careers in later years. Hessel left for America a year later. The group had been blown apart.

By the way, for a few days I was concerned that Holz really would set the Gestapo on to me. As time passed I realised that he had obviously not done so. It was decent of him really!

Thirty-One

No, retiring into private life was not an option. However far one retreated, everywhere one was confronted with the very thing one had been fleeing from. I discovered that the Nazi revolution had abolished the old distinction between politics and private life, and that it was quite impossible to treat it merely as a 'political event'. It took place not only in the sphere of politics, but also in each individual private life; it seeped through the walls like a poison gas. If you wanted to evade the gas there was only one option: to remove yourself physically – emigration. Emigration: that meant saying goodbye to the country of one's birth, language and education and severing all patriotic ties.

In that summer of 1933 I was prepared to take even this final step. I had become accustomed to leave-taking all around. I had lost my friends, had seen harmless acquaintances changed into virtual murderers or enemies, threatening to deliver me to the Gestapo. I had seen all my small daily pleasures vanish. Solidly based institutions like the Prussian justice system had caved in before my eyes. The world of books and discussion groups had dissolved. Opinions, points of view, theoretical systems had had to be abandoned as never before. Where were the career plans and ideas I had so confidently entertained just a few months before? The adventure had begun. Already the basic tenor of my life had changed. The pain of leave-taking was followed by numbness and exhilaration: I no longer felt firm ground beneath my feet, but rather seemed to float or swim in empty space, strangely light and free as a bird. Partings no longer caused much pain, just a feeling of 'Let it go,' and 'Well then, you can dispense with that too,' and I felt myself becoming ever poorer, but also ever lighter. Even so, this final parting – mentally taking leave of my own country – was difficult, strenuous and painful. It advanced by fits and starts, with many relapses; sometimes I felt I would not have the strength to go through with it.

Once again, in telling my story I am not recounting just my own unimportant experience, but what thousands of others also went through.

True, in March and April, as I had witnessed the nation leap into the quagmire to the accompaniment of patriotic jubilation and shouts of triumph, I had angrily declared that I would emigrate, and have nothing more to do with 'this country'; I would rather run a tobacconist's shop in Chicago than be a German secretary of state, and so on. But these had just been outbursts. There was not much thought and little serious reality behind them. Now, in the chilly, airless coolness of these months of parting, it was quite a different matter to consider leaving my country in earnest.

To be sure, I was not a German nationalist. The nationalism of the sports clubs that had been the dominant feeling of the years following the Great War and is now the spiritual basis of Nazism, the childish delight of seeing one's own country represented by ever larger blobs of colour on the map, the feeling of triumph over 'victories' and the pleasure in seeing people humiliated and subjugated, the relish of the fear aroused in others, the bombastic national self-praise in the style of the 'Meistersingers', the hysteria about 'German' thought, 'German' feeling, 'German' constancy, 'German' manhood, 'being German!' – all of that had long been abhorrent and repugnant to me. It was no sacrifice to forgo it. However, that did not prevent me from being a fairly good German, and I was conscious of it often enough, if only for the shame I felt at the excesses of German nationalism. Like most members of any nation I felt proud of the better points that one sees here and there in German history and the German character; offended by the insults in word or deed sometimes aimed at Germany by the nationalists of other countries; gratified when Germany was unexpectedly praised; and ashamed when compatriots of mine, or worse still my whole country, behaved badly. In a nutshell, I belonged to my country as one belongs to one's family: more critical than outsiders, not always on the best of terms with all its members, certainly not prepared to make it the centre of my life with a cry of 'my family first and foremost'; but belonging to it after all, and making no secret of it. To give up this sense of belonging, to turn away and learn to look on one's home country as an enemy is no small matter.

I do not 'love' Germany, just as I do not 'love' myself. If there is a country that I do love, it is France, but I could love any country more easily than my own – even without the Nazis. However, one's own country plays a different and far more indispensable role than that of a mistress; it is just one's own country. If one loses it, one almost loses the right to love any other country. One loses the prerequisites for the delightful game of international hospitality – exchange, mutual invitations, getting to know one another, showing off to each other. One becomes, well, 'stateless', a man without a shadow, without a background, at best tolerated somewhere – or if, voluntarily or involuntarily, one fails to follow inner emigration with the real thing, utterly homeless, an exile in one's own country.

To undergo this operation, the internal detachment of oneself from one's country of one's own free will, is an act of biblical savagery: 'If your eye offend you, tear it out!' Many who came as close as I did balked at this step and have since stumbled along, spiritually and morally lamed, shuddering at the crimes committed in their names, unable openly to deny responsibility for them, caught in a net of apparently insoluble conflicts: Do they not owe it to their country to sacrifice their greater wisdom, their morals, their human dignity and their conscience? Does not what they call the 'incredible rise of Germany' show that the sacrifice is worth it and that it all adds up? They forget that it is no better for a nation than for a single man to gain the whole world if it loses its soul; and they also forget that they are sacrificing not just themselves for their patriotism (or what they think is patriotism) but also their country.

For – and this is what made the parting finally almost inevitable – Germany did not remain Germany. The German nationalists themselves destroyed it. It gradually became clear that the conflict was only superficially about the question of whether it was necessary to leave one's country in order to keep faith with oneself. The real conflict beneath the surface, hidden by the common clichés and platitudes, was between nationalism and keeping faith with one's country.

The Germany that was 'my country' and the country of those like me, was not just a blob on the map of Europe. It was characterised by certain distinctive attributes: humanity, openness on all sides, philosophical depth of thought, dissatisfaction with the world and oneself, the courage always to try something fresh and to abandon it if need be, self-criticism, truthfulness, objectivity, severity, rigour, variety, a certain ponderousness but also delight in the freest improvisation, slowness and earnestness but also a playful richness of invention, engendering ever new ideas which it quickly rejects as invalid, respect for originality, good nature, generosity, sentimentality, musicality, and above all freedom, something roving, unfettered, soaring, weightless, Promethean. Secretly we were proud that in the realm of the spirit our country was the land of unlimited possibilities. Be that as it may, this was the country we felt attached to, in which we were at home.

This Germany has been destroyed and trampled underfoot by the nationalists, and it has at last become clear who its deadliest enemy was: German nationalism itself and the German Reich. To stay loyal to it and belong to it, one had to have the courage to recognise this fact – and all its consequences.

Nationalism, that is national self-reflection and self-worship, is certainly a dangerous mental illness wherever it appears, capable of distorting the character of a nation and making it ugly, just as vanity and egoism distort the character of a person and make it ugly. In Germany this illness has a particularly vicious destructive effect, precisely because Germany's inner-most character is openness, expansiveness, even in a certain sense selflessness. If other peoples suffer from nationalism it is an incidental weakness, beside which their true qualities can remain intact; but in Germany nationalism kills the basic values of the national character. That explains why the Germans – doubtless a fine, sensitive and human people in healthy circumstances – become positively inhuman when they succumb to the nationalist illness; they take on a brutal nastiness of which other peoples are incapable. Only the Germans lose everything through nationalism: the heart of their humanity, their exis-tence, their selves. This illness, that damages only the external features of others, corrodes their souls. A nationalist Frenchman can still be a typical (and otherwise quite likeable) Frenchman. A German who yields to nationalism is no longer a German. What he achieves is a German Empire, maybe even a Great or Pan-German Empire – but also the destruction of Germany.

Admittedly, you should not imagine that in 1932 Germany and its culture were in a flourishing, magnificent state which the Nazis demolished at a single blow. The history of Germany's self-destruction through poisonous nationalism goes further back than that. It would be worth writing about. Its great paradox is that every act of this self-destruction consisted of a victorious war, a great outward triumph. One hundred and fifty years ago Germany was in the ascendant. The 'liberation wars' against Napoleon of 1813 and 1815 were the first setback, the wars of 1864 to 1870 the second. Nietzsche was the first to recognise prophetically that German civilisation had just lost its war against the German Reich. For a long time Germany was prevented from finding its political shape by the straitjacket of Bismarck's Prusso-German Reich. From then on it had no political representation (except perhaps in its Catholic sector): the nationalist Right hated it, the Marxist Left ignored it. Yet it remained mutely and stubbornly alive – until 1933. You could still find it in a thousand homes, families, and circles of friends, in the editorial offices of some newspapers and publishers, in theatres, concert halls and in odd corners of public life from churches to cabarets. It was only the Nazis, radical and thoroughly organised as they were, who rooted and smoked it out wherever it was to be found. The first country to be occupied by the Nazis was not Austria or Czechoslovakia. It was Germany. It was just one of their now so familiar tricks that they occupied and trampled on the nation in the name of 'Germany' itself – that was part of the mechanism of destruction.

A German who felt attached to this Germany – and not to any structure that happened to be erected in a particular geographical location – had no alternative but to leave, however forbidding this step must appear which would outwardly deprive him of his country. On the other hand, the expansiveness and openness that lie in the original German character made this loss perhaps a little easier than it would have been for others. One came to feel that any foreign country would seem more like home than Adolf Hitler's 'Reich'. Perhaps it might be possible – one thought with timid hope – to save a little bit of Germany here and there 'abroad'.

Thirty-Two

Yes, people in Germany had vague hopes that something positive would come from the emigrants. There was not much basis for these hopes, but since the situation was hopeless at home, and since it is difficult to live without some hope, they placed their hopes abroad.

One hope, which a few months before would have been a fear, and which many still were not sure whether they should call hope or fear, was directed towards 'foreign countries'. In Germany, that meant France and England. Could France and England idly contemplate what was happening in Germany for long? Would not the humanitarian Left in both countries be appalled by the barbaric tyranny that was taking place on their doorsteps – and would not the nationalist Right be alarmed by the preparations for war that were not even kept hidden, and the open rearmament that had been pursued almost from the very first day of the new regime? Whatever the shade of their governments, surely these two countries would soon lose patience with the Nazis and use their still infinitely superior military might to stop the mischief in a week? If the politicians there were not totally blind, no other course of action was conceivable. One could not expect them to sit idly by while the knives were being sharpened for use against their countries – they would hardly be fooled by a few 'peace speeches' when every schoolchild in Germany could see straight through them.

In the meantime the political emigrants in France and England would certainly be favoured and cultivated by sensible statesmen. They would form the backbone of the organisation of the future German Republic, which would have learned from the mistakes of its predecessor and be truly effective. Perhaps everything would seem to have been a bad dream, as after a cleansing thunderstorm, or the quick, decisive lancing of a boil. We would begin again at the point where a false start had been made in 1919, a bit more wisely and with fewer prejudices.

Those were the hopes. Admittedly, they had little foundation, except that their realisation would have been sensible and desirable. These hopes, coupled with my overwhelming feeling that everything in life had become unpredictable anyway and that I could only act on the spur of the moment, replaced any properly thought-out plans for emigration that I might have made. I would just leave, or so I thought. Where to? Paris, of course. For as long as it was permitted I would arrange to have 200 marks a month sent to me, and then I would take stock. There would doubtless be something for me to do. There was, after all, no lack of things that needed to be done.

The naiveté of this plan was in part an expression of my situation at the time, that of a young person who has never lived away from home and feels the time approaching when he must 'fly the nest'. That in this case 'flying the nest' meant going into exile, that it was a step into the unknown, an adventure, did not bother me very much. The strange counterpoint of a certain numb desperation ('It can't get much worse') and a youthful spirit of adventure made the decision easier for me. One should also not forget that, like all Germans of my generation, the feeling that everything was so uncertain was deeply embedded in my mind. It is a commonly held belief that caution is just as dangerous as recklessness, and that caution deprives one of the pleasure of taking risks. Incidentally, everything I have experienced in my life reinforces the truth of this perception.

Thus, one day, when my training period at the *Kammergericht* had ended, I declared to my father that I wanted to 'leave'. I could not see anything worth while for me here; in particular it was impossible and senseless to try to become a judge or administrative civil servant in the current circumstances. I wanted to get out, go to Paris for the time being. Would he give

me his blessing and send me 200 marks a month as long as that
was possible?

It was almost suprising how weak my father's opposition was.
In March he had brushed aside emotional outbursts like this
with a quiet smile of superiority. In the meantime he had grown
very old. He no longer slept at night. The drumming and
alarms at the nearby SS barracks kept him awake, but more so
perhaps, his thoughts.

It is harder for an old man to bear the destruction and
disappearance of everything he has worked for than it is for a
young one. For me leave-taking, even in its most radical form,
meant a new beginning; for him it was final. His dominant
feeling was that he had lived in vain. There had been great
pieces of legislation in his administrative area, on which he had
worked closely. They were important, daring, thoughtful,
intellectual achievements, the fruits of decades of experience
and years of intense, meticulous analysis and dedicated refine-
ment. With a stroke of the pen they had been declared null and
void. It had not even been a major event. Not only that, but the
foundations on which such things could be built or replaced had
been washed away. The whole tradition of a state based on the
rule of law, to which generations of men like my father had
devoted their lives and energies, which had seemed so firm and
permanent, had disappeared overnight. It was not just failure
that my father experienced at the end of a life that had been
severe, disciplined, industrious and all-in-all very successful. It
was catastrophe. He was witnessing the triumph, not of his
opponents – that he would have borne with wise acceptance –
but of barbarians, beneath consideration as opponents. In those
days I sometimes saw my father sitting at his desk for long
periods, just staring into space, without a glance at the papers
before him. It seemed as though he were surveying a vast,
baleful scene of destruction.

'And what do you intend to do abroad?' he said, his old
scepticism still showing in the question, and his canny lawyer's
instinct for the decisive point. But the voice was so tired that its

tone suggested the question had only been asked as a formality, and that he would accept almost any answer.

I put the best gloss I could on my lack of plans.

'Well,' he said with a small, sad, kindly smile, 'that doesn't sound very promising, does it?'

'True,' I said, 'but what can I look forward to here?'

'I'm just afraid,' he said, beginning to warm to his argument and take a firmer stand than he had perhaps intended, 'that you are deluding yourself. They're not just waiting for us over there, you know. Immigrants are a burden for any country, and it's not pleasant to feel you are a burden. There's a great difference between entering a country as a kind of ambassador, with a purpose and something to show, and coming as a refugee looking for shelter. A great difference.'

'Don't we have something to offer?' I said. 'If the entire German intelligentsia, all the artists and scientists were to emigrate – which country would not feel privileged to be given all that as a present?'

He raised his arm a little and let it sink tiredly. 'Bankrupt stock,' he said. 'You lose your value if you become a refugee. Just look at the Russians. The Russian refugees were also an elite. Now their generals, politicians and writers are glad if they are allowed to be waiters or taxi-drivers in Paris.'

'Perhaps they prefer being waiters in Paris to being ministers in Moscow,' I said.

'Perhaps,' said my father, 'perhaps not. Such things are easy to say beforehand. Afterwards, when you're faced with reality, things look different. Starvation and destitution are easy to contemplate when you have enough to eat.'

'Should I perhaps become a Nazi for fear of starvation and destitution?' I said.

'No,' he said, 'you shouldn't. Certainly not.'

'And do you think I can become a judge without becoming a Nazi?'

'I don't suppose you could be a judge,' said my father, 'at least for the time being. Who can tell what lies in the future? But I thought you could at least become a lawyer. And anyway, aren't you beginning to get some money for the stuff you write?'

That was true. A well-respected newspaper, in which I had occasionally published short pieces, had written to me suggesting a closer collaboration. At that time the great newspapers that had formerly been democratic offered surprising opportunities for young, Aryan, non-Nazi people who were not handicapped by a leftist record, or better still were unknown quantities. I had not rejected the offer. I had gone to the offices and to my delight had found an editorial staff that was not in the least Nazi, that thought and felt as I did. It was pure joy to sit in the offices, exchange pieces of news and slander; it was pleasant to dictate articles and watch them being passed to the messengers to be taken to the typesetters. It sometimes felt like being in a nest of conspirators. The only thing that made me uneasy was that, in spite of all the allusions concealed between the lines of the articles we had written, which had produced such laughter in the office, the next morning when the paper appeared, it seemed to be a committed Nazi organ.

'I think I may actually be able to write for the paper from abroad,' I said.

'That makes sense,' said my father. 'Have you spoken to the editors yet?'

I had to admit that I had not.

'I suggest,' said my father, 'that we let the matter rest for a few days, and think about it a bit more carefully. You must not think that it would be easy for your mother and me to let you go, and into such uncertainty at that. In any case I expect you to sit your exams first. If only from a sense of propriety.'

That he continued to insist on. After a few days he put forward a plan of his own.

'First you will take your *Assessor* examination as intended. You cannot simply throw twenty years of education overboard and run away just before your finals. That will take about another five months. Then you have six months in hand to write your doctoral thesis. After all, you can write that as easily in Paris as here. So if you still feel the same way then, you can take six months' leave and go where you like, let's say to Paris, and work on your thesis. You can look around while you're doing that. If you think that you can gain a foothold, well and good. If not, you haven't lost anything and you can still come back. That will be about a year from now and who knows what things will be like in a year's time.'

After a little to-ing and fro-ing, that was the agreed-upon plan. I thought it was unnecessary to sit the *Assessor* exams, but recognised that I owed it to my father to do so. My main fear was that war might break out in the next five months, while I was still here. It would be the inevitable preventive war of the Western powers against Hitler and I would be forced to fight on the wrong side.

'The wrong side?' said my father. 'Do you think the French side would be the right side for you?'

'Yes,' I said firmly, 'in this case I do. As things are now, Germany can only be liberated from abroad.'

'Oh dear,' said my father bitterly, 'liberated from abroad! You probably don't seriously mean that. Anyway you can't be liberated against your will. That's an impossibility. If the Germans want freedom, they will have to work for it themselves.'

'But do you see any means of doing that, in chains as we now are?'

'No.'

'So the only option is –'

'That "so" is illogical,' said my father. 'Just because one path is blocked, it does not follow that another must be open. We should not seek comfort in illusions. Germany took refuge in illusions in 1918 and the result is the Nazis. If German liberals again resort to self-delusion the result will be that we will have a foreign government.'

'Maybe that would be better than a Nazi government.'

'I don't know,' said my father. 'The more distant of two evils always seems the lesser. It may not be the lesser in reality. I myself would not raise a finger to bring about a foreign government.'

'But then you see no possibilities and no hope?'

'Hardly any,' said my father, 'not at the moment.'

Again his eyes took on that vacant, staring look of forlorn self-control, as if he were surveying a scene of vast desolation.

Now and again associates from his old department would visit my father. He had retired several years ago, but he still had personal contacts there, and he enjoyed hearing how this or that matter was developing, or how this or that young colleague was shaping up. He liked to feel he was still part of things and give the occasional hint or piece of informal advice. The visitors still came, but the conversations had become dreary and unchanging. My father would ask about a colleague, speaking his name. The visitor's answer was a laconic 'Clause 4' or 'Clause 6'.

Those were clauses from a recent law. It was called 'the Law for the Re-establishment of the Civil Service' and its individual paragraphs allowed civil servants to be demoted, involuntarily retired, laid off with a lump sum, or sacked without any pension or lump sum. Every clause contained a destiny. 'Clause 4' was a devastating blow. 'Clause 6' was demotion and humiliation. These numbers dominated conversations between civil servants.

One day the president of the department called. He was much younger than my father and they had had their quarrels. The president had been a Social Democrat; my father had been far more to the right. More than once they had clashed, and things had not been helped by the fact that the younger man had the senior position. Nevertheless, they had respected each other and they had not completely lost touch.

This time the visit was painful. The president, a man in his late forties, looked as old as my father did at seventy. His hair had gone completely white. My father told me afterwards that he had often lost the thread of the conversation, not answered and looked absent-mindedly down at the floor. Then he had burst out, 'It's dreadful, my friend. Just dreadful.' He had come to say goodbye. He was leaving Berlin to 'crawl away somewhere in the country'. He had just come from a concentration camp.

He was 'Clause 4.'

As I said, my father himself had retired long ago. He had no official powers any more and he could have done nothing to harm the Nazis, even if he had wanted to. It seemed as though he was out of the line of fire. But one day he too received an official letter. It contained a detailed questionnaire. 'Under Clause X of the Law for the Re-establishment of the Civil Service, you are required to answer the following questions truthfully and in full . . . Under Clause Y, refusal to answer will entail loss of pension . . .'

There were a lot of questions. My father had to state which political parties, organisations and associations he had ever belonged to in his life, he had to list his services to the nation, explain this and excuse that and finally to sign a printed declaration that he 'stood behind the government of national uprising without reservations'. In short, having served the state for forty-five years, he was required to humble himself again in order to continue to receive his well-earned pension.

My father stared silently at the questionnaire for a long time.

Next day I saw him seated at his desk, the form in front of him. He was staring past it.

'Are you going to fill it in?' I asked.

My father looked at the questionnaire, grimaced and said nothing for a time. Then he asked, 'Do you think I should?'

Silence.

'I wonder what you and your mother would live on?' he said at last.

'I really don't know,' he repeated after a while. 'I don't even know,' and he tried to smile, 'how you will be able to go to Paris to write your thesis.'

There was an uneasy silence. Then my father pushed the questionnaire aside, but he did not put it away.

It lay on his desk for several days. Then one afternoon as I entered the room I saw my father filling it in, slowly and laboriously, like a child writing a school essay. Half an hour later he went out himself and took it to the letter box before he could change his mind. He showed no outward change in his manner and spoke no more excitedly than usual, but it had none the less been too much for him. With people who are used to restraint in word and gesture, some part of the body is invariably affected by severe mental stress. Some have heart attacks in such cases. My father's weakness was his stomach. He had hardly sat down at his desk again when he jumped up and began to vomit convulsively. For two or three days he was unable to eat or keep down any food. It was the beginning of a hunger strike by his body, which killed him cruelly and painfully two years later.

Thirty-Three

*T*he longer this summer of 1933 lasted, the more unreal everything became. Things gradually lost their substance, changed into bizarre dreams. I began to live in a state like that of a mild fever, pleasantly limp, slightly dazed and free of all responsibilities.

I registered for the *Assessor* examination, the great final examination of a German lawyer's training which confers the right to become a judge or a higher civil servant. I did it without any intention of ever making use of that right. Whether I passed or failed the exam was a matter of complete indifference to me. Normally, you will agree, examinations are stimulating things that put you on your mettle. People even speak of examination fever. I felt nothing of the kind. The fever I experienced was of a very different nature.

I worked on the preparatory homework tests, which are part of the *Assessor* examination, in the 'legal archives', a library on the top floor of a large office building. It had airy studio rooms with glass partitions, beneath a blue, windy summer sky. There I wrote my answers, as lightly and carelessly as one writes a letter. I simply could not take them seriously. The questions and points for discussion assumed a world that no longer existed. They still covered the Civil Code, and even the Weimar state constitution. I read obsolete commentaries on these dead and buried clauses, which only yesterday had been much quoted. Instead of picking out the sentences that were important for my answers, I read on and began to daydream. From downstairs I could hear tinny march music. If you leaned out of the window you could see columns of brown uniforms rolling through the streets, punctuated by swastika flags. Wherever the flags were, passers-by on both sides of the street would raise their arms in salute (we had learned that those who did not were beaten up). What was the occasion this time? Oh, they were marching to the Lustgarten, a parade ground in the centre of Berlin. Herr Ley had left the International Labour Office in Geneva because he had disagreed with something, and now the SA was parading to the Lustgarten to slay the dragon once and for all, with singing and shouting.

You saw these marches and heard this singing every day, and you had to be careful to disappear into a house entrance in time to avoid having to salute the flags. We lived in a state of war, though it was a rather peculiar war, in which victories were achieved by marching and singing. The SA, SS, Hitler Youth, Workers' Front or whatever would march through the streets singing 'Do you see the sunrise in the East?' or 'Heathlands of Brandenburg', form ranks somewhere, listen to a speech and thunder 'Heil!' from a thousand throats, and another enemy would bite the dust. It was paradise for a certain kind of German, and there was a definite 1914 feeling about it. I saw old ladies with shopping bags pause and watch such a brown column of marching, lustily singing men. With a gleam in their eyes they said, 'You can see, yes, you can just see that things are looking up.'

Sometimes more substantial victories were won. One morning a strong force of police surrounded and occupied the artists' quarter in Wilmersdorf, which had been home to many left-wing literati and still was to a few. Victory! There was great booty. Dozens of enemy flags fell into the hands of our troops, subversive literature, from Karl Marx to Heinrich Mann, was loaded on to the lorries by the kilogram, and the number of prisoners was respectable. That really was the style in which this event was portrayed in the press, as though it were a second Battle of Tannenberg. Another time all traffic on road and rail was brought to a standstill 'at a stroke' at midday, and every vehicle was searched. Victory! What things were uncovered! From jewels and currency to 'propaganda material of enemies of the state'. It was really worthy of a 'spontaneous demonstration' in the Lustgarten.

At the end of June all the papers had banner headlines, 'Enemy Planes over Berlin!' No one believed it, not even the Nazis, but no one was particularly surprised either. That was the current style. A 'spontaneous demonstration' followed: 'Germany needs the freedom of the air.' Marches and flags, the Horst Wessel Song, 'Heil'. About the same time the minister of culture deposed the Church authorities, and appointed the Nazi military padre Müller as 'Bishop of the Reich'.* At a demonstration in the Sportpalast this was celebrated as a victory for German Christianity, with Adolf Hitler as the German Messiah, flags, the Horst Wessel Song, and 'Heil'. This time the celebrations concluded with a rendering of Luther's chorale, 'Ein feste Burg ist unser Gott' ('A solid castle is our God'), perhaps in honour of the institution that was being buried, or for some other tasteful reason. Then there were 'Church elections'. The Nazis ordered all their nominally Christian followers to the ballot, and next day the press reported an overwhelming election victory for German Christianity! That evening, as I rode through the city, there was a swastika flag on every church tower.

The Nazis were to encounter serious resistance to this attack, but that could not yet be discerned at all outside Church circles. It had not been without qualms that I had participated for the first time in an issue of the governance of the Church, and placed my ballot paper in the box labelled with the solemn words 'Bekennende Kirche' (Confessing Church).† I did not feel very committed. I had always respected rather than venerated the Church, but I felt strongly that it should be

---

* Ludwig Müller, a former naval chaplain, chosen as prospective 'Reich Bishop' by Hitler in May 1933. He failed to gain the position in the Church elections of 26 May 1933 but his election was forced through on 27 September 1933.
† A Protestant movement upholding the traditions of scripture and the confessions of the Reformation against the aryanising changes proposed by the German Christians under Müller.

respected, even by those who did not venerate it. The blasphemous fancy-dress cavortings of the 'German Christians' disgusted me, but I was utterly convinced of the futility of any kind of resistance, particularly in the Church. For decency's sake, I thought, one should 'commit' oneself to a defeated and violated institution. I felt a certain sympathy for the conservative old gentleman whom I heard at this time saying, 'For pity's sake, now we even have to fight for the faith which we don't have.'

Emotions became less intense in the course of the summer, the tension dropped, even the feeling of disgust weakened. It was all covered by a narcotic cloud. For many, who had to remain in Germany, it was a time of acclimatisation, with all its dangers. For my part, I half felt as if I had already left. A few more months and I would be in Paris – I never considered the possibility of return. This was just a waiting period. It did not count any more.

Indeed there was not much left worth experiencing. My friends had all gone – or they were no longer my friends. Sometimes I got postcards with foreign stamps. There were occasional letters from Frank Landau. These letters became gloomier as time went by. At first they sounded decisive and hopeful. Then they became shorter and more ambiguous, and once in the middle of August there was a veritable bundle of a letter, twelve or fourteen pages written as they came to mind, like a soliloquy. The tone was tired and despondent, even desperate. It was all no good. Things had gone as badly as possible with Ellen and they were going to part. There were no opportunities for Frank in Switzerland, nothing on the horizon after his doctorate. He could not forget Hanni, and our talks.* There was nothing to replace what he had left behind, nothing to connect with the past which might give him strength. 'I'm not writing this to ask for your advice, because I know there is none . . .'

A little later Ellen suddenly came back. She simply appeared.

---

* Hanni, like Lisl, was one of the circle of tennis club friends.

The relationship was over. She had capitulated. She wrote to me and I visited her two or three times in Wannsee, sat with mixed feelings in the garden of the house I had been in on the 1st of April. She wanted me to explain it all to her and give her solace and advice. She was in a bad state, confused and off balance: she loved Frank, but she no longer thought she could live with him. It had all been terribly hasty and now it was spoiled for ever. If only they had had time to let things develop slowly and see where they were leading! But that was the terrible thing. Everything always had to be decided immediately. You stood at so many crossroads. Here and now you had to make up your mind, and the roads led in such different directions, towards an unknowable future. Her family was preparing to emigrate to America. Should she go with them? That would mean never seeing Frank again. Should she go back to Zurich? That meant tying herself to him permanently, and this summer had not been propitious. But she loved him. 'You know him. Tell me what he's really like. Tell me what to do.'

I had spoken to Hanni at the beginning of April. She had lain in a darkened room for a few days, eating nothing and crying all day. Later we had traipsed from one consulate to the next, written letters to various Czech ministries and had interviews at police stations. It had all been to no avail. The question of her nationality was hopelessly tangled. Hanni was a prisoner in Germany.

I led a strange existence, almost like being a receiver in charge of a bankrupt life. In-between-times I did the preparatory tests for a certificate that meant nothing to me and that belonged more to that bankrupt life – which had once been my own. Also in-between-times I wrote newspaper articles, little things with as much bitter wit as I could muster – and was surprised to see them in print a few days later in that slightly schizophrenic paper with its enforced, stolid Nazi opinions, a paper that had had an international reputation only a few months ago. How proud I would have been to belong to it then! Now it was of little concern to me, it was temporary and did not count.

Of all the people I had been close to, only Charlie remained – strangely enough, since it had started as a carnival fling. She stayed. She wandered like a silken thread through the weave of that unreal summer. A slightly painful, not quite happy love affair – but still a love affair with a little sweetness.

She was a good, simple, young Berlin girl and in happier times our story might have been simple, trite and sweet. As it was, misfortune bound us more tightly together than was good for us, and demanded more of us than we were able to give each other; namely, to be precise, compensation for the loss of a whole world and for daily painful, choking distress. That was too much for both of us. I could hardly bear to speak to her about what was going on inside me; after all, her own position was much worse and much more dangerous, more immediate, more urgent. She was Jewish, she was persecuted, she was in daily fear for her life and that of her parents and the large family she belonged to, and to which she was very close. So many terrible things were happening to the Jews, but I had difficulty telling them all apart. Like many other young Jews she considered what was happening to them almost to the exclusion of all else, and who can blame her? She reacted in all innocence, becoming a Zionist from one day to the next, a Jewish nationalist. It was a common reaction, and one that I could sympathise with but observed with regret. It so closely followed the Nazis' intentions. It contained so much weak-hearted acceptance of their hostile assumptions. If I had argued with her, I would have robbed her of her only consolation.

'But Peter, what are we to do?' she asked with large sad eyes, the one time I tried, as gently as I could, to hint at my scepticism. She studied Hebrew and thought about Palestine, but she had not arrived there yet. She still went to work in the shop – it had been re-allowed, but who knew for how long? – and helped to feed her family. She was touchingly caring about her father and all her relatives, went to work, and suffered. She lost weight and cried a great deal, but sometimes she let me comfort her and laughed again, at least for one evening. Then she would be charmingly silly and boisterous, but it did not last long. In August she became seriously ill, and she had her appendix removed. That was the second time that year that I saw appendicitis apparently caused by mental stress.

All the while we continued our little affair as well as we could. We went to the cinema and drank wine together, tried to be merry and in love, in the normal way. We parted late at night. I took the last underground from her distant part of town to mine and sat around on empty platforms where the only movement was the escalators.

On Sundays we often went for walks in the woods, or lay around by the water's edge or in some clearing. Berlin's surroundings are beautiful, rather untamed and wild. Even within the range of the suburban railway you can, if you leave the well-trodden excursion routes, still reach areas that seem untouched, magnificently lonely, unchangeable, and romantically sad. We searched them out and wandered down long alleys of dark green firs, or we lay in a meadow beneath a threateningly blue sky. The sky was beautiful, and so were the long, densely packed rows of tall trees, the grass, the moss, the ants and the buzzing summer insects. It was all infinitely, lethally soothing. Only we should not have been part of the picture. Without us it would have been even more beautiful. We were intruders.

That summer the weather was wonderful, the sun tireless, and an ironic God arranged that 1933 of all years would be a vintage of which connoisseurs of wine would speak with reverence for many years.

Thirty-Four

*A*n unexpected letter arrived, from Teddy in Paris. It was hardly to be believed. She wrote that she was coming – very soon, next week. My heart began to beat like a drum. She was coming to try to get her mother out of the country, she wrote, and she wanted to see how things were close up. She was a little anxious, but she was looking forward to many things and she hoped to see a lot of me.

As I put the letter in my inside pocket I had a feeling as if life were returning, an overwhelming tingling as though ants were crawling all over me. I suddenly realised that all the while I had been stiff, numb and cold, almost dead. I ran around the flat, whistled and smoked one cigarette after another. I did not know what to do with myself. In my present condition it was almost unbearable to feel such pleasure in anticipation.

The next day the headlines were 'Training Camps for *Referendars*'. All *Referendars* who were about to take their *Assessor* examinations, and had finished their preparatory tests, would be required to go to training camps where they would take part in military and sporting exercises and ideological indoctrination sessions to prepare them for their great task as the German people's judges. The first batch would receive their call-up papers in the next few days. There followed an editorial comment, full of praise and 'Heil': 'Every young German lawyer will be grateful to the Minister of Justice ...'

That was the first time, I think, that I threw a real temper tantrum. The cause may seem rather slight, but the reactions of us frail and weak human beings are not always strictly commensurate with the general importance of the occasion. I beat the walls with my fists as though I had been locked up, I screamed and sobbed and cursed God and the world, my father, myself, the German Reich, the newspaper, everyone and everything. I was about to hand in my last preparatory homework test, and so could reckon on being part of the first contingent. I saw red and went berserk. Then I collapsed and wrote a short, despairing letter to Teddy. She should come as quickly as possible so that we could see each other at least for a day or two.

The next day or the day after that I dutifully submitted my final homework test, with a broken feeling of having had a thorough drubbing.

Then, praise be to Prussian red tape, nothing happened. My tests were probably gathering dust in some office. First they must be processed there, then my name had to be ticked off on some list and transferred to some other list, then the contingents for the camps had to be assembled, the call-up papers printed and sent off, and marvellously, each of these stages took a few precious days. When some days had passed without any reaction, I calmed down and remembered the way that Prussian departments work. I saw that there was some hope; indeed I could hope for two, maybe even four weeks of freedom. True, any day could see an end to it, but it was not inevitable. Every day I checked the post for official letters, at first anxiously and with relief, then with quiet confidence, and finally, as it became more critical, with an ever more confident, sacrilegious certainty that there would not be one. It could have arrived any day, but it did not. Teddy arrived instead.

She came, and it was as if she had never been away. She brought a whiff of Paris with her: Parisian cigarettes, Parisian magazines, Parisian gossip, and irresistible as a perfume, the air of Paris, air that could be breathed – and I breathed it greedily. In Paris the fashion that summer, the summer in which uniforms had become so horribly fashionable in Germany, was for women to dress *à l'uniforme*. Thus Teddy wore a little blue lancer's jacket with insets and brass buttons. It was unimaginable. She came from a world where the women wore that kind of thing for fun, and nobody thought anything of it. She had many stories. Parisian students of all nationalities had just been on a six-week trip through France. There had been Swedes, Hungarians, Poles, Austrians, Germans and Italians. They had danced the folk dances of their countries in their national costumes and sung folk songs. Everywhere they had been received like princes with cries of 'Bravo' and 'Bis' and fraternal speeches. In Lyon, Herriot* himself had delivered a speech that had almost had them all in tears, and then the city had given them a such a meal that they had all felt overfed for two days ... I sat there and just let her tell me everything, eagerly asking for more. Such things still existed! Yes they existed – less than a day's journey away. And Teddy was here sitting next to me, really next to me, on my chair, telling me all this as though it were nothing out of the ordinary.

This time I had nothing to show her in exchange, absolutely nothing. Before, when she had come, there had still been a few things worth seeing in Berlin: an interesting film, that was the talk of the town; a few major concerts; a cabaret or small theatre with a special 'atmosphere'. This time there was nothing of the kind. You could almost see Teddy gasping for air. Innocently she asked about cafés and cabarets that had long since been closed, asked about actors who had not appeared for many months. Of course she had read the news in the press, but now the reality seen face to face was rather different, less sensational perhaps, but much harder to comprehend and much harder to endure. The swastika flags everywhere, the brown uniforms that one could not get away from: not in buses, cafés, in the streets or even in the Tiergarten park. They were everywhere, like an army of occupation. The never-ending march music and drums – strange, Teddy still noticed it, and asked what the reason was. She did not know yet that there would have been more reason to ask if there had been no music. The red posters with the announcements of executions on the poster pillars almost every

* Edouard Herriot, French politician, variously foreign minister and prime minister in the 1920s.

morning, next to the cinema programmes and the posters for summer restaurants; I did not even notice them any more, but Teddy shuddered as she studied them innocently. On one walk I suddenly pulled her into a house entrance. She did not understand and asked with a start, 'What's up?'

'There's an SA flag passing our way,' I said, as though it was completely obvious.

'So what?'

'You don't want to salute it, do you?'

'No. Why?'

'You have to if they pass by and you're on the street.'

'What do you mean: have to? You just don't do it.'

Poor Teddy, she really did come from another world. I did not answer, but just pulled a long face.

'I'm a foreigner,' said Teddy. 'Nobody can force me.' Again I could only smile ruefully at her illusions. She was an Austrian.

There was one day when I was seriously concerned for her safety, just because she was Austrian. The night before, the Austrian press attaché had been dragged from his bed, arrested, and expelled. 'We' were angry with Austria because it had refused to unite with us. Dollfuss* in Vienna reacted by expelling one or maybe more Nazis – I do not remember exactly; but I do remember how the press bayed with one voice at the enormity of this provocation by the Austrian regime. 'This will not go unanswered,' they wrote. Given the style of our government, what could a response consist of but the expulsion of all Austrians? But fate was kind to us. Hitler found a problem with the idea, or put it aside for something else. This time it did go unanswered, and Teddy was allowed to stay.

'This really is my last visit,' said Teddy. I told her that I intended to come to Paris soon, and we immediately began to make plans: a little international theatre appeared, like a castle in Spain, run perhaps by students or emigrant actors. 'How are the German emigrants doing?' I asked hopefully, but Teddy

---

* Engelbert Dollfuss, right-wing Chancellor of Austria, suppressed the Austrian Nazis in June 1933 and was assassinated in a bodged Nazi coup attempt on 25 July 1934.

only answered evasively. 'Those poor people are not on their best form, it's only to be expected,' she said mildly.

A few days passed in this way. Then there was a thunderbolt. Teddy told me – or rather she let me surmise and deduce – that she was about to be married, very soon after her return. 'Mr Andrews?' I asked, with sudden inspiration (he had not played a major part in her reports). She nodded. 'Very good,' I said. We were sitting on the terrace of the Romanisches Café, opposite the Gedächtniskirche at the end of the Kurfürstendamm. Once it had been the meeting place of literary Berlin. Now it was deserted. The squat stone towers of the church seemed to close in on me like dungeon walls.

'*Mon pauvre vieux*,' said Teddy, 'is it very bad?'

I shook my head.

Then she said something that sent a sweet wave of pain through my head. There had never been a question of anything like marriage between us, and our love affair had always been interrupted just at the critical moment. I had never been very certain that I was not just a friend among others for her and I had never told her what she meant to me. It would have been difficult to express. It would have sounded too grandiloquent and sentimental. Even our most intimate moments had had a light playful tone.

'We would not have been able to marry now anyway,' she said. 'How would you have managed here with me?'

'You thought about it?' I said mawkishly.

'Of course,' she laughed. Then with a gesture of infinite warmth, 'And for now I'm still here.'

Parting. Another parting, but such a resounding, moving parting, like none of the others. Everything seemed to be all right again, as though it had all just been a preparation for these three weeks that remained to us. Everything had moved aside and made room for me. There were no other friends, and no duties, to prevent me from being with Teddy from early till late, and to be there for her entirely. She also seemed to have come just to see me – even if it was only to say goodbye.

At this moment the world seemed to withdraw, as if by

agreement, to free these three weeks. The German Reich generously took its time before it finally laid its hand, already hovering, on my shoulder. There was no official letter to call me away. My parents went on holiday. Poor Charlie became ill and had to go to hospital; she seemed to be doing me a terrible favour that I could hardly accept. I know I should not have felt that way.

The three weeks passed like a single day. Yet they were no idyll. We hardly ever had time to act like a pair of lovers or to talk about our feelings. Teddy had to arrange her mother's emigration. She was a little old lady, sitting quietly and hopelessly among her pieces of furniture, no longer able to understand the world. So we passed our time at consulates, and government offices and removal companies, spent hours in the waiting room of the government currency exchange office. Every day we had to make plans and organise things. Then we had to oversee the packers and the removal men. Departure and leave-taking. It was a familiar scenario. But these three weeks of departure and leave-taking were all the time we had left in the whole of eternity to express all the long-held feelings of our bashful, tender love. We were as inseparable as if we were newly betrothed, and as familiar and easy as an old married couple. There were no wasted moments. Even sitting in the waiting room of the currency office, discussing what we would tell the officials, was full of sweetness.

That office's final verdict was that a certain proportion of the family money would not be permitted to leave the country. 'There's nothing to be done,' said Teddy, 'I'll have to smuggle it. I'm not going to let them steal it from us –'

'But if you get caught!'

'I won't get caught,' she said, beaming with confidence. 'By the way, I know how to bind books.' So for a few days we sat in Teddy's long unused bedroom and fabricated book bindings using a lot of cardboard, art paper and glue. Inside they were made of 100-mark notes. Looking up from our work, we suddenly saw our faces in the mirror. 'Old jailbirds,' said Teddy and work stopped for a couple of minutes. One day our work

was interrupted by the doorbell. There were two SA men
at the door. This time they only rattled collection boxes
menacingly. I said, 'Sorry!' rudely and shut the door in their
faces. With Teddy behind me I felt an indescribable, gay
confidence.

But sometimes I would wake up at night and the world would
seem grey as a gallows yard. In those hours, but only then, I
knew that it was all over. Mr Andrews was waiting for Teddy in
Paris. When I arrived there, she would be Mrs Andrews and I
liked Andrews far too much to cheat him. Perhaps they would
have children. This thought made me feel sick to death. I saw
Andrews before me as I had sometimes seen him two years
before. It had been a peculiar time. Teddy had remained in
Paris against her family's wishes, a prodigal daughter with no
money but lots of friends who all wanted to tear off as large a
piece of her for themselves as they could get, and who were all
incapable of really helping her (I was not much better than any
of the others). At that time the quiet Mr Andrews had
occasionally come to Teddy's tiny, untidy hotel room, put his
feet up on the mantelpiece and had an unnecessary and
ineffective language lesson. Then he would unexpectedly say
something really clever and helpful, smiling slightly before he
left again, quietly and unobtrusively. A patient man. Now he
was going to marry Teddy. An Englishman. The English always
seemed to have all the luck. They got everything worth having
in the world: India and Egypt and Gibraltar and Cyprus and
Australia and South Africa, the gold countries, Canada, and now
also Teddy! A poor German like me had the Nazis instead.
Those were the miserable thoughts I had if, by some misfortune, I awoke during the night.

The next day it would all be forgotten and I was happy. It was
autumn, an early, golden autumn. The sun shone every day.
There was still no official letter. Today we had to go to the
finance ministry, then to the police and the consulate. If we
were lucky there might be an hour free in the afternoon for a
walk in the Tiergarten. We might hire a rowing boat. And
Teddy all day.

Let us not look forward
Nor back. Be cradled, as in
A swaying boat on the sea.

Friedrich Hölderlin, *Mnemosyne*

Thirty-Five

*F*our weeks later I was wearing jackboots and a uniform with a swastika armband, and spent many hours each day marching in a column in the vicinity of Jüterbog. Along with all the others, I chorused 'Do You See the Sunrise in the East' or 'Heathlands of Brandenburg' and other marching songs. We even had a flag – with a swastika, of course, and sometimes this flag was carried before us. When we came through villages, the people on either side of the road raised their arms to greet the flag, or disappeared quickly in some house entrance. They did this because they had learned that if they did not, we, that is I, would beat them up. It made not the slightest difference that I – and, no doubt, others among us – ourselves fled into entryways to avoid these flags, when we were not marching behind them. Now we were the ones embodying an implicit threat of violence against all bystanders. They greeted the flag or disappeared. For fear of us. For fear of me.

I still feel dizzy when I consider my predicament then. It was the Third Reich in a nutshell.

Thirty-Six

*J*üterbog is a barracks town in the south of Brandenburg. One fine autumn morning fifty or a hundred other young men and I blown together from all over Germany found ourselves on the platform of its station. We had coats over our arms, suitcases in our hands and embarrassed expressions on our faces. None of us knew what was in store for us; each of us wondered what was the point of being here. We intended to take our *Assessor* examinations – and for that reason we had been ordered, unasked, to this unwelcoming provincial platform. Not a few of us would have armed ourselves with quiet reservation and irony against the 'ideological training' that we had been promised. But surely none had foreseen the strange, disturbing, outlandish picture we presented standing around with our little suitcases in this dismal part of the world, faced only with the problem of presenting ourselves at a place called the 'New Camp', which no one knew of, for purposes that were unclear to all of us. Obviously we were not going to be met. After a while we hired a car to take our cases to the camp. The driver told us where it was: a few kilometres down a highway. Some of us suggested hiring more cars to drive us there. Others rejected that out of hand: what kind of impression would it make in the camp if we drove up in hired cars like upper-class gentlemen! Some among us wore SA uniforms. One of these, clearly a born leader, gave the command, 'Form up in threes. Quick march!', and since none of us had a better idea, we obeyed, and after a little jostling set off in the direction of the highway. The situation had suddenly acquired a typically German air: we were recruits marching to the depot.

The SA men, six or eight in number, formed the vanguard. The others muddled along behind them, more or less in step: a picture full of symbolism. Those up ahead tried to start up a song: at first they tried SA songs, then infantry songs and finally folk songs. It turned out that most of us did not know the words, or at best just the first verse. So they finally gave up singing and we marched along the highway in silence. To the right and left of us the bare land lay in the autumn sun. During the march I let my mind wander and marvelled at the detours that would, I hoped, take me to Paris.

On arrival at the camp, we first had to wait. We stood 'at ease' but perplexed and watched other *Referendars* who were already installed there sweeping the dust in the yard to and fro between the huts. (A week later we knew perfectly well that this was called 'cleaning the precincts' and was the normal Saturday occupation.) While they were doing this they sang curious songs in a special, jerky, disjointed style that had been introduced by the Nazis. I tried to understand the texts, and gradually recognised that they were satirical verses on the 'March casualties' – those people who, after the Nazis had won, had suddenly become Nazis too. For a few moments I yielded to uncomprehending, hopeful illusions. Then I realised that the satire came from the opposite side to the one I had naively assumed.

> 'In nineteen thirty-three,' they sang,
> 'The battle had been fought . . .
> In nineteen thirty-three
> The gentleman went out
> And from his tailor bought
> An outfit, made to measure.
> Now see the arsehole strut about . . .'

They were obviously pithy SA songs for the party faithful. It was ironic, though, that most of those singing these songs were themselves 'March casualties' – or perhaps not even that . . . one could no longer tell the difference. They were all wearing the same grey uniforms with swastika armbands and they all sang equally jerkily. With hesitant glances, I tried to gauge my neighbours, all still wearing civilian clothes and not yet singing; they were probably doing the same with me ... 'Is he a Nazi? Anyway, better be careful...'

Thus we waited, waited with interruptions for three or four hours. In the interruptions we were given boots, tin food cans, swastika armbands and a ladle of potato soup ... After each of these events we had to wait another half an hour. It was as though we were inside a large cumbersome machine that creaked into movement once every half-hour. Then there was a medical, one of those rough and insultingly summary military check-ups: 'Stick your tongue out. Drop your trousers. Have you ever had a venereal disease?' The doctor briefly put his ear to your chest, shone a torch between your legs and hit you on the knee with a little hammer. That was all. Then we were assigned to 'dormitories', large barrack rooms with forty or fifty bunk beds, little lockers and two long dining tables with benches on either side. It was all very military; the only thing was, we were not training to be soldiers, we just wanted to pass our *Assessor* examinations. Indeed, nobody said anything about our becoming soldiers; even now it was not mentioned, though we did get a speech.

Our dormitory head man made us form up. He was an SA man, but not just an ordinary SA man, a *Sturmführer*. (He had three stars on the collar of his uniform, and I learned that day that that denotes a *Sturmführer*, the SA equivalent of a captain. Apart from that he was a *Referendar* just like us.) I cannot say that he made an unpleasant impression. He was a small, dainty, brown-haired young man with lively eyes, not a bully-boy. But I noticed a peculiar expression on his face – it was not even particularly disagreeable; but it reminded me of something and it bothered me. Suddenly I remembered: it was exactly the expression of brazen audacity that Brock had worn ever since he had become a Nazi.

He gave the order, 'Attention!' and then, 'At ease!', or rather he did not give the orders, but spoke them in a gently cajoling tone, as though he were saying, 'Look, we are playing a game here, and in this game I have to give the orders, so don't be spoilsports and do what I say.' So we did him the favour of obeying him. After that he gave a speech that made three points.

First, since it still seemed to be unclear, here in the camp there was only one form of address, namely the comradely *Du* and not the more formal *Sie*.

Second, this dormitory would be the model for the whole camp.

Third, 'If one of you has smelly feet, I expect him to wash them thoroughly every morning and every evening. That is a rule of comradeship.'

And with that, he declared, our duties for today and tomorrow were over. (It was Saturday afternoon.) Furlough would not be available yet, but we could spend our time as we pleased inside the camp. 'Dismiss!'

So, apart from all the obscure and disturbing impressions that the day had brought, we now had the difficult task of filling one and a half days of nothingness.

We began to make hesitant acquaintances. Hesitant, because none of us knew whether any of the others was a Nazi or not, and so caution was necessary. Some people openly tried to strike up with the SA men, but they maintained a proud reserve towards their civilian colleagues. They clearly thought of themselves as a sort of aristocracy here in the camp. On the other hand, I started looking for faces that did not have a Nazi air. But could you rely on mere physiognomy? I felt uncomfortable and indecisive.

Then someone spoke to me. I glanced at him quickly; he had a normal, open blond face – but sometimes one saw such faces beneath SA caps.

'I have the feeling that I have met you before,' he said, stumbling a little because he started to say *Sie* and had to change to *Du*.

'I'm not sure,' I said. 'I have a bad memory for faces. Are you,' stumbling in the same way, 'a Berliner too?'

'Yes,' he said, and introduced himself with a little civilian bow, 'Burkard.'

I also gave my name and then we tried to find out where we might have met. That provided a safe topic of conversation for about ten minutes. Once we had determined that we really could not have met anywhere, silence descended. We cleared our throats.

'Well anyway,' I said, 'then we have met here.'

'Yes,' he said.

Silence.

'Is there a canteen anywhere around here?' I asked. 'Shall we have a cup of coffee?'

'Why not?' he said. We both avoided addressing each other directly.

'One has to do something, after all,' I said. Then tentatively, 'Funny set-up here, isn't it?'

He looked sideways at me and answered even more carefully, 'I haven't formed a definite impression yet. Rather military, eh?'

We looked for the canteen, had a coffee and offered each other cigarettes. The conversation dragged. We avoided saying 'you', and we avoided saying anything compromising. It was a strain.

'Do you play chess?' he asked at last (correcting himself from *Sie* to *Du*).

'A little,' I said. 'Shall we play a game?'

'I haven't played for a long time,' he said. 'But there seem to be chess boards here. We can give it a try.'

We borrowed a chess set at the bar and started to play. I tried to remember what I could of opening theory. I had not played for a long time, not for many years, and looking at the pieces and the development of the game irresistibly brought back a long-vanished era when I had been an ardent chess player: my first student years, 1926, 1927, and the atmosphere of the period with all its youthful, unquestioning radicalism, its freedom and spontaneity, its open, heated discussions, its laughter and its exuberance ... For a moment I saw myself sitting here like a stranger, seven years older, and playing chess again, for want of anything better to do, with an opponent I did not know, but had to address with the familiar *Du*, in a strange, remote place to which I had been ordered to go without knowing what for. I felt the humiliation and also the outlandishness of my position as I carefully moved a pawn to prepare for castling. A giant Hitler portrait stared sullenly down at me from the wall.

The radio crackled in the corner. Military music as usual. Six or eight people were sitting at other tables, smoking and drinking coffee. The others were probably strolling round the camp. The windows were open; autumn sunlight slanted in.

Suddenly the radio broke off. The banal march tune that had been playing seemed to stop with one foot in the air. There was a strained silence, in which we still waited for the foot to make contact with the ground. Instead, an oily-voiced anouncer said, '*Achtung, Achtung*! Here is a special announcement from the wireless service.'

We both looked up from our game, but avoided looking at each other. It was Saturday October 13th 1933, and it was the announcement that Germany had walked out of the disarmament conference and resigned from the League of Nations. The announcer used the style of speech that had been introduced by Goebbels. He had the oily smoothness of a trainee actor playing a conspirator.

There were a lot of other special announcements. The Reichstag was dissolved: yes, the harmless, docile Reichstag which had given Hitler every dictatorial power. For what reason? At the new election there would only be one party: the NSDAP, that is, the Nazis. This still astonished me, in spite of all I had experienced. An election where there was no choice. An audacious idea. I glanced briefly at my opponent's face. It was as non-committal as he could possibly make it. The parliaments of the *Länder* were also dissolved but they would not be re-elected. This piece of news was an anticlimax after the others and seemed uninteresting, even though it entailed the end of such historical entities as Prussia and Bavaria. Hitler would make a speech to the German people that evening. My God, one would

probably have to listen to that here, in public, with everyone
else. 'After that special announcement of the wireless service we
return to our regular programme of music. Dadum-da-da,
Dadum-da-da . . .'

No one jumped up and shouted 'Heil' or 'Hooray'. Nothing
else happened either. Burkard bent his face so low over the
pieces that he gave the impression that nothing in the world
interested him as much as our game. At the other tables, people
sat in silence and blew the smoke from their cigarettes, their
serious faces giving nothing away. But there was so much to say!
I felt sick with contradictory emotions. I was happy that now
the Nazis had obviously gone too far, and I felt a despairing
rage that I was caught on the wrong side, and I felt disappointed
because the cause of the Nazis' downfall would be something
where they were really in the right. The good old republicans
had also all wanted 'equal rights' and the 'freedom to arm', and
that in itself would have been quite all right. I noted with
impotent irritation their cunning combination of a vote of
confidence with a motion that nobody could disagree with;
while the announcement of 'elections' at which there would be
only one party to vote for left me quite speechless, helplessly
searching for some expression adequate to express their colossal
effrontery and provocation. All that cried out for expression and
discussion. Instead I said, 'Quite a lot at once, don't you think?'

'Yes,' said Burkard, bent over the game, 'the Nazis never take
half-measures.'

Ha! He'd given himself away. He'd said 'Nazis'. If you said
'the Nazis', that meant you were not one of them. He was
someone you could talk to.

'I think they'll come a cropper this time,' I began eagerly. He
looked up with an expression of total incomprehension. He had
probably noticed that he had given himself away.

'Difficult to tell,' he said. 'By the way, I think you're going to
lose your bishop.' In his confusion he used the formal *Sie*.

'Do you think so?' I said (also using *Sie*), and tried to
concentrate on the game. I had lost my thread.

We ended our game with no further conversation except the occasional 'check' or 'gardez'.

That evening we all sat in the same canteen and listened to Hitler speechifying on the radio, while his giant portrait stared sullenly down at us. The dominant figures were the SA men, laughing or nodding at the appropriate places almost as well as the members of the Reichstag. We sat or stood closely packed, and this closeness contained a horrible confinement. I was more at the mercy of the words that came from the loudspeaker than usual, packed in between neighbours whose opinions I could not be sure of. Some of us were obviously enthusiastic. Most were inscrutable. Only one person spoke: the invisible man in the radio.

The worst came when he had finished. A fanfare signalled the national anthem, and we all raised our arms. A few hesitated like me, it was so dreadfully shaming. But did we want to sit our examinations or not? For the first time I had the feeling, so strong it left a taste in my mouth: 'This doesn't count. This isn't me. It doesn't count', and with this feeling I too raised my arm and held it stretched out ahead of me for about three minutes. That is the combined length of 'Deutschland über alles' and the Horst Wessel song. Most of us sang along, droning jerkily. I moved my lips a little and mimed singing, as one does with hymns in church.

But we all had our arms stretched out, and in this pose we stood facing the radio set, which had pulled these arms out like a puppeteer manipulates the arms of his marionettes, and we all sang or pretended to do so, each one of us the Gestapo of the others.

Thirty-Seven

As we know, there was no allied reaction to Hitler's resignation from the League of Nations, or to German rearmament, which from this moment onwards was demonstratively pursued (though it was still occasionally denied in speeches). In the following days I experienced that blend of cowardly relief and deep disappointment that would become the common feeling of the next few years for me and those like me. It was repeated *ad nauseam*, and made life wearisome.

These days marked the beginning of our 'ideological training'. It took a remarkably indirect and subtle form.

We had been prepared for lectures, speeches and interrogations in the guise of discussion groups. None of that occurred. Instead, on the Monday we were given proper uniforms: grey, blowsy uniforms, rather like the ones worn by the Russians in the Great War, with caps, belts and shoulder straps. In this military gear we tramped around the barracks yard, our only duty being to sit the written law examinations – martial, field-grey examinees.

Once that was over, something began that was called 'drill'. Superficially it was a little like military drill, the more so since our superiors – SA *Sturmführers* and the like – deliberately employed the classical tone of army sergeant-majors. However, we received no weapons training. We exercised a bit, and were taught to march and salute. For example, saluting occupied a full morning in the following manner.

We formed up in threes. At a command each row in turn marched forward. The platoon leader – as he was officially called – marched backwards a few steps in front of and to one side of the row, checking posture and alignment. Suddenly the platoon leader would bark, 'Heil Hitler!' in a voice like an exploding bomb. At that the three men had simultaneously to snap their left hand thumbs under their shoulder straps, spreading the other fingers of that hand, thrust out their right arms so that the tips of the fingers of the right hand were exactly at eye level, and jerk their heads to the left. Then, after mentally counting 'two, three', they had to bellow 'Heil Hitler! Platoon leader' in perfect unison, again as loudly as an exploding bomb. If it was not satisfactory, the whole procedure was repeated with the order, 'Repeat. Quick march!' Otherwise, it was the next row's turn, and the three who had just finished had no more to do for ten minutes until it was their turn again. This lasted two or three hours.

Or we just marched, marched around the countryside for one, two, three, sometimes four hours. These marches had no aim or recognisable purpose. While we were marching we sang. There were three kinds of songs, which we were taught in lessons in the afternoons and sang on these marches. The first was SA songs, literary constructs of the type that shop assistants sometimes send in to local papers: usually they contained dire threats against the Jews combined with sentiments like:

> 'The last few rays of
> the golden setting sun . . .' and so on.

Then there were infantry songs from the last war, gentle, sentimental bits of nonsense, richly provided with obscene variants, but not lacking a certain balladesque charm. Finally there were strange *lansquenet* songs, in which we might declare that we were Geyer's black band and would put a red cock on the monastery hall (Florian Geyer was a leader of the peasants' uprising of 1525). These songs were the most popular and were more ruggedly and more fiercely sung than the others. I am certain that at least half these German *Referendars* and future judges marching through the surroundings of Protestant Jüterbog really felt as though they were Geyer's black band, who would put a red cock on the monastery hall. Like children absorbed in a game they sang these songs with wild delight. Sounding like a troop of club-carrying, ancient Germanic tribesmen their gruff voices roared:

'Lord on high, we cry to you,
Hey-ho! Hey-ho!
To death the clergy we shall do.
Hey-ho! Hey-ho!
Up and at them!
One and all!
Put a red cock on the monastery hall!'

Of course I sang along. We all sang along.

That was the sum of our ideological training. By acceding to the rules of the game that was being played with us, we automatically changed, not quite into Nazis, but certainly into usable Nazi material. Why then did we accede to them?

There were many reasons, some major and some minor, some mitigating and some aggravating. The most superficial one was that we wanted to pass our examinations, and that this had become a requirement to do so. Certainly the mysterious hints that the 'camp report' would play a major part in determining the outcome of the examinations, and that weak performance in the written papers could be compensated for by keenness in marching and singing, must have increased the motivation of some of us. It was more decisive that we had been caught completely off guard, and had had no idea of what would be done with us, or how to resist it. Mutiny? Simply leaving the camp and going home? That would have needed to be organised, and, under a thin coat of rough and hearty camp comradeship, we all mistrusted one another deeply. Finally, there was a typically German aspiration that began to influence us strongly, although we hardly noticed it. This was the idolisation of proficiency for its own sake, the desire to do whatever you are assigned to do as well as it can possibly be done. However senseless, meaningless or downright humiliating it may be, it should be done as efficiently, thoroughly and faultlessly as could be imagined. So we should clean lockers, sing and march? Well, we would clean them better than any professional cleaner, we would march like campaign veterans and we would sing so ruggedly that the trees bent over. This idolisation of proficiency for its own sake is a German vice; the Germans think it is a German virtue. In any case, it is deeply ingrained in the German character. We could not help ourselves. We are the worst saboteurs in the world. If we do something it has to be done scrupulously. The voice of conscience and self-respect are powerless against this attitude. We find a deep, numbing, sinful pleasure in doing anything, be it a decent and important job, a wild adventure or a crime, as well as can be. This feeling robs us of the ability to think about the significance of what we are doing. Faced with a particularly thoroughly and methodically burgled house, a policeman may say admiringly, 'That's a first-class piece of work.'

That was our weakest point – whether we were Nazis or not. That was the point they attacked with remarkable psychological and strategic insight.

It came into full effect only when after one or two weeks the training personnel was changed. The SA *Sturmführer*s, who had been in charge of us so far, left to go for further 'training' in some 'camp' themselves; in their place there appeared a lieutenant of the *Reichswehr* with a dozen petty officers.

One morning this attractive young man suddenly appeared just as we had formed up for a march in the pouring rain. 'What dismal faces you've all got,' he said, 'in such glorious weather – and with such a satisfying occupation!' That had a friendly, human sound. He even used the formal *Sie*. He left us in no doubt about his opinion of the SA in general and our previous SA leaders in particular. The petty officers were even more outspoken. 'Now we're going to do something sensible here,' declared Corporal Schmidt that very afternoon, as he took charge of our platoon. We were handed rifles, and were quickly taught their seven component parts, and then how to use them. That was a real relief. Now we really were recruits, and we were inclined to view that as an improvement. At least we knew what was going on, and what we were supposed to be learning. The implicit general humiliation of doing senseless things, whose purpose was unfathomable, all day long, was over. How glad we were! Our ideological training really was beginning to take effect.

There is a saying ascribed to Hitler: 'I will press my opponents into service – in the *Reichswehr*.' There is more truth in this than in most of Hitler's sayings. The *Reichswehr* has indeed become the great collection point for almost all of non-Nazi Germany: here average Germans can follow their instinct for proficiency, their need for action and also their intellectual and moral cowardice. Here is an arena where you do not continually need to raise your arm, where you can even let yourself go a little and permit yourself a coarse word or two about Hitler or the Nazis in general without too much danger; an arena where you are effectively and thoroughly kept occupied, where everything runs like clockwork and you do a 'good job'; best of all, you need only do your duty in silence and so you are relieved of the need to think or take moral responsibility for your actions; you do not have to ask yourself for whom and for what you will one day have to use your weapon. For many years, those who needed an additional sedative also persuaded themselves that 'one day the *Reichswehr* will make an end of the whole sham'. They carefully failed to see that it was just the *Reichswehr* that formed the channel through which their capabilities were pressed into Hitler's service. This is an important, decisive process. In Jüterbog I experienced a tiny sliver of it, but I saw it in magnified close-up, with all its psychological details.

We were eager recruits. After a couple of weeks we had almost entirely forgotten how strange it was that we should be learning to shoot in order to pass our legal examinations. Military life has its own rules. Once you are immersed in it, you are no longer free to ask how you got there in the first place. We were fully occupied in cleaning our rifles and our boots, aiming and taking cover properly, marching in proper formation and in step. Besides, we were far too exhausted to think.

The petty officers were extremely kind – the opposite of the harsh sergeant-majors of tradition. We were heartily glad to have escaped Nazi lectures, and felt we had got off very lightly. Indeed, when one afternoon (it was even a Saturday afternoon) a co-*Referendar*, who occupied some middling position in the party, tried to organise such a lecture there was a riot. The lecture was continually interrupted by foot scraping and restless shuffling, and that night the *Referendar* was almost beaten up. Quite open criticisms in unparliamentary language were voiced, not quite of the content of the lecture itself, but certainly of its quality, which was called an insult to our intelligence. Being soldiers, we could say such things. In the first few days, when we had only been *Referendars*, we would not have dared to.

Thus we believed we had escaped ideological training, even while we were thoroughly immersed in it. Then one day we had a lecture that capped it all. This time it was not party propaganda, nothing about the Jews, or the 'System', or the Führer's magical powers, or the shameful peace treaty of Versailles. None of all that. No, it was something much more effective. Our lieutenant and commander-in-chief gave us a talk about the Battle of the Marne.

Had he been a professional propagandist, he could not have made a more subtle or cunning choice. Probably he acted entirely instinctively in choosing his topic and honestly believed the opinions he wanted to impart.

The Germans have a very different picture of the Battle of the Marne from the rest of the world. Elsewhere people argue whether the victory was primarily due to Gallieni or Joffre or Foch, but that question is completely meaningless in Germany, because there it is not even admitted that it was an allied victory. Rather the picture that is firmly fixed in the German mind is one of a battle where a German victory was only prevented by abandoning the field, because of unfortunate misunderstandings, just as the decision was going their way. What is more, without these misunderstandings, not only the battle but the whole war would have been irrevocably won. It was because of these misunderstandings that the war now became one of attrition, in the trenches. The Germans would have won that, too, if it had not been for . . . At this point further legends set in.

This picture, which they have drawn for themselves, tortures the Germans. It is like a thorn in their flesh.

They are not nearly as interested in the question of war guilt, which is so important for other nations. Secretly they would not mind being guilty of starting the war, though it is, of course, not done to admit that. What vexes and torments them is that they *lost* the war. They try to explain away the final collapse – either by the legend of the 'stab in the back' or by claiming that Germany voluntarily laid down its arms, trusting in Wilson's fourteen points, only to find itself shamefully betrayed. Yet that does not pain them as much as the loss of the Battle of the Marne. For at that moment, so the legend goes, the Germans let slip the glorious final victory that was already within their grasp, all because of stupid misunderstandings, confusion, and ridiculous little errors of organisation. That they cannot bear. Almost every German has the battle sketch of the positions of the armies on the 5th and 6th of September 1914 before his inner eye, and almost every one of them has desperately moved the black marks this way or that: if only the second army had turned just a little – or if only the reserves had been brought up this tiny bit – the war would have been won! Why did the generals fail to make these moves? Even today they discuss whose fault it was, that the disastrous, unnecessary order to retreat was issued, General Moltke's, Colonel Hentsch's, or General Bülow's . . . An inevitable consequence of this picture is the idea: 'That must be corrected . . . We must start the contest over, just as it was then, and this time we will make no mistakes . . .' Not even the shameful treaty of Versailles calls as strongly for a rematch and revenge as this technical incompetence, this accidentally lost battle that was really a victory.

Our lieutenant let the whole affair roll past our eyes, just as the German legend describes it. He let the first army make its famous manoeuvre, wheeling away from Paris. He described Gallieni's flank attack from that city and how the first army turned to the north-west in forced marches and brought

Gallieni to a standstill, but how in doing that it opened the infamous gap between itself and the second army – at this point the second army's reserves should have . . . Instead there was the infirm commander-in-chief, far from the front and ill-informed, Colonel Hentsch had a crisis of nerves, and so on, right up to the unbearable incorrect and unacceptable end.

In this mood, tormented and dissatisfied, he left us. Immediately military discussions broke out. 'If Bülow . . . If Hentsch . . . If Kluck . . . At this point the second and third armies should have started a pincer movement against Foch . . .' We were all eagerly correcting the Battle of the Marne, nineteen years after the event. Almost unnoticeably the discussion moved to the prospects for a new war, and how it would be done better next time. 'Just wait till our rearmament is complete!' 'But they won't let us complete it,' said someone. 'Oh, yes they will,' said another. 'They know only too well that we may not have enough soldiers yet, but we do have enough aeroplanes, so that before we are done for we can mount a night attack on Paris and flatten it.'

And we thought that we had not been undergoing ideological training – that we had not become Nazis!

Thirty-Eight

What about me? I notice that I have not had occasion to use the word 'I' in my story for quite a while. I have used either the third person or the first person plural; there has been no opportunity to use the first person singular. That is no accident. It was one of the points – perhaps *the* point – of what was happening to us in the camp that the individual person each one of us represented played no part and was completely sidelined. That just did not count. Things were quite deliberately arranged so that the individual had no room for manoeuvre. What one represented, what one's opinions were 'in private' and 'actually' was of no concern and was set aside, put on ice, as it were. On the other hand, in moments when one had the leisure to think of one's individuality – perhaps if one awoke at night in the midst of the multifarious snoring of one's comrades – one had a feeling that what was actually happening, in which one participated mechanically, had no real existence or validity. It was only in these hours that one could attempt to call oneself morally to account and prepare a last position of defence for one's inner self. Perhaps thus.

Well, this will last another four, six or eight weeks. I have to get through it without drawing attention to myself, then there will be the exams. After that I shall go to Paris, and it will all be forgotten, as though it had never happened. In the meantime, it is a kind of adventure and certainly an experience. There are some things I must never do: never say anything that I would be ashamed of later. Shooting at targets is all right. But not at people. I must not commit myself, or sell my soul . . . Anything else?

Oh dear! It dawned on me that I had already relinquished and lost everything. I wore a uniform with a swastika armband. I stood to attention and cleaned my rifle. But that did not count; I had not been asked before I did it; it was not me that did it; it was a game and I was acting a part.

Only what if, dear God, there was some court that did not recognise this defence, but simply wrote down everything as it happened; that did not look into my heart, but simply noted the swastika armband. Before that court I was in a wretched position. Dear God, where had I gone wrong? What should I say to the judge who asked, 'You wear a swastika armband and say that you do not want to. Then why do you wear it?'

Should I, perhaps, have refused on the very first day, when the armbands were handed out? Stated immediately, 'I will not wear such a thing', and trampled it underfoot? That would have been sheer madness, and ridiculous as well. It would only have landed me in a concentration camp, and not in Paris, and I would have broken my promise to my father to take my exams. I would probably die – for nothing, for a quixotic gesture, not even made in public. Ridiculous. Everybody wore the armbands here, and I was certain that there were many whose private views on the matter were the same as mine. If I had made a fuss, they would only have shrugged their shoulders. It was better to wear the armband and maintain my freedom for a later, greater purpose. It was better to learn how to shoot. That way I might be able to use the skill in a more important cause . . .

But the nagging voice remained, 'All that does not change the fact that you have worn the armband.'

My comrades snored, tossed and turned in their sleep and made other noises. Only I was awake and alone. The air was stuffy. I ought to open a window. The moon shone in. I ought to go back to sleep.

Getting back to sleep was no longer easy. It was not good to wake up in the dormitory. I rolled over. My sleeping neighbour's breath smelled bad, and I rolled back.

Different thoughts, more night thoughts. When that was said about 'flattening Paris', didn't you feel a stab in your heart? Why didn't you say anything?

What should I have said? Perhaps 'That would be a pity'? I might actually have said that. Did I? I'm not sure any more. Anyway, the answer would only have been, 'Of course it would be a pity'. And what then? Saying something as mild as that was more cowardly and dishonest than silence. What should I really have said? 'That's dreadful, it's inhuman. You don't know what you're saying . . .'? That would have had just as little effect. They wouldn't even have been angry, just irritated. They would have laughed or shrugged their shoulders. What should I have said that would really have been appropriate, really effective, that would have broken through their armour of deafness, and saved my soul?

I strained to find something, without success. There was nothing. Silence was better.

Or the other day when somebody else – otherwise a pleasant comrade – had talked about the trial of those accused of starting the Reichstag fire and said, 'I don't really believe they're guilty. But what does that matter? There are enough witnesses against them. So why not just chop off their heads and be done with it? A few more or less don't make any difference.' (He said it pleasantly, without rancour.)

What can one say to that? There is no answer. The only reaction is to take an axe to the person's head who said it. Just so. But me with an axe? Besides, the man who said it is quite decent otherwise. The other day when I felt sick, he got up and helped me to the latrines and hung a bathrobe round my shoulders. I can't take an axe to his head . . . Anyway, who knows if that is his 'real', 'private' opinion? Perhaps it just slipped out . . . What great difference is there between saying something like that, as he did, and listening to it without retort, as I did? It's almost the same.

I tried another position and my thoughts shifted a little. What if you actually had to *do* something? Yes, that is the decisive point . . . Would any of us, would *I*, find a way out, if actions were demanded of us? If the war suddenly did break out, and we were ordered into battle, just as we were now – into battle, where we would be required to use our rifles for Hitler ... Well? Would you throw aside your rifle and desert? Or shoot at your neighbour, who only yesterday helped you clean your weapon? Well, would you? *Would you*?

I groaned and tried to force myself to stop thinking. I realised that I was well and truly in a trap. I should never have come to the camp. Now I was in the trap of comradeship.

Thirty-Nine

*D*uring the daytime you had no time to think, no opportunity just to be yourself. During the daytime comradeship brought contentment. It is indubitable that a certain kind of happiness thrives in such camps, it is the happiness of comradeship. It was a pleasure to go for a cross-country run together in the morning, and then to go naked into the communal hot showers together, to share the parcels that one or other received from home, to share too the responsibility for misdemeanours that one of your comrades had committed, to help and support one another in a thousand little ways. We trusted one another without reserve in all the actions of the day, and had boyish battles and fights. We were all the same. We floated in a great comforting stream of mutual reliance and gruff familiarity ... Who would deny that that brings happiness? Who would deny that men yearn for this, a yearning that is rarely satisfied in ordinary, peaceful, civilian life?

I, for my part, do not wish to deny it. And yet I know for certain, and emphatically assert, that this very comradeship can become the means for the most terrible dehumanisation – and that it has become just that in the hands of the Nazis. They have drowned the Germans, who thirst after it, in this alcohol to the point of *delirium tremens*. They have made all Germans everywhere into comrades, and accustomed them to this narcotic from their earliest age: in the Hitler youth, the SA, the *Reichswehr*, in thousands of camps and clubs – and in doing this they have driven out something irreplaceable that cannot be compensated for by any amount of happiness.

Comradeship is part of war. Like alcohol, it is one of the

great comforters and helpers for people who have to live under unbearable, inhuman conditions. It makes the intolerable tolerable. It helps us cope with filth, calamity and death. It anaesthetises us. It comforts us for the loss of all the amenities of civilisation. Indeed, that loss is one of its preconditions. It receives its justification from bitter necessities and terrible sacrifices. If it is separated from these, if it is exercised only for pleasure and intoxication, for its own sake, it becomes a vice. It makes no difference that it brings a certain happiness. It corrupts and depraves men like no alcohol or opium. It makes them unfit for normal, responsible civilian life. Indeed it is, at bottom, an instrument of decivilisation. The general promiscuous comradeship to which the Nazis have seduced the Germans has debased this nation as nothing else could.

Observe how centrally and fatally this poison attacks the soul. (I reiterate that poisons can bring happiness, body and soul can crave for them, they can even be indispensable in their place. They are, nevertheless, poisons.)

To start with the essential point, comradeship completely destroys the sense of responsibility for oneself, be it in the civilian, or worse still, the religious sense. A man bedded in comradeship is relieved of all personal worries, and of the rigours of the struggle for life. He has his bed in the barracks, his meals and his uniform. His daily life is prescribed from morning to night. He need not concern himself with anything. He lives, not under the severe rule of 'each for himself', but in the generous softness of 'one for all and all for one'. It is one of the most unpleasant falsehoods that the laws of comradeship are harder than those of ordinary civilian life. On the contrary, they are of a debilitating softness, and they are justified only for soldiers in the field, for men facing death. Only the threat of death justifies and makes this egregious dispensation from responsibility acceptable. Indeed, it is a familiar story that brave soldiers, who have been too long bedded on the soft cushions of comradeship, often find it impossible to cope with the harshness of civilian life.

It is even worse that comradeship relieves men of responsibility for their actions, before themselves, before God, before their consciences. They do what all their comrades do. They have no choice. They have no time for thought (except when they unfortunately wake up at night). Their comrades are their conscience and give absolution for everything, provided they do what everybody else does.

> 'Then the friends took the jug
> And bewailed the sorrowful ways of the world
> And its bitter laws,
> And threw the boy down.
> Close, foot by foot, they stood
> At the edge of the chasm
> And threw him down *closing their eyes,*
> *None more guilty than his neighbour.*
> And they threw sods of earth
> And flat stones
> After him.'

That is by the German communist poet Brecht, and it is meant as praise and commendation. In this, as in so much else, the Communists and the Nazis are of the same opinion.

It was comradeship, which in a few weeks in a camp at Jüterbog had moulded us – *Referendars* after all, with an intellectual, academic education, future judges – into an unthinking, indifferent, irresponsible mass, in which sayings like those about Paris or the Reichstag fire were commonplace, went unanswered and set the intellectual tone. Comradeship always sets the cultural tone at the lowest possible level, accessible to everyone. It cannot tolerate discussion; in the chemical solution of comradeship, discussion immediately takes on the colour of whining and grumbling. It becomes a mortal sin. Comradeship admits no thoughts, just mass feelings of the most primitive sort – these, on the other hand, are inescapable; to try and evade them is to put oneself beyond the pale. How familiar were the attitudes that governed our camp comradeship absolutely and

irrevocably! They were not really the official Nazi party line –
but they certainly had a Nazi character. They were the attitudes
we had had as boys during the Great War, which had
dominated the Rennbund Altpreussen and the athletics clubs in
the Stresemann era. A few Nazi-specific ideas had not yet taken
root. For instance 'we' were still not virulently anti-Semitic. But
'we' were not prepared to make an issue of it. That was a trifle.
Who could take it seriously? 'We' had become a collective
entity and with all the intellectual cowardice and dishonesty of a
collective being we instinctively ignored or belittled anything
that could disturb our collective self-satisfaction. A German
Reich in microcosm.

It was remarkable how comradeship actively decomposed all
the elements of individuality and civilisation. The most important part of individual life, which cannot be subsumed in
communal life, is love. So comradeship has its special weapon
against love: smut. Every evening in bed, after the last patrol
round, there was the ritual reciting of lewd songs and jokes.
That is a hard and fast rule of male comradeship, and nothing is
more mistaken than the widely held opinion that this is a safety
valve for frustrated erotic or sexual feelings. These songs and
jokes do not have an erotic, arousing effect. On the contrary,
they make the act of love appear as unappetising as possible.
They treat it like digestion and defecation, and make it an object
of ridicule. The men who recited rude songs and used coarse
words for female body parts were in effect denying that they
had ever had tender feelings or been in love, that they had ever
made themselves attractive, behaved gently and used sweet
words for these same parts ... They were rough, tough and
above such civilised tenderness.

Naturally, it fitted the style that civilian courtesy and manners
were an easy prey to comradeship. Gone were the times when,
blushing and awkward, we had bowed and displayed our good
upbringing. Here the normal expression of disapproval was
'Shit!'; 'Well, you arseholes' was a friendly form of address and
'arse-kicking' was a popular pastime. The need to be an adult
had been dispensed with here, and replaced by an obligation to

be childishly boyish. For example, it was customary to attack a neighbouring dormitory at night with 'water bombs', drinking mugs filled with water to be poured over the beds of the defenders ... A battle would ensue, with merry 'ho's and 'ha's and screaming and cheering. You were a bad comrade if you did not take part. If the night patrol appeared, everyone disappeared into their beds as quickly as possible. There we lay, snoring and pretending to sleep. It was taken for granted that comradeship prevented those who had been attacked from telling tales. They would declare to the authorities that they had seen and heard nothing, and would rather admit to having wet their beds than accuse their comrades. The next night, however, we had to be prepared for a revenge attack ...

This leads me to certain dark and bloody aspects of comradeship that could not be absent. If someone had committed a sin against comradeship, or 'acted superior' or 'shown off' and exhibited more individuality than was permissible, a night-time court would judge and condemn him to corporal punishment. Being dragged under the water pump was the punishment for minor misdemeanours. However, when one of us was proved to have favoured himself in distributing butter rations – which were still quite adequate at that time – he suffered a terrible fate. Darkly, the procedure to be used was debated in his absence. That evening there was a heavy atmosphere of anticipation in the dormitory. The evening round passed. Even the obligatory smut was recited only briefly and half-heartedly, and did not raise the usual titters. Suddenly, the fearsome, wrathful voice of the self-appointed chief judge intoned, 'Meier, we have something to say to you!' Before much could be said the unfortunate man had been dragged from his bed and spreadeagled on a table. 'Every man will whack Meier once, no one is excused,' the judge thundered. From outside I heard the slapping noise of the blows. I had got myself excused after all. I had claimed not to be able to stand the sight of blood, and had been graciously allowed to be the lookout. The victim seemed to accept his destiny. By the dark laws of comradeship that governed us, independently of our individual wills, a complaint would have put him in danger of his life. Somehow, the matter was allowed to be forgotten and a few days later he was one of us again, almost as though nothing had happened. Even the rules of honour and self-respect were no match for the corrosive power of comradeship.

It is clear that there is something demonic, deeply dangerous, in this widely praised, harmless male comradeship. The Nazis knew what they were doing when they made it the normal way of life for an entire nation. And the Germans, with their lack of talent for individual life and happiness, were so dreadfully ready to submit to it, so willing and eager to exchange the delicate, hard-to-reach fruits of freedom for the juicy, swelling, close-at-hand intoxication of general, undiscriminating, vulgar comradeship.

It is said that the Germans are subjugated. That is only half true. They are also something else, something worse, for which there is no word: they are 'comraded', a dreadfully dangerous condition. They are under a spell. They live a drugged life in a dream world. They are terribly happy, but terribly demeaned; so self-satisfied, but so boundlessly loathsome; so proud and yet so despicable and inhuman. They think they are scaling high mountains, when in reality they are crawling through a swamp. As long as the spell lasts, there is almost no antidote.

Forty

Nevertheless, the condition of comradeship, dangerous as it is, has its weak point – as does every condition that is based on deception, doping and mumbo-jumbo. The moment, namely, that its external requisites are missing, it disappears into thin air. That has been observed many thousands of times, even with genuine, legitimate, wartime comradeships: men who in the trenches would have given their lives for one another and more than once shared their last cigarette, feel the greatest shyness and inhibitions when they meet again as civilians – and it is *not* the civilian meeting that is deceptive and illusory. Our comradeship at Jüterbog had been an artificial fit of drunkenness fabricated by the Nazis, and it evaporated with eerie rapidity, in the space of a single week between two parties.

The first was our leaving party at Jüterbog. It was, to put it briefly, an orgy of comradeship. There was an alcoholic, heightened atmosphere of community and if we had not already used *Du* to greet one another, we would have sworn brother-hood and started doing it that evening. There were speeches, and in his the camp commandant, an SA *Standartenführer*, who had survived the departure of his men and the arrival of the *Reichswehr*, finally revealed the secret of our 'ideological training'. We did not need great orations, he said, or interminable lectures and explanations. Being young German men, all that we needed to show, quite automatically, that we were at heart National Socialists, was to be removed from our deceitful bourgeois environment and our dry-as-dust legal files and put in the right surroundings. That was the secret of the success of

National Socialism, that it appealed to something that was part of every German's make-up. Those of us who were not yet National Socialists knew now that it was in their blood. The rest would look after itself.

The appalling thing was that there was some truth in this speech, if you interpreted it correctly. It really was true that you had only to place us in the right circumstances for a kind of chemical process to corrode our individualities and turn us into an unthinking mass, easily arousable for any cause whatever . . . This process reached its climax that evening. There was universal brotherhood. Everybody praised and proposed toasts to everybody else. The lieutenant praised our military prowess. We praised the lieutenant's strategic genius. A petty officer, replying humorously to a toast, stated in his gruff manner that he had never dreamed that lawyers and academics would make such good soldiers. 'Sieg Heil.'

There were humorous poems written for the occasion, and read out by their authors to general acclaim from the undiscerning, tipsy audience. We sang that we were Geyer's black band one last time, and at the *hey-ho*s beer glasses and chairs were smashed. We were like a tribe of self-satisfied cannibals at a victory celebration. Then some dormitory or other was attacked with water bombs and there was a battle royal. Suddenly some of us had the drunken idea that somebody ought to be dragged under the water pump – not because he had committed an offence, just as a kind of symbolic human sacrifice to the god of comradeship. The chosen victim demurred, and several others immediately offered themselves, but that did not satisfy the sacrificial priests. So they started to persuade him that he should accept it, of his own free will, for his comrades' sake, and so that the party would not end on a sour note. It was rather spooky, but also transfigured by high spirits, alcohol and madness. The victim finally agreed, 'I'll do it. But only douse my head,' he said. 'I don't want to sleep in wet pyjamas again.' They promised, but of course, once he was under the pump they doused his whole body. 'You arseholes,' he shouted, but the

Homeric laughter that greeted this left him no choice but to join in. It was an orgy of barbarity.

The next day we left for Berlin, and during the following week we took our oral examinations. Everything was different. We wore civilian clothes again, used flushing toilets and knives and forks at table and said 'thank you' instead of 'shit'. We bowed to the old gentlemen who were our examiners, and answered their questions in educated, literary German, mentioning such things as the law concerning mortgages or joint property. Some failed their examinations and some passed. A deep gulf opened up between these two groups.

We saw our own acquaintances again, and greeted them with 'good day' rather than 'Heil Hitler'. We had conversations again, real conversations. We rediscovered our own existences, and got to know ourselves again. Asked about our experiences in the camp, we felt embarrassed, mumbled, 'It could have been worse', and explained briefly that we had learned to shoot and been taught strange songs. I began to think of Paris as though it actually existed. In the camp it had had no reality. On the other hand, the camp itself receded like a dream ... With mixed feelings I made my way to the beer hall on the Kurfürstendamm where we had agreed to meet for our farewell party. I felt uneasy, but I did at least go. The spell was still strong enough for that.

That was an uncomfortable evening. It was only one week since the orgy in Jüterbog had taken place and the same people were there – except those who had failed, who stayed away in bitterness – but it was as though we were meeting for the very first time. We all looked different in our civilian clothes. Indeed, there were a few I did not recognise at all. I noticed that some of us had intelligent, sensitive faces while others looked coarse and brutal. The difference had not been visible in the camp.

Conversation was slow to start. We did not want to talk about the examinations (nobody likes talking about examinations once they are safely over), but strangely we also did not want to reminisce about the camp. A few who made hearty remarks in this vein found little resonance or understanding, and soon gave up. It was a little like the first day at Jüterbog. The most awkward thing was that we still felt obliged to use the familiar *Du*. It would have been easier if we could have addressed one another as colleagues with the customary *Sie*.

We made enquiries about plans for the future and proposed half-hearted toasts. There was a rather loud band and its rattling, sentimental music filled the long gaps in the conversation. Soon the SA men formed a group of their own, and started discussing higher SA politics. They grumbled about the party and the paper work and toasted *Gruppenführer* Ernst.* We others kept aloof. We saw no reason to participate.

It was not long before the whole company had split into little groups. I sat with a young man with whom I had occasionally had pleasant conversations about music, outside the camp at Jüterbog on Sundays. It turned out that we had both been to the Furtwängler concert the Sunday before. We exchanged our views. 'Look at those eggheads,' said somebody who had observed us for a while. We just looked at each other and ignored it.

The evening became gloomier and gloomier and by midnight we were all surreptitiously looking at our watches. Then it fell apart completely. A group of girls of doubtful virtue settled down at the next table and some of us began to flirt with them and gradually moved over to that table or drew the belles over to our table ... 'Now it's getting boring,' somebody said loudly, and as he prepared to leave several of us joined him. I went too.

On the street, one person suggested we move on somewhere, but his suggestion was met with total silence. As for me, I saw a bus approaching. 'That's my bus,' I shouted, 'goodbye,' waved, and jumped aboard.

I left the group still standing around. I never met any of them again. The bus carried me swiftly away. I felt cold, ashamed and relieved.

---

* Gruppenführer Karl Ernst (1904–1934) Leader of the SA in Berlin, executed in the Night of the Long Knives (30th June 1934).

Afterword

Here the manuscript breaks off. In a notebook of jottings written by my father in 1946 I have found a list of section headings for a possible revision of the book to be entitled *Dance in the Lions' Den*. They give a tantalising hint of what might have followed. The headings are:

Catastrophe as Adventure (1933)
Glorious Failure (1934)
Resignation with Obstacles
Unwanted Career
Escape in Slow Motion

My parents did not speak much about this period of their lives, so it is a lasting sadness to me that the later chapters were never written. I can only add very little to flesh out the details.

As the reader has seen, my father had intended to follow a career in law, devoting his spare time to literature. By 1933 he had already written two novels and many shorter pieces, a few of which had been published in the intellectual press. The book describes how he abandoned this plan in 1933, and at his father's suggestion decided to write his Ph.D. thesis in Paris, away from the Nazis and close to the girl he loved, Teddy. It was intended as a first step towards emigration, but Teddy had married another man, and my father failed to gain a foothold in Paris. So he returned to Berlin in 1934.

He made his living by writing for the arts pages of the better newspapers and for non-political magazines. Many of these had been owned by Jews and were now controlled by the Nazis, but the censorship was subtle. The political pages were, of course, heavily censored, but the arts pages could completely ignore the Nazis if they wished. They must only avoid direct criticism. In this atmosphere my father wrote harmless, slightly snobbish (his own word) pieces about fashion, or horses, or places he had visited. When talking about this period he used to say that he had seen no possibility of direct resistance to the Nazis, but that he was determined to write nothing that he would have to be ashamed of when they had been defeated. In the editorial offices almost all of his colleagues were anti-Nazis; initially there were even still some Jews among them. They relished the sly hints of opposition which they smuggled into their texts, but when the paper appeared the following day, it was evident that the insider references failed to subvert the Nazi impression of the paper as a whole.

Some time after his return from Paris my father met my mother, who was Jewish (by race, though not by tradition or religion) and had recently separated from her first husband, a press colleague of my father's. She had a young son, my half-brother Peter. Although he was of Jewish descent, Peter was blond and blue-eyed and was quite often photographed as the ideal 'Aryan' child. My mother had been the librarian of the Hochschule für Politik (an institution a little like the London School of Economics) and had lost her job because of her race. My father soon moved into her flat but, of course, they could not marry because of the race laws. Indeed even cohabiting with a Jew was an offence, but for some reason the Nazi block warden responsible for their flat liked and protected them.

My father made a good living and even became editor of one of the magazines he had been writing for. Politically, however, life became progressively more difficult. The ambivalence of his position rankled more and more and the free space for manoeuvre became ever narrower.

Early in 1938 my mother became pregnant (with what would become me) and this made my parents' situation truly dangerous, quite apart from the fact that the war was looming. I think my father had been planning to emigrate, but that his experience in Paris in 1934 had caused him to hesitate. Now hesitation was no longer an option. The clock was ticking. My mother's brother Kurt Hirsch had emigrated to England in 1934 and had completed a Ph.D. at Cambridge and embarked on a university career there. I am not absolutely sure of the details of my mother's emigration, but I believe she first tried to get a visa for Britain armed with a phoney job invitation and a promise from her brother to cover her costs. I know that she was flatly turned down and came home in despair. My father comforted her and told her to try again with a direct appeal to the truth. She might come before a sympathetic official. So a little later she made herself up to look as smart as she could, took Peter along and tried again. This time she was successful and at the beginning of June she left for England.

My father remained in Germany and had to find a different method of escape, without acknowledging his liaison with my mother. He arranged for a commission to write a series of articles on some harmless English topic. On the basis of this commission he obtained a six-week visa and arrived in England on the 29th of August 1938. The first thing my parents did was to marry, and I was born a few weeks later, in October 1938. I have a letter in which my father reveals to his mother (living as a widow in Berlin) first that he has married, then that he has a son, then that his wife is Jewish, and finally that he has left Germany for good.

British officials did not view the manner in which my father had come to this country with favour and he had difficulty renewing his visa, even though by marrying my mother he had lost his German nationality and committed a felony under German law. It was at first renewed for a month or two at a time, but by the winter the excuse about the series of articles had worn thin, and there was a real possibility that he might be deported.

In the meantime he had to make a living somehow. In the spring of 1939 he wrote to Frederic Warburg with a synopsis of this book. In the second volume of his memoirs, Warburg recalls:

By the spring of 1939 he [Haffner] was almost at his wits' end, and in desperation had written to me, sending the synopsis of a book he planned to write. [. . .] Haffner's book was to be a political autobiography. I remember it as the most brilliant synopsis ever put before me.*

In spite of the financial difficulties his publishing house Secker & Warburg was experiencing, Warburg offered my father a retainer of £2 per week to complete the book. After the war my father wrote to Warburg, 'Never in my life, before or after, did I feel such relief.' Warburg also helped with the problem of my father's visa. In a family letter of 13th June 1939 my father writes:

Today I have been rescued from great fear and depression. The Home Office has relented after representations by Ursel [a sister of my mother's, O.P.] and a 'very strong letter' from Warburg 'in praise of my literary capacity and sterling character(!)'. They have given me a year on condition that I 'do literary work solely on behalf of Messrs Secker & Warburg'.

With the outbreak of the war, understanding why the Germans had become Nazis became a somewhat academic question. More urgent was the problem of how to deal with them. My father abandoned this project and started a new book. It was written in German but from an English point of view. Its subject was how the war might be won, and what should be done after victory had been achieved.

Warburg writes 'This book [*Defying Hitler*] was never completed. When Haffner was halfway through it the war broke out, and he felt he must write something less private and more directly political.

In the late autumn of 1939, he sent me several chapters of *A Survey of Germany*. [. . .] I also suggested a change of title to

* Frederic Warburg, *All Authors are Equal*, Hutchinson, London, 1973, p. 6.

Germany, Jekyll and Hyde, which suited the book to perfection.'*

A letter of my father's dated the 6th of October 1939 gives more detail:

> Personally, I have now started a second book of at most 200 pages beside my main one [*Defying Hitler*] which is already 270 pages long. It is to be called *Germany: A Survey* [. . .] It is intended as a handbook for English propagandists, who have to know about Germany, but also for the general reader. I will keep the tone calm and unpolemical and not make my heart a nest of vipers. What do you think?

At that time my parents were living in a tiny terraced house in Cambridge. Soon Germans in Britain, now 'enemy aliens', were interviewed and categorised according to the danger they might represent. My uncle and my mother came into the safest category C, but because of the manner of his entry my father was classed in the riskiest category A and was interned in a holiday camp in Seaton in south Devon at the start of 1940. It was run by the army, who appointed the only real Nazis among the internees as block leaders. That was the most unpleasant thing about internment: living under the very people he had emigrated to get away from. It was well organised and the detainees were well fed, but the camp was designed for summer holidays; it was January and the chalets in which they were housed were unheatable. In February 1940 during a morning muster my father was called forward and handed a telegram announcing the birth of my sister Margaret (now Sarah Haffner). My father was released from Seaton in April after Warburg had made representations to the home office. Not long afterward the Battle of Britain began and enemy aliens of all categories living within a certain distance from the coast were interned, this time on the Isle of Man. Organisation was a shambles, because the island was not prepared for such a large

* Ibid., p. 7.

influx. The men and women were at opposite ends of the island and had little communication. However, the atmosphere appears to have been friendly, and the weather was warm.

My father had completed the new book just before his internment in January, and Warburg published it in June. Because he feared reprisals against his relatives in Germany, my father dropped his real name, Raimund Pretzel, and chose a pseudonym, Sebastian Haffner, which he kept for the rest of his life. When asked about it, he would explain that the name had to satisfy three conditions: it must be clearly German, not Jewish, and easy to pronounce for English speakers. The names themselves are from Johann Sebastian Bach, and Mozart's Haffner Symphony.

Germany, Jekyll and Hyde was a critical success. There were even questions in the House of Commons as to why the author of such an important work was still interned. My father was one of the first internees to be released, in August 1940, arriving in London on the night of the first air raid on the city.

On the 9th of September 1940 Hans Lothar (also a liberal German journalist) and my father sent a *Memorandum on 'Die Zeitung'* to the foreign office, proposing that the government subsidise the publication of a German language paper for emigrants. It appears that the idea came from Hans Lothar, who also became editor-in-chief, while my father became its main political commentator. Although the paper was primarily aimed at German emigrants, it was also intended to be air-dropped over Germany. At that time my father dreamed of forming a German exile faction, like the Free French, which would help the Allies and eventually play a role in rebuilding Germany after the war. My father left *Die Zeitung* after sixteen months because of internal differences, perhaps also because he saw that his dream would not become reality.

A little later David Astor invited him to work for the *Observer*. This offered the opportunity to influence British policy far more directly than *Die Zeitung*. My father used to say that at the *Observer* he became a 'virtual Englishman'. He learned to write a beautiful, clear English and analysed events from the British point of view. He rose rapidly and from 1942 onwards wrote most of the editorials and many policy articles under various pseudonyms. It would not be an exaggeration to say that he determined the paper's political line. David Astor himself was in the army and could not play a part in the normal running of the paper. By the late forties the name 'Sebastian Haffner' was very well-known and respected in British journalism.

In the early 1950s political differences with David Astor arose, and in order to stay with the *Observer* but avoid conflict, my father returned to Germany as a foreign correspondent. Generously, the paper continued to pay him his full salary. He sent reports from Germany, but also made occasional forays into the German press and television. Gradually these became more frequent and he became quite well-known in his own country as a 'British journalist'. He left the *Observer* in 1961 over differences in policy towards the Soviet Union in general and the British stance on Berlin in particular. A year later he began to write a series of popular political columns in *Stern* magazine. These and further television appearances made him very famous. He could no longer travel by train or bus in Germany without being accosted by name and drawn into political discussions.

For *Stern* he also wrote features on historical topics, such as why Germany had lost the First World War, or the abortive 1919 revolution in Germany. These were subsequently published as books, which were widely read and translated. In 1978, a publisher asked him to write a short book on Hitler. This he did, with the German title *Anmerkungen zu Hitler* (Notes on Hitler). The book was an outstanding success and sold nearly a million copies. It was translated into English (as *The Meaning of Hitler*, a title he did not like) and many other languages. In the 1980s he continued to write books on history, but age was beginning to creep up on him.

Reunification in 1989 found my father a sick and weary man. He was profoundly uneasy about the way in which East Germany was 'annexed', and worried about the stability of Eastern Europe, especially the Balkans. The article in which he expressed his concerns was almost his last. It ran against the grain of the general euphoria of the time, and was not well received, but it showed once again his sound instinct and political foresight.

After 1990 he became progressively weaker and stopped writing altogether. Frail and housebound, his main pleasure was intellectual discussions about history, the world and the politics of his (short) century (1914–1989). He was not much given to personal reminiscence, but he did refer to the manuscripts that he kept in a side cupboard of his desk. He was particularly keen on one of his early novels, which he thought showed signs of talent. He suggested I go through his papers after his death, but forbade me to read any of them during his lifetime.

When he died in January 1999, I started looking through the manuscripts, mainly searching for the novel. It was not among the papers in his desk, but later turned up serendipitously, hidden in a chest of drawers. While searching for the novel, I stumbled across the manuscript of this book. It came as a complete surprise. I was immediately fascinated by it and read it at a single sitting, but I was unsure whether my interest was due to personal involvement. So I gave it to a German journalist friend, Uwe Soukup, to read. He was equally enthusiastic and that decided me to publish it in Germany. There were, however, two large gaps in the manuscript, covering the whole of chapters 10 and 25. Uwe told me he knew what had happened to chapter 25. An abbreviated version had been published in *Stern* in 1983 on the fiftieth anniversary of the events it relates. No doubt the other chapter had been cannibalised similarly, but I was unable to find where it had been published. Luckily my father's papers also contained a clumsy translation of the first third of the manuscript into English. It was written in an unidiomatic style through which one could almost hear the original German. I retranslated chapter 10 back into German from this source, completing the manuscript for publication.

When the book appeared in Germany in the summer of 2000 it had an astonishing reception, receiving rapturous reviews and going straight to the top of the non-fiction bestseller list, where it stayed for 42 weeks. This completely confounded my expectations and it was some time before I found a plausible explanation. Now I think it was because the book offers direct answers to two questions that Germans of my generation had been asking their parents since the war: 'How were the Nazis possible?' and 'Why didn't you stop them?' The usual replies had been evasive. Frequently those questioned declared that they had known nothing until it was too late. My father's vivid account makes the rise of the Nazis psychologically comprehensible, and it shows how difficult resistance was, but it also demonstrates that it was plain from the outset what they stood for.

Some Germans appear to have found that unpalatable, for a year after its publication, allegations began to appear in the press that the book had been assembled or modified after the war. At first they were based on claimed anachronisms in the text. One by one, these claims were refuted. But then a more vicious attack appeared, asserting, on the flimsiest grounds, that the text had been extensively rewritten and engineered in the final years of my father's life in order to secure his posthumous reputation. It provoked a flood of articles in his defence. Nevertheless, the archives holding the original felt that the charge was too serious to ignore. They sent the manuscript to the German state forensic laboratories for analysis. After two months, during which they examined every page, the laboratories issued a report. It completely vindicated my father, confirming that the typescript had been entirely produced before the war and showed no signs of any later manipulation.

Had my father really made any later changes, they would have been the opposite of those his detractors allege. He would have toned the text down, removed some of the more personal passages and generally lowered its temperature. However he would not, I am certain, have revised his conclusions.

I thought that would be the end of the excitement and that the book was now settled in its final form. Then in March 2002 a young historian, Jürgen Peter Schmied, working on my father's papers in the German state archives, made two discoveries. The first was the complete manuscript of chapter 25. My father had obviously just pushed it in a drawer with other papers when it was returned by *Stern* magazine. The second was really thrilling: it was a handwritten draft of six additional chapters (35 to 40), which bring the manuscript to the 270 pages mentioned by my father. The manuscript now really is, I believe, in its final form, as my father abandoned it in 1939.

Although still incomplete, the book also has a more satisfactory ending. Instead of the earlier final note of unreal bliss, it now concludes with a powerful close-up of Nazi methods in action.

Oliver Pretzel
London 2002

Index